ALSO BY JOHN PORTMANN

When Bad Things Happen to Other People

In Defense of Sin (Palgrave Macmillan)

S
a
Hea

Sex
and
Heaven

Catholics in Bed and at Prayer

John Portmann

First published 2003 by PALGRAVE MACMILLAN™
175 Fifth Avenue, New York, N.Y. 10010 and
Houndmills, Basingstoke, Hampshire, England RG21 6XS.
Companies and representatives throughout the world.

PALGRAVE MACMILLAN is the global academic imprint of the
Palgrave Macmillan division of St. Martin's Press, LLC and of
Palgrave Macmillan Ltd. Macmillan®is a registered trademark in the
United States, United Kingdom and other countries. Palgrave is a
registered trademark in the European Union and other countries.

ISBN 0-312-29488-3

Library of Congress Cataloging-in-Publication Data
Portmann, John.
    Sex and heaven
        p. cm.
    Includes bibliographical references.
    ISBN 0-312-29488-3
        1. Sex—Religious Aspects—Catholic Church. 2 Heaven. I
Heaven.

BX1796.S48 P67 2003
241'.66—dc21
                                                            2002030753

A catalogue record for this book is available from the British Library.

Design by planettheo.com

First edition: March 2003
10 9 8 7 6 5 4 3 2 1

Printed in the United States of America.

Ad majorem Dei gloriam

Michelangelo, "The Original Sin" detail. Sistine Chapel, Vatican Palace, Vatican State.
© Alinari/Art Resource, NY

CONTENTS

ACKNOWLEDGMENTS

Gayatri Patnaik and Michael Flamini, both outstanding editors, have left me in their debt. It is a pleasure to express my appreciation here. Alan Bradshaw oversees production for Palgrave Macmillan, and I profited from his attention to detail. Once again, Sonia Wilson's careful comments sharpened my final draft.

Daniel Ortiz sparked the idea for this book in a conversation on a California freeway, and I cannot overstate my gratitude to him. He sets a strong scholarly example.

Virginia Germino read over an early draft of the project and offered useful suggestions. Mark Jordan and Colleen McDannell, two experts I have never met, read the manuscript for Palgrave Macmillan and saved me from various errors. Mark Jordan in particular has my thanks.

SEX CRIMES AGAINST GOD

What does it take to get into heaven? It is hard to say for sure. Good behavior will certainly improve our chances. If there is one thing that will ruin them, it is sex.

As a Catholic schoolboy, I feared sex could trigger my downfall. I absorbed stories of saints who had endured mutilation, torture, and death in order to avoid that sin. The moral gap between a virgin and a sexual explorer rivaled the distance between heaven and hell. Sex threatened my eternal reward and earthly success.

As vulnerable as I felt, priests and nuns seemed to walk a tightrope more daunting. Adultery infuriated God. If an ordinary husband or wife could unleash divine fury by cheating, what havoc would a wayward priest or nun create in heaven? Sex crimes against God outran any other sin in my adolescent mind. If you were going to marry God, you'd better be prepared *never* to drop your guard. Years later, the shrill tone of public debate suggested to me that gay people must be committing sex crimes against God. Gays and lesbians had to live like priests and nuns, for gay sex upset God even more than ordinary adultery. In 1964 the Vatican welcomed Jews to heaven; nearly forty years later, the Vatican still hasn't opened the pearly gates to romantically attached gays and lesbians, even if these sexual minorities are otherwise model Catholics.

Catholics aren't the only ones who see great risk in physical intimacy; Protestants, Jews, and Muslims do as well. As an adult, I see the power of sex more clearly than ever. What fascinates me are people who will convert from one religion to another in order to follow a faith that gets sex right, as it were.

The word "sex" carries two distinct meanings in English: it signifies whether one is male or female, or the use to which we put genitals. This book revolves around these two senses of what has become the most incendiary word in religious debates today.

Gender, another word that distinguishes male from female, mattered to ancient Jews and Christians, who feared that women would inevitably distract men from prayers. Women might even spark erotic fantasies. For this and other reasons, there could be no such thing as a female rabbi or priest. In order to contain sex, our forebears reasoned, we had to regulate gender.

In the closing years of the twentieth century, something dramatic happened to women: they were allowed ordination in some denominations—Conservative Judaism and Episcopalianism, for example. At roughly the same time, something dramatic happened to church-going gays and lesbians. Here and there, we would find Baptists, Methodists, or Presbyterians marrying same-sex couples. This prompted some of the faithful to migrate into new religions or new branches of their old religion. Getting sex and gender right became so important that some of the faithful put sex concerns before theological ones. What a religion had to say about God mattered less than what it had to say about sex. In England alone, over four hundred male clergy have resigned from the Anglican ministry since 1993 out of opposition to the ordination of women priests. We have no count of how many lay Anglicans have converted for the same reason.

I found the increasing preoccupation with sex and gender so intriguing that I decided to write a book about it. Religious devotion now revolves around sex. Whereas God once rested at the center of the spiritual universe, genitals do today.

The book was largely finished when, in January 2002, a sex scandal in the Roman Catholic Church catapulted onto the front pages of newspapers throughout the Western hemisphere. For months afterward, Catholics agonized over the barrage of articles, exposes, and television reports on a problem that kept unfolding. The secrecy and mystery of sexual union dovetailed with the distant, larger-than-life aura of Catholic priests: one enigma seemed to fuel the other. Erotic yearning for minors and religious authority collided in a terrifically painful way, right before our eyes. Just as ancient cults offered up precious crops or special animals in fertility rituals, so did contemporary clerics sacrifice our children. Under a cloak of piety, sex found fertile soil. This book does not seek to document or detail the scandal, only to indicate how we got here. Sex and heaven have known each other well for a long time.

I offer observations and raise questions in this work, which is more suggestive than conclusive. In some places I do not pursue extensive interfaith comparisons; fleshing out the commonalties between the three major religions of the West would require much space and would frustrate many readers who care less about details than emerging trends. By no means have I presented a comprehensive survey of two enormous subjects—sex and heaven—or of their intersection.

The risk of overgeneralization looms here. Even in a work written for a broad audience, it is irresponsible to speak patly of "the Islamic tradition" or "the Jewish tradition," much less "the Christian tradition." Each of these traditions derives from multiple, sometimes conflicting, sources. In Islam, for instance, one must consider not just the Koran (which Muslims take to be the word of God) but also the Sunnah, Hadith, Fiqh or Madahib, and Shari'ah. It is already hard enough to focus on Catholicism, given its vast array of parishes, schools, hospitals, social services, and universities. Although I believe the Catholic hierarchy's refusal to ordain women or embrace the sexuality of gay people finds parallels in Protestantism, Judaism, and Islam, the scope of this book prevents me from exploring these parallels fully. I do not address the thorny question of how people become gay (referred to as the essentialism/constructivism debate in scholarly circles), important though it is. It is simply not possible within the span of a 200-page book to explain how the various sources (many of them disputed) of three faiths pertain to the complex roles of sex and gender in determining a person's suitability for divine favor. I hope to indicate that sex has become the stairway to heaven in Roman Catholicism. I see this book as a sustained argument, not a polemic.

A movement sixty-three million strong in the United States and growing virtually everywhere (one billion worldwide), Roman Catholicism possesses a clear center, even though it lacks clear boundaries. In matters of doctrine, one can responsibly speak of "the church" in the singular. When it comes to real, live Catholics, though, one cannot. Ecumenism will become ever more feasible as Catholicism gradually loses its distinctive identity. Old battle lines will be redrawn, and former adversaries who locked horns over God's nature will find a passionate cause in a common enemy: defiantly unorthodox genitals, coupled occasionally with intractable women. All hands on deck rally to man the sex debates.

Meanwhile, a bulging class of believers struggles to reconcile its passion for God with its lust for other people of the same sex.

Hasn't sex always dominated Western religious thought? Is there anything new under the sun? I hope to show there is. Religious morality has long fastened on sex, but the sexual revolution of the 1960s pulled sex ever closer to dead center. Although something dramatic happened at the end of the twentieth century, it was perhaps less a shift than an acceleration. Sex was always on its way to dominating religious morality, which is not to say that it has to stay there.

The older our civilization gets, the less shielded we are from sex. Now we spy mighty Eros on billboards, confront it on television, and spot it on the Internet. The test of heaven lurks in these signs and sounds.

ONE

On Earth as It Is in Heaven

Across so many stormy seas! Life isn't easy, not even for those born healthy and beautiful into loving, affluent families. So many problems can beset us from year to year that worry may seem a natural state of mind. What will happen tomorrow? Will things get better? How could they get worse?

For nearly two thousand years, downtrodden Christians have steeled themselves to the slings and arrows of fortune by contemplating heaven. In heaven, God will reward us lavishly for having behaved well in spite of hardship. Throughout eternity, we will savor a gift beyond any pleasure found in this fleeting world. Because celestial bliss will vastly exceed earthly suffering, we need not dwell on today's problems. Heaven heals all wounds.

Following the September 11, 2001 terrorist attacks on the Pentagon and the World Trade Center, the media pumped into living rooms around the globe reports that those radical Muslims who had sacrificed their lives that day counted on immediate entrance into heaven. In fact, it was the promise of heaven that motivated their attacks. Americans initially struggled to understand how evildoers could bomb their way into paradise, but perhaps remembered that heaven is a contested territory.

Although Muslims and Christians disagree on what heaven will look like, they share an abiding sense that it rewards devotion to God. Protestants, particularly in the United States, have leaned on hell in order to reinforce a notion of heaven as the ultimate payoff for good behavior.[1] Sermons such as Jonathan Edwards's classic "Sinners in the Hands of an Angry God" serve up a fire-and-brimstone warning about Hades, thus doubling our motivation to get to heaven. And the steady diet of saint stories that nourishes many Catholic schoolchildren relies on the same link between righteousness and heaven. As a heroic nun or priest expires in these stories, admirers crowd around the likely saint's body and report basking in bright rays from above. In 1958, for example, the newspaper *L'Osservatore Romano* described the funeral of Pope Pius XII as the greatest Rome had ever witnessed—more magnificent even than that of Julius Caesar. "Inferring that Pacelli [Pope Pius XII] was already enjoying the beatific vision, the Pope's secretary for briefs, Monsignor Antonio Bacci, said in his eulogy: 'With his death a great light went out on earth, and a new star lit in heaven.'"[2] Writers with a religious audience in mind learn early on that arrival in heaven makes for the most dramatic ending of all.

Early Christians didn't spend much time musing about what heaven would be like because they kept thinking that Christ would return tomorrow. They would find out soon enough. Not surprisingly, the New Testament comes up short on heavenly details. Subsequent Christian thinkers have devoted a bit more time to pondering the afterlife. They have argued over what heaven is like and what it means. Saint Thomas Aquinas maintained that heaven is not so much a reward as the very end for which human beings were created.[3] Before him, Augustine had claimed that, as an embodied intellect, our very purpose is to return to the contemplation of God in a resurrected body. (This is what Augustine means when he says we are *capax Dei*). Since Augustine's teaching on the city of God, Latin theologians have regularly denied that every visible member of the Catholic Church is bound for heaven, just as they have regularly allowed that some who appear to be ex-members or even non-members may end up in heaven. Although Catholic teachers working in the trenches may suggest otherwise, church membership is not a prerequisite for gaining heaven. Technically speaking, anyone can get there. Who knew?

So why bother to obey Catholic rules if anyone can make it to the top? As it turns out, Catholics have been less than entirely generous in admitting foreign souls into paradise (or at least canonizing them as saints). This may be an unfair way of putting the matter; there are rules to follow and conditions to meet if one is to pass the final judgment. Those who fail will find the doors of heaven barred to them. This is the cold, hard truth. Or is it? In this age of affirmative action, we moderns labor to extend equal opportunities to those who have rarely enjoyed the advantages and privileges that sweeten our short stay in this world. Here in this life, we continue to struggle to make human society more just. Who will take up the challenge of democratizing heaven? Of goading Christians, Jews, and Muslims to admit anyone into their preferred corner of eternity?

That is the organizing question of the next chapter. Here I want to probe the grand prize of existence—not sex, as the media would have us believe, but heaven.

HEAVEN: WHAT IT'S LIKE

Christianity remains a major cultural force around the globe. Christians constitute the clear majority in America, and the United States ranks as the most demonstrably religious country in the West. According to a 1996 Gallup poll, 96 percent of American adults believe in God, 90 percent in heaven, 79 percent in miracles, and 72 percent in angels.[4] These figures will likely remain constant for at least another generation.

Both within and across religious traditions, the faithful in the modern West disagree on virtually every aspect of the supernatural and morality. In an effort to avoid tediousness and at the risk of miffing specialists, I will ignore many details of this disagreement. Heaven shouldn't ever bore us.

And despite Chateaubriand's reasonable worry about boredom in paradise—"No one is interested in beings who are perfectly happy"—enthusiasm for heaven endures.[5] Most Christians, particularly those on a deathbed, will allow their imaginations to run wild when it comes to paradise. Saint Paul encourages such reveries even as he assures us of their futility: "Eye has not seen, nor ear heard the things that God has prepared for those who love him."[6] For many Christians, all of earthly life is a test, a trial to see whether one will get to heaven.

Even today, Catholics wear sacred medals, set out on pilgrimages, recite novenas, and diligently stockpile indulgences, all in the name of getting to heaven. Since the start of the Christian era, countless books and legends have pondered the mystery of the afterlife. Heaven steeped Christian sensibility with the logic that temporary acts carry eternal consequences. Reverence for rules came to absorb much of the sense of duty contained in Jewish attitudes toward mitzvot, or good deeds.

Two rival visions of the ultimate goal pit Eden, the earthly paradise, against the sky, a celestial paradise. Christians have generally endorsed the latter. Spatially and literally, Christians refer to heaven as up. The sky is where, for example, Catholics believe the Ascension took Christ, and where the Assumption later delivered his mother. Myriad paintings present angels swooping down to the earth from out of the sky. The Christian version of heaven, to the extent it can be considered uniform, contrasts with earlier versions of a euphoric afterlife, such as the Elysian fields and ancient Egyptian paradise.[7]

Christian theology borrowed extensively from its Jewish parent, which is hardly surprising given that Christianity began as a Jewish sect. But heaven really only surfaced in later Judaism, a religion that seems to show much less sustained interest in the afterlife than Christianity. Christianity deliberately spiritualized a realm for which many Jews saw a largely practical significance. For example, according to Jewish scholar Daniel Jeremy Silver, "Rabbinic Judaism never let go of redemption as a purely political category. 'There is no difference between this world and the World to Come except the end of our political subjugation.'"[8]

A number of Jewish writers, in any event, have woven heaven into their fiction. In "Yom Kippur," Eliezer Rosenthal depicts an Orthodox Jewish man wracked with guilt over having stolen money from a rabbi in order to finance a daughter's wedding. Pondering the humiliation he'd feel upon admitting his deed, the character Berel thinks, "I risk my world to come." Later, "He pictures how his soul flew up to heaven while he slept, and entered everything in the eternal book. . . ." Realizing that his time is running out, Berel assures himself "that the door of heaven will stand open a little while longer, his repentance may yet pass through. . . ."[9] And Steve Stern's short story "Lazar Malkin Enters Heaven," like Bernard Malamud's "Angel Levine," details a visit from the angel of death to an old man who simply refuses to die.[10] Perhaps most notably of all, Isaac Bashevis Singer, the 1978 Nobel laureate in literature, peppered his stories with references to heaven. That they do not think of it in Christian terms does not mean that Jews disallow heaven. That they may not dwell on heaven does not mean that Jews disavow it.

Although we read about heaven in the New Testament, we do not find a single, coherent account of it there. We find the most useful sources in the early Christian moralist Tertullian (circa 162–224) and in Augustine's *City of God.* Dante's *Paradiso* continues to mold popular imagination, seven centuries after its publication.

Tertullian emphasized the bodily aspect of resurrection that remains central to Roman Catholic belief. Due to a fervent belief in the resurrection of the body (and therefore in its sanctity), Christians only cremated their dead in extraordinary circumstances, such as battle or plague. Although Protestants generally allowed cremation after the Reformation, Catholics continued to eschew the practice until it was formally permitted in 1963 by Pope John XXIII. It is no accident that medieval paintings of heaven feature people with bodies; on the contrary, this fact is highly significant and reflects submission to Catholic theology. For better or worse, in heaven we get back the body we had in this world—with some improvements. Children and fetuses rise perfected, and amputees find their limbs restored. According to Augustine, men will rise as men, women as women. Black people will still be black in heaven, and the tall will still be tall. Curiously, there should be no difference between straight people and gay people, because there is no sexual desire in heaven. Gay identity, to the extent that it issued from desire, not the body, would thus disappear. We will all be about thirty years old, supposedly the age of prime vigor.

According to Catholic theology, our cosmetically restored bodies will no longer be vulnerable to lust. And missing organs will be reinstated in heaven, which must mean that those men who made themselves "eunuchs for the kingdom of heaven" (as Christ counseled in Matthew 19:12) will become anatomically correct again. Why bother, we might wonder, if there is to be no lust. The penis must have an important aesthetic role to play in the next world. (Whether circumcised penises are more decorative than others remains open to debate; it seems safe to assume, though, that discarded foreskins will reunite with their members.)

There will be countless attractive bodies in paradise, but no yearning to explore them. That we will all be naked in heaven makes the absence of lust all the more remarkable. Maybe the nudist-camp enthusiasts really mean it when they insist there's nothing lascivious about their cookouts and volleyball games; nudists might be providing us with a sunburnt preview of heaven.

Most of the famous artistic depictions of heaven center on the Last Judgment or the coronation of the Virgin. In paintings of Christ's birth, we regularly see angels and perhaps as well a dove, representative of the Holy Spirit. The angels are never naked, either in nativity scenes or heaven. The saints are another story. Some artists clothe the heavenly saints, as in major works such as Giotto's *Last Judgment* (ca. 1305, Cappella degli Scrovegni, Padua); Fra Angelico (*The Last Judgment*, ca. 1433, Museo di San Marco, Florence or *The Coronation of the Virgin*, ca. 1433, Musée du Louvre); Signorelli (*Procession of the Elect into Paradise*, 1499-1504, Orvieto Duomo); or Michelangelo (*The Last Judgment*, 1537-1541, Sistine Chapel, Vatican). These splendid portrayals create some confusion over nudity, for the saints are supposed to go about their business unencumbered by garments. We get a technically more accurate view of heaven in Michelangelo and Signorelli than in Fra Angelico and Giotto, the latter of whom add garments mistakenly (Michelangelo, finding the *via media,* tactfully drapes the problem spots). Other painters showcase the plain nakedness of the saints: Lucas Cranach (*The Golden Age,* Alte Pinacothek, Munich) and Hans Memling (*Last Judgment,* ca. 1471, Muzeum Narodowe, Gdansk). Although it is difficult to ascertain what motivated painters more, the spirit of time and place or theology, it seems reasonable to conclude that artists feared the very real power of the church.

Religious authorities naturally worried that the faithful would become sexually aroused by artistic depictions of nude people. The reason for clothing the saints in paradise likely came down to politics: painters, serving prelates who, after all, paid their wages, knew better than to challenge the faithful with images that might stir lust. Hagiography should not be pornography. Some artists may well have agreed that representations of heaven, the big payoff for good behavior, should not distract us into thinking our reward will be sensual. Naked images threaten to seize our imaginations and hold them captive, making religious devotion a tiring mental sideshow. Beyond that risk, Catholic eyes could not bear the sight of the Virgin naked, nor could they understand any depiction of heaven which excluded her. Curiously enough, even those painters who clothe the saints will leave the damned naked. This is unfortunate, for the damned rarely seem to be at all attractive (Signorelli paints with exception here).

Love will rule in a heaven from which lust will be absent. Love differs from lust, Augustine explains in *On the Christian Doctrine,* in the ends to which each leads: "I call love [*caritas*] the activity of the soul that aims at enjoying God for His own sake as well as oneself and one's neighbor with reference to God. Lust [*cupiditas*], on the other hand, aims at enjoying oneself and one's neighbor and any object whatsoever without reference to God."[11]

No one will work in heaven—everyone will be in retirement. There will be no plants or animals, Aquinas tells us. According to one scholar's interpretation of Augustine, saints will not talk to one another: they already know everything, so what is there to talk about?[12] Plenty, if we choose Dante's *Paradiso* as our model instead. There is much conversation in Dante's paradise, so who can say for sure?

Two histories of the place, *Heaven: A History* and *A History of Heaven: The Singing Silence,* have argued that heaven evolves as mankind does. This in itself would be a fairly pedestrian thesis, but these richly detailed studies make for lively reading. They demonstrate the unwieldy difficulty of covering the details of heaven we find in the three major monotheistic traditions—Judaism, Christianity, and Islam. One emerges from these studies impressed by the energy our forebears have devoted to exploring what lies ahead.[13]

No talk, no work, no pets, no sex—Chateaubriand's worry about eternal boredom seems reasonable. And yet Catholics yearn for their heaven, just as Protestants, Muslims, and some Jews do theirs.

THE OPPOSITE OF HELL

As is often the case with learning, we come to understand one thing through examination of its opposite. Early on, we use the example of a woman to understand manhood, the taste of sweetness to grasp sour, and night to appreciate day. Hell, the opposite of heaven, only increases our desire for paradise.

What are we to make of the fact that Christians have focused on hell to a greater extent than Jews or Muslims? In any event, Christian development of hell might be a function of either morally suspect enthusiasm (because hell is where our enemies will be sent) or gripping fear (because we don't want hell to happen to us). To be sure, we find references to hell in Judaism (specifically, Gehenna, the place of fire), although nothing so carefully thought out as what we find in Christianity.[14]

Christians conceptualize heaven in eternal terms—once you make it in, you never have to worry about failing again. Whereas hell is similarly immutable in most Christian theology (once you're damned, you're damned for eternity), it isn't for Mormons or Muslims. In the Mormon and Muslim afterlife, those who are suffering in a state resembling hell are free to liberate themselves gradually. Even after death, Mormons will continue proselytizing the misguided. Once properly converted, newly enlightened souls may join paradise.

Much more can be said of hell, but I introduce it here only as a way of thinking about heaven and as a motivation to get there. Hell emerges as a confusing doctrine in Catholicism. Particularly in places like chapters 12 and 13 of the gospel of Luke, Jesus scares us with dramatic references to the horror and finality of hell. He admonishes:

> that we fear God, because he has the power to cast us into hell;
> that those who blaspheme against the Holy Spirit will never be forgiven;
> that those who store up treasure in this world, instead of heaven, will perish;
> that many will try to enter heaven and will fail.

Catholics may puzzle over hell, specifically because of information handed down from Fatima. The Virgin Mary appeared episodically to a group of young children in Fatima, Portugal in the early twentieth century. The children who listened to the Virgin were allowed a glimpse of hell, a glimpse from which they suffered traumatic effects. This is not to say that the children actually saw anyone in hell (as readers of Dante's *Inferno* do). Jesus never actually said that anyone was in hell or would be sent there. Following Jesus, the Catholic Church acknowledges only the *possibility* that people may suffer eternally in hell.[15] When it comes to heaven, though, the Vatican does not hold back. People are there now, it is said, and the point of canonization is to publicize arrival in heaven.[16]

WHAT IT TAKES TO GET TO HEAVEN

Jews, Christians, and Muslims all revere the Hebrew Bible, often referred to as the Old Testament. It is in the Hebrew Bible that we find the all-important Ten Commandments, the best known distillation of moral conduct in the West. Christians share with Muslims some sense of minimum requirements to pass through the heavenly gates, and both rely on the Ten Commandments. Jews, on the other hand, have generally been leery of the very idea of qualification standards.

In the New Testament, Christ responds to a man who inquires about what it takes to get to heaven by simplifying all requirements as follows: love God with all your mind, strength, soul, and heart; and love your neighbor as yourself (Matthew 19:16-19). About one thousand years later, the distinguished Muslim philosopher Walid ibn Ahmad ibn Rushd (1126-1198), known in Europe as Averroës, warned that the acceptance of certain truths was essential to salvation—a novel view in the Islamic world. These are the truths he enumerated:

> The existence of God as Creator and Sustainer of the world.
>
> The Unity of God.
>
> The knowledge, power, will, hearing, seeing, and speech attributed to God throughout the Koran.
>
> The uniqueness and incomparability of God, clearly asserted in Koran 42:9: "There is nothing like unto him."
>
> The creation of the world by God.
>
> The validity of prophecy.
>
> The justice of God.
>
> The resurrection of the body on the Last Day.[17]

To obtain salvation, believers must embrace each of these doctrines. It is worth noting that the Koran contains these truths, that they are not the speculation of some authoritative body (such as an assembly of mullahs or the Roman Catholic Curia).[18]

Ibn Rushd inspired the influential Jewish philosopher and Talmudist Rabbi Moses ibn Maimon (1135-1204), known as Maimonides. Averroës (1126) and Maimonides (1135) were both born in Cordoba; these two influential scholars defended human freedom, albeit from different perspectives. Ironically, both died in exile: first Averroës in 1198 in Marrakech, and then Maimonides in 1204 in Egypt.

The canonical Jewish thinker's philosophical text, *The Guide for the Perplexed,* also includes a host of basic requirements the faithful must meet if they are to gain salvation. Maimonides's list closely resembles his predecessor's:

The existence of God.

The unity of God.

The incorporeality of God.

The eternity of God.

The prohibition of idolatry.

The validity of prophecy.

Moses was the greatest of the prophets.

The divine origin of truth.

The eternal validity of the Torah.

God knows the deeds of men

He judges them accordingly.

He will send a Messiah.

The resurrection of the dead.[19]

The idea of a threshold, of certain minimum requirements one must meet, was a peculiar innovation in Judaism that never became entirely accepted. Even today, the idea of being "saved" carries little meaning in Judaism. And yet, it must be true that Jews possess a vivid sense of a sacred threshold as well, particularly as regards circumcision. In the book of Genesis, God establishes a pact with Abraham and makes the mortal promise to honor their covenant by seeing to it that every male in every generation be circumcised on the eighth day (Genesis 17:10-13). Keeping the covenant, if not explicitly qualifying for heaven, began with attention to a sexual organ.

Striking a notably sympathetic tone, Maimonides broadened the idea of threshold: "The righteous of all peoples have a part in the world to come."[20] Centuries ahead of his time, Maimonides illustrates ecumenical goodwill. The Christian tipping point, endlessly elaborated throughout successive centuries, always included recognizing Jesus as the son of

God, the essential vehicle to salvation (John 6:51-58). This criterion refused to budge until the late twentieth century, when Vatican II eliminated it for humanitarian reasons. This is a point to which I'll return again and again.

If a threshold specifies only the minimum a believer must do, the picture remains dangerously incomplete. For certain acts or attitudes may disqualify an infinite number of good works. Saint Paul warns us to avoid his own version of the big sins. Make no mistake about it, he exhorts, heaven is off limits to the following classes of people (1 Cor 6:9-10):

1. fornicators
2. idolaters
3. adulterers
4. the effeminate (Challoner-Rheims version) / male prostitutes *(Revised Standard Version)*
5. sodomites
6. thieves
7. the greedy
8. drunkards
9. revilers / gossips
10. robbers

Why does Paul include the effeminate on his list? Sissy boys beware. The good news for effeminate men is that the *Revised Standard Version* has superseded the Challoner-Rheims version, the rendering used by Catholics for centuries. Modernity has made life easier for effeminate men, because a sin has apparently been lost in translation. (Much more about this will be said later.)

Despite Christ's handy simplification of leading a moral life and remaining a candidate for eternal life, Christians argue amongst themselves about getting the rules right, and a separate book remains to be written about precisely how these visions differ among Christian sects. I'll continue to stick with Catholicism. Catholics must acknowl-

edge the authority of the pope and accept papal *ex cathedra* pronouncements as obligatory dogma (so far, there have been only two: the
Immaculate Conception of the Blessed Virgin Mother and her
Assumption into heaven in lieu of bodily death and decay). Catholics
must endorse the Nicene Creed, to which the Congregation for the
Doctrine of the Faith has added clauses in the last two decades. These
clauses profess general submission of intellect to the extraordinary and
ordinary Magisterium of the church (that is, teaching authority), so
that much more is included than just the extraordinary, infallible
statements contemplated by Vatican I (1869-1870). Catholics enjoy
freedom of conscience, to be sure, but each individual conscience must
submit to the infallible church, which also disciplines the enthusiasm
of charismatics.

This truncated synopsis of what Catholics must do in order to attain
heaven neglects much. I haven't even mentioned purgatory, a Catholic
way station to which some souls are assigned en route to heaven. Early
Christians smiled on a notion of a second chance at heaven—purgatory
accepted the souls of those who had fallen short of the excellence required
for heaven, but who deserved better than hell. Calvin asserted that
purgatory is a deadly fiction of Satan, one that "nullifies the cross of
Christ." The later Lutheran and Reformed rejection of purgatory raised
the psychological stakes of salvation: whereas Catholics could console
themselves and others with the idea of a "second chance" realm, early
Protestants could not.

Purgatory seems to pose a logical problem, one Shakespeare gives
voice to in *Twelfth Night*. The beautiful young Olivia mourns the death
of her brother and dismisses an intrusive, passing fool as unworthy of
serious conversation. He challenges her:

CLOWN: Good madonna, give me leave to prove you a fool.
OLIVIA: Can you do it?

The fool's trap centers on purgatory, we learn.

CLOWN: Good madonna, why mourn'st thou?

OLIVIA: Good fool, for my brother's death.

CLOWN: I think his soul is in hell, madonna.

OLIVIA: I know his soul is in heaven, fool.

CLOWN: The more fool, madonna, to mourn for your brother's soul,
           being in heaven.[21]

The clown then pretends to summon men to take away Olivia, who is proven the fool. He raises the question of why we pray for the dead: those in heaven hardly need our prayers, and those in hell can't be helped. It must be because of purgatory that we pray.

Various Catholic societies have left us with accounts, some of them quite idiosyncratic, of what it takes to get out of purgatory. The prayers of the faithful on earth can help lessen the sentence. So can horrible physical pain, medieval Spaniards believed. They feared easy deaths, for they believed that each hour of pain before death would lessen by a year the sentence in purgatory. The creative idea that illness could martyr a person testifies to the zeal with which these Spaniards wanted to reach heaven. In this desire, they have hardly been alone.[22]

There is such a thing as going beyond the call of duty: martyrdom exemplifies this industriousness. Preparation for death, and thus for heaven, dominated the stories of early martyrs. This preoccupation remained important in late medieval spirituality, even though there were few occasions for martyrdom apart from the Crusades. According to Thomas à Kempis (ca. 1379-1471), all Christians were obliged to stand ready to sacrifice their lives for Christ, just as the martyrs had done:

> How shouldest thou sinful creature think that thou shouldest go to heaven
> by any other way than by the plain, right and high king's way, that is to
> say the way of the cross. . . . Now since the leader of life with all his martyrs
> have passed by the way of tribulation and the cross, who so ever intend to
> come to heaven without the way of tribulation and the cross they err from
> the right way, for all the way of this mortal life is full of miseries and crosses
> of tribulation.[23]

Of course, one only becomes a martyr if an infidel threatens to take your life. What becomes of the soul of the infidel who makes martyrs?

In 1964, the Second Vatican Council proclaimed in "Dogmatic Constitution of the Church" (*Lumen Gentium*) that non-Christians who, through no fault of their own, do not know Christ but who nonetheless seek his truth, can go to heaven. The next year, the Council addressed the chances of non-Christians getting to heaven in the "Declaration on the Relationship of the Church to Non-Christian Religions" (*Nostra Aetate*). Here again, we see the Vatican moving in a bold new direction. According to *Nostra Aetate,* non-Christians can find salvation, even though their religions are not on an equal footing with Christianity. Error mixes with truth in certain non-Christian religions, and so these other faiths have to be purified. What is remarkable about *Nostra Aetate* is that it concedes a kernel of truth in a few other religions and so reaches for common ground.

The German Jesuit theologian Karl Rahner (1904-1984) had coined the phrase "anonymous Christian" in a work published in Germany in 1963, *Hearers of the Word.* Rahner meant to show through this term that non-Christians who live morally share something sacred with Christians. This creative solution seems to suggest that Jews and Muslims are basically Christian, even though they don't realize or admit it.

Of course, Jews and Muslims may object to Rahner's honorific, such as it is. In any event, Catholics are hardly alone in restricting heaven to their own kind, and Rahner's attempt to shoehorn in the spiritually different no doubt reflects genuine goodwill. For the record, the Mormon belief about entering heaven is no less harsh than the Catholic. And various Protestant leaders have gone on record, particularly in the twentieth century, as saying that Catholics do not even qualify as Christians. Southern Baptists, for example, bar the heavenly doors to Catholics.

Pope Urban II had already launched the First Crusade of 1096-99 by the time Ibn Rushd and Maimonides formulated their respective lists.

Many Muslims and Jews already lived in the shadow of Christian contempt. By Augustine's time, Jewish communities had prompted Christians to wonder whether toleration was in order. And anti-Muslim polemic started shortly after the arrival of Muslim armies in Christian lands. From the time the Crusaders conquered Jerusalem in 1099, European Christians regarded Jews and Muslims as the enemies of God. This psychological mindset must have colored Christian notions of the acts and attitudes God demanded.

The three moralists I've surveyed purposely skipped over details in order to simplify the criteria for pleasing God. What's missing from any list—Jewish, Christian, or Muslim—may have been deliberately overlooked or simply implied. Christian doctrine would also include the Augustinian notion of baptism, an essential step to salvation. Just as notably absent from the Jewish and Muslim summaries is mention of sex. Ibn Rushd and Maimonides seem either not to have known the work of Augustine or to have deliberately discounted his sexual warnings. The absence of sex may well have surprised educated Christians, who had already grown accustomed to think of sex as a dangerous disqualifier.

WILL THERE BE SEX IN HEAVEN?

Lovers dancing beneath the moon wish the night could last forever, implying that they believe themselves already to be in heaven (in fact, it's often just lust). The irony is that what they ache to do to one another is prohibited in heaven. German director Wim Wenders spun an enchanting 1987 film out of an angel's sexual frustration and subsequent return to earth to pursue a fleshy woman (*Der Himmel über Berlin*, translated as *Wings of Desire*).

There is no such thing as a marriage made in heaven (Matthew 22:30), unless one thinks of oneself as marrying God at death (God is himself both agape and eros, according to 1 John 4:8). Taking religious vows in Roman Catholicism conjures up the classic marriage drama, and nuns have long referred to themselves as "brides of Christ." Saint Teresa of Avila (d. 1582) and Saint Thérèse Martin de Lisieux (d. 1897) both described their burning desire for union with Christ in diaries. Of the various examples men have left us, one of the most haunting must be the poem "Batter My Heart, Three Person'd God" by the English metaphysical poet John Donne (d. 1631) in which Donne beseeches God to "ravish" him.

Just what do religious people want from God? Ecstatic union, achieved through prayers here on earth, doesn't exactly amount to sex. The emotions arising from the two experiences seem to overlap, though. While in heaven, souls will likely fixate on God. But with so many comely bodies hovering about, it only seems natural to inquire about our relationship to other saints. The answer to the question of whether there will be sex in heaven depends on whom you ask. Mormons and Muslims maintain they will enjoy sex in the afterlife. (But notably, Muslim women will not have sex in heaven; Muslim men will have all their sex with *houris,* voluptuous angels.) For Catholics and Protestants, the idea of sex in heaven is nearly unthinkable.[24]

Children will continue to be born in the Mormon spirit world; they will age and die as well, but without suffering or pain. "While the details of this eternal reproduction are not known, it is suspected that the residents of the celestial heaven reproduce 'after the same manner that we have here' but without sorrow, pain, or distress. Since the Latter-Day Saints believe that God has a body and is not spirit, it makes sense that the gods [or saints, in roughly Catholic terms] reproduce in a human manner."[25] Only Mormon marriages will continue into the next realm, for ordinary civil and other religious marriages expire at death ("until death do us part"). Only the properly married can attain the highest rung of heaven, only they can become gods. Those who lived as celibates in this world, indeed all unmarried persons, can only become angels in the next world. Who wants to settle for being an angel? Particularly if you can't have sex?

Sex will take place in Muslim heaven, but not between spouses. The point of sex in Muslim paradise *(Janna)* is not reproduction but pleasure. Men will enjoy the services of seductive attendants who conjure up images of modern-day Playboy bunnies (the *houris*). According to Koranic commentator Al-Ash'ari (d. 935), "Each time we sleep with a *houri* we find her virgin. Besides, the penis of the Elected never softens. The erection is eternal; the sensation that you feel each time you make love is utterly delicious and out of this world and were you to experience it in this world you would faint. Each chosen one will marry seventy *houris,* besides the women he married on earth, and all will have appestising vaginas."[26] Muslim attitudes toward sex here on earth seem similarly enthusiastic. To please God, Muslim men may abstain from sex with their wives. However, the sacred significance of intercourse punctuates this dry period:

> An *īlā* is an oath by which the husband makes his wife unlawful for a given period. The Quran accepts the validity of such an oath, but limits its duration to four months, at the end of which the husband who does not return to the marriage bed, is *ipso facto* separated definitively from his wife.
>
> This is another aspect of *nikāh,* the obligation to satisfy one's spouse. *Nikāh* and unconsummated marriage are mutually exclusive. Abstinence of a hundred and twenty days is a maximum not to be exceeded in any circumstances.
>
> Sexual intercourse is one of the pillars of *nikāh.* What is now understood is that the parallel between the sacral and the sexual is beyond question.[27]

The Muslim idea that people deserve sex applies both in this life and the next, although women are owed none after death.

Could it make sense for a Christian to envy Muslims a heaven in which sex takes place? Consider the following literary attempt of a man to seduce a woman in this life. He refers to the Muslim afterlife perhaps to recommend haste to her—"we Christians won't be able to do it after death, so we'd better get going." Thinking of his mistress, John Donne reasons in the poem "On Going to Bed":

> Now off with those shoes, and then softly tread
> In this love's hallow'd temple, this soft bed.

In such white robes, heaven's angels us'd to be
Receiv'd by men; thou angel bring'st with thee
A heaven like Mahomet's paradise; and though
Ill spirits walk in white, we eas'ly know,
By this these angels from an evil sprite,
Those set our hairs, but these our flesh upright. (*Elegy XIX* 17-24)

That a Christian woman might be seduced through an appeal to Muslim theology seems unlikely. That a Christian man might regret the restrictiveness of his own moral tradition seems more plausible. Whether anyone would convert from a restrictive tradition to a less restrictive one raises far-reaching questions about personal values and how individuals choose beliefs. Such a conversion could happen; we'll see in subsequent chapters that sex can tip the scales.

In the Muslim paradise the righteous feast with one thousand beautiful women. Not in the Christian paradise. For most Christians, there certainly will not be sex in heaven, although there will be plenty of people who've had sex. To the extent that the point of sex is the reproduction of life, sex would be wholly unnecessary in heaven. To the extent that sex satisfies intrinsically sinful desire (that is, lust), sex would have no place in heaven. Because no one in heaven will be having sex, we should strive to follow their example: on earth as it is in heaven.

The irony here is plain: whereas lovers here on earth frequently compare the act of physical union to paradise, there is no sex in paradise. And so it makes no sense for a Christian to envy a Muslim his paradise, for paradise enchants Christians in part because lust dies there. If it turned out that a Christian had never even considered the possibility of having sex in heaven, he might be surprised and delighted to entertain the thought. A Christian who enjoyed sexual arousal, as opposed to one who yearned to escape it, might well feel envy.

We seem to know more about the next world than ever before, for people who emerge from near-death experiences come back to life and report what they have seen. To date no one has reported spying sex in paradise. Maybe it's just a matter of time.

Protestant writers, particularly Emanuel Swedenborg (d. 1772), worked to broaden the Christian view of heaven in the eighteenth century. Influenced by the Romantics, some thinkers reasoned that heaven might include lovemaking. As long as it happened between husbands and wives, some Protestants seemed to come around to the idea. William Blake, for example, favored the idea that people carried their passions with them into heaven; he condemned people who denied their own passion and crushed the passion of others.[28]

In sum, religious believers here on earth differ over sex in heaven. How God views sex—whether as a necessary evil, a harmless pastime, or the summit of pleasure—will become clear once we glimpse paradise ourselves. Until then, we continue to worry about getting there, which is to say nowadays that we worry about sex.

SEX, THE DEAL BREAKER

Sexual sins are not like other sins. Aquinas allowed stealing when times got tough, despite a commandment not to steal. In times of famine and poverty, Aquinas argued, property becomes common. The poor man may take from the rich man in order to survive. No matter how tough things got, though, women are never allowed to dabble in prostitution, which was forbidden. Sins of the body were a case apart.

Catholic schoolchildren study and celebrate the lives of saints. As David Herlihy has noted, "Saints' lives typically express abhorrence at sexual relations, and seem never to depict a happy, holy marriage, with normally frequent intercourse."[29] The Catholic high school (in Hagerstown, Maryland) nearest to my own home town was named after a twelve-year-old Italian girl, Maria Goretti (d. 1902), who had died some years earlier after choosing death over rape. Rape is not the victim's fault, and a teacher or parent might recommend enduring the horror in order to remain among the living. In any event, the lesson I internalized as a child was that people who avoid sex deserve our admiration. Other saint stories, having nothing to do with rape, will communicate the general unpleasantness of the carnal act. Sexual intercourse caused Saint Francesca of Rome (d. 1440) to vomit, to the point of throwing up blood. And so on.

Modern critics have taken to portraying Augustine as the original spoil sport of sex, but it is unfair to pin all the blame on him. Writing at the beginning of the third century, Clement of Alexandria (d. ca. 215) insisted that intercourse take place only for the begetting of children. He preceded by a century Augustine's disapproval of taking pleasure in the sensual delight of sex. The late second-century church father Tertullian took a similarly dour view of sex. Objecting to the Roman practice of punishing early Christian women by forcing them to work in brothels, he wrote in a rhetorical address, "In condemning a Christian woman to a brothel instead of to death by being mauled by a lion, you were admitting that to us such a fate is more terrible than any punishment and any death."[30] Such a remark might have surprised Christians who had heard Tertullian refer to women as "the Devil's gateway." It doesn't take a psychiatrist to spot the ambivalence here.

In sexual attitudes, we can see Christianity starting to distinguish itself more and more from its parent, Judaism. Certainly, religious Jews would have found brothel work repulsive. They were more willing to smile on marital intercourse than early Christians, though. In Judaism, moral focus rests more on purity than on sex (although sex is certainly important). Women could not enter the temple while menstruating; after menstruating, they had to visit the mikvah, or ritual purification bath, before returning. We find this same aversion to menstruating women in Islam and Christianity.[31] Despite the abiding importance of ritual purity in Judaism, the parent religion never valued virginity as the Christian offspring did. Sexual renunciation marked the higher path even when diocesan clergy could, and did, marry (monks and nuns had always been celibate, in theory at least) for roughly the first eleven centuries of Catholicism. In 1954 Pope Pius XII issued the encyclical *Sacra Virginitas* which reiterated the traditional Catholic teaching that celibacy is a higher calling than marriage. This is somewhat surprising, given that marriage enjoys the status of a sacrament in Catholic theology, whereas virginity does not. In any event, those really interested in getting to the Catholic heaven are well advised to remain virgins.[32] Luther regularly faulted the Catholic Church for declaring virginity superior to the married state.

Sexual purity and virginity matter to Catholics a lot. In their churches, Roman Catholics tend to use candles made of beeswax. The traditional reason might have been that bees produce offspring without having sex, according to popular belief: "in this they were symbols of the church, married to God alone and prolific in its children and in the graces it provides for them."[33] Catholics, for whom the unchaste thoughts or sexual acts of an individual can defile a building, have pressed purity far. A devoutly Catholic husband and wife attending Vatican II (1962-1965), Pat and Patty Crowley, were forbidden from staying together in a seminary, even though there were no seminarians present.[34] While perhaps not entirely representative, this example is hardly extreme. Sex, even permissible intercourse between a man and wife, poses a threat to the integrity of a place. Anyone interested in researching the ethics of fantasy, of our interior life, could hardly do better than to scour the gold mine of Roman Catholic theology, particularly the work of moral theologians (for example, Bernard Häring, the most influential moral theologian of the twentieth century).

Other examples seem as fascinating as they are weird. Saint Thérèse of Lisieux, notable in part for the erotic dimension of her prayers, quickly became one of the most celebrated saints of the twentieth century. Her parents, Louis and Azélie Guérin Martin, are now being looked over by the saint-makers in Rome. Saint Thérèse's parents remained celibate for nine months after their marriage, until a priest convinced them that their vocation was to raise children for God. All of their surviving children became nuns. Despite having given five daughters to God (that is, to a cloistered Carmelite convent), these parents might stand a better chance of being declared saints had they never married at all. The Vatican squirms at the thought of canonizing the sexually active.

Rome does, however, embrace the sexually contrite. On May 15, 2002, for example, Pope John Paul II oversaw a ceremony in Saint Peter's Square for five hundred women, each of whom was swearing off prostitution for good. The harlot saints demand mention here, and they make for unusual contemplation. Debauched women could still make it to heaven, but only if they renounced their sex lives in dramatic terms: "Above all others, Mary Magdalene is the prototype of the penitent whore, but she has colleagues in this particular brand of hagiography, which so neatly condenses Christianity's fear of women, its identification of physical beauty with temptation, and its practice of bodily mortification."[35] The harlot saints came in handy during the Reformation, when early Protestants challenged the validity of the sacrament of confession and questioned whether sins really can be forgiven. Fourth-century Saint Mary of Egypt became a poster child for the cause. Having lived as a prostitute from the ages of 12 to 17, she wanted to make a pilgrimage to the Holy Land. Having no money, she struck a deal with the ship's crew—she would provide all of them with sexual services in exchange for free passage.[36] Once in the Holy Land, she melted before a statue of the Virgin, kissed a relic of the True Cross, and set off for the desert, where she lived as a hermit for forty-seven years. A priest came across her one day and witnessed her walking on water and levitating. Who could doubt the holiness of a woman who walks on water? It is not hard to understand the appeal of Saint Mary of Egypt to subsequent generations of Catholics: her lapses humanized her. Like Augustine, though, she turned her back on bodily pleasures and subsequently became a useful vehicle for church leaders with an ascetic agenda.

Prostitutes may well have rejoiced over religious intervention in their professions. It was the church that openly opposed popular prejudice against these women, even promoting the cause of taking a prostitute as a wife. Pope Innocent III (1198-1216) not merely permitted those marriages but "promised spiritual rewards for men who married loose women, provided of course that the husbands of former prostitutes kept close watch over their wives to make sure that they remained sexually faithful and did not return to their wanton ways."[37] Perhaps in answer to Innocent III's call, Europeans would sometimes devote an entire convent to reforming prostitutes. Such havens sprang up in the thirteenth century, the most successful of which was the Order of St. Mary

Magdalene (whose members were often called White Ladies). Ludovica Torelli, countess of Guastalla, consecrated her widowhood to God and founded the Angelicas in Milan in 1549. She and the sisters who eventually joined her supervised houses for repentant prostitutes in Vicenza.[38] Such places of refuge gave rise to secular equivalents.[39]

In ways both obvious and obscure, the church has quite literally transformed individual lives. Prostitutes make an excellent example. A Roman museum, the Crypta Balbi, offers an unusual glimpse of the church's beneficence. In the middle of the sixteenth century, on Ignatius Loyola's initiative, the area around Santa Maria Domine delle Rose was transformed to provide space for a new building designed to host the daughters of Roman prostitutes. In 1559, due to a papal bull by Pius IV, the Confraternita delle Vergini Miserabili di S. Caterina (Confraternity of Santa Caterina's Pitiful Virgins) was created. Its main task was to protect the "spinsters," but the association also wanted to get them married. To that end, the confraternity provided recovering streetwalkers with a dowry and taught them domestic skills. They were paraded around the city annually on the first of May and the twenty-fifth of November in the hope that someone would propose to them. Sadly, these hopes were almost invariably dashed, but who could fail to find this example of the church's generosity moving?

Surely the lives of most prostitutes were dreadful. Catholics deserve real credit for intervening in a dismal cycle. But the real lesson here is that the church will forgive our sexual transgressions. The cost of forgiveness, though, may strike some as unreasonably high. Even if priests and nuns did levy a high price (her sex life) every time they rehabilitated a streetwalker, prostitutes were no doubt better off. Rescuing a prostitute invariably creates a job vacancy, yet the church provided a valuable social service to women (and likely to men as well) whose names we'll never know.

Any attempt to portray sex as a deal breaker, in Catholicism specifically or Christian thinking in general, must attend to reconciliation, which has a robust history of its own. Depending on the Christian church in question, forgiveness is possible (Calvinism is an exception).

No matter what you've done, you can be forgiven. In Catholicism, priests hold the power to bind or forgive sins; in Protestantism, individuals request forgiveness directly of God. The point is that you can wipe the slate clean, once you renounce sincerely what you've done and perform some penance.

A rich background of theological detail looms over this generalization and threatens to subvert any pat summary. And a myriad of sociological variables presents another daunting obstacle, for popular beliefs can vary widely according to time, place, culture, and class. In crude terms, heaven is the reward waiting for those who have followed the rules. God makes a deal with people, and the terms of the deal are more or less straightforward. Because God loves his people so very much, he grants them free will. He then moves to the sidelines of life, watches, and waits. As people die, he judges how well they have followed the rules and compensates them accordingly.

But some rules are more important than others, and some infractions are consequently graver than others. Catholics prize both heaven and celibacy more than Jews. For Catholics, sex is indeed a deal breaker: if a person steps over the line, he forfeits God's favor. The deal is off, unless one repents. We cannot defend Catholic preoccupation with sex by claiming that Catholicism remains faithful to the Old Testament in a way that Protestantism, Judaism, and Islam have not. But neither can we say that obedience to the New Testament explicitly guides Catholic decisions about, say, priestly celibacy or the ordination of women.

It's not so difficult to understand why Catholics have long prized virginity. Well into the twentieth century, an unmarried pregnant woman was a ruined woman. No one would marry her (think of the anxiety of Joseph in the story of Jesus's birth and the enduring relevance of this concern). But now that women in the West enjoy an unprecedented sexual liberty (thanks in large part to the birth control pill), the old rules about sex seem outmoded. True, we might still emphasize the intrinsic value of sexual purity. But given how many other strictures have fallen by the wayside (for example, lending money at interest, eating meat on Fridays, covering a woman's head in church), it is hard to understand the renewed enthusiasm for sexual purity. Perhaps the crescendo of sexual liberty, manifested in part by incessant talk about sex, accounts for the Vatican's vigilance.

The practical risks of sexual sins came back into vivid focus in the late 1980s and early 1990s, when American Catholic bishops debated whether to allow the distribution of condoms (to heterosexuals) in order to stem the spread of AIDS. Initially, the bishops decided it was morally acceptable; under a subsequent firestorm of criticism, they relented and declared that, much as they regretted the potential loss of lives, they feared even more the loss of souls. The use of condoms or contraceptives qualifies as a mortal sin in Catholicism, and, in making a pronouncement that enraged many Americans, the bishops strongly implied that people could indeed be excluded from heaven because they had used condoms.

Sexual transgressions receive more attention and inspire more fear than other sins, in part because of the mythical might of the libido. In 1961 the assumption that young men needed sexual intercourse led an American professor to examine the "problem" of male virgins, who, he claimed to document, experienced teasing and a lack of support from family and friends.[40] What if it could be proven that young men, and perhaps young women as well, think about sex constantly and suffer not only physical frustration but teasing when they swear off sexual activity? Virginity would then seem all the more extraordinary, and expecting it of young people would seem perhaps perverse.

Until they can bring themselves to defy their elders, obedient adolescents whose parents want them to grow up Catholic swim against the tide. Parents and children alike turn for support to Mary, about whom more books have been written than any other woman in the Western hemisphere. Catholic reverence for the virginity of Mary manifests itself across virtually the entire spectrum of practicing Catholics and fuels the threat sex poses to piety in Catholic culture. As former priest Eugene Kennedy has written: "Any effort to explore Mary as a sexual being, or even to open the possibility that this eradication of generative sexuality in her life may have wounded her reality and the sexual sensibility of the untold generations who have called her blessed, would be rejected angrily by institutional officials who would judge this to be sacrilegious and heretical."[41]

Kennedy is no doubt correct. There is simply no chance that the Vatican will consider the possibility of certain sex lives (the Virgin's or her son's) anytime soon. Some Catholics bristle at this intransigence, just as they do while watching Isabella refuse to sleep with the king in order to save her brother's life in Shakespeare's *Measure for Measure*. Even though forgiveness is possible for virtually every sin, certain transgressions still strike more fear than others in the hearts of Catholics who hope for heaven.

ARE THERE JEWS IN CATHOLIC HEAVEN?

There didn't used to be Jews in Catholic heaven but now there are, according to Catholic theologians. According to some, the heroes and heroines of the Hebrew Bible (or "Old Testament"), all of whom predated Jesus, number among the Catholic saints. Catholics view the moral figures in Hebrew Scriptures as early Catholics: Jews who eagerly awaited the arrival of their messiah. Jews who lived after Jesus are in another category: it is these Jews who were barred from heaven because they ignored the arrival of Jesus, the Catholic messiah.

For nearly two millennia, salvation came through membership in the universal church, outside of which there was no hope. In the anti-Semitic play *The Merchant of Venice*, we find several references to the question of whether there are Jews in Catholic heaven. Referring to Jessica, the daughter of Shylock, Lorenzo remarks to Gratiano and Salarino:

> If e'er the Jew her father come to heaven
> It will be for his gentle daughter's sake. (II.4)

Later in the play, Lancelot tells Jessica that the sins of the father are to be laid upon his children. Therefore, her one hope for salvation is that another man, presumably a Christian, impregnated her mother (according to Jewish belief, religious identity is passed on through the mother, not the father). Judiciously, Jessica responds by chirping that then the sins of her mother would consequently have been visited on her. Jessica's way out of this logical impasse:

> I shall be saved by my husband.
> He hath made me a Christian. (III.5)

To the extent that we can rely on a beloved play as a reliable gauge of popular belief in sixteenth-century England, Catholics did not anticipate meeting Jews in heaven. Lutherans certainly didn't either, as Martin Luther's 1543 anti-Semitic piece "On Jews and Their Lies" would indicate.[42] Dante placed Abraham and Moses in limbo, a place that is emphatically not hell. And according to various Christian theologies, Abraham, Moses, David, Elijah, and many other historical Jewish religious figures may be in Catholic heaven. These luminaries and others (for example, Lazarus and the contrite thief crucified next to Jesus) entered God's kingdom upon the Crucifixion. The Crucifixion in a sense "Christianized" good Jews who lived before Christ. But did the Jews want to be? Catholics have named churches after a number of these "pre-Christians," and it is not so surprising to find a church named Saint Moses, Saint Job, or Saint Daniel the Prophet. That Catholics have converted Jews such as Moses and Elijah troubles many Jewish people.[43]

Among all those groups traditionally excluded from Catholic heaven, Jews have been the most salient.[44] For generations, Holy Week Masses included priestly references to "the perfidious Jews." A recent surge of scholarly attention to Catholic anti-Semitism has saddened many contemporary Catholics, even as they feel more committed to a church that can admit its mistakes.[45] Given all the persecution and cruelty Jews have endured, Catholic heaven may well seem the least of their worries. And yet heaven has been the source of the problem.

Susan Zuccotti has judiciously summed up what she calls "the Church's traditional position regarding the Jews" as follows: "The Jews are in error, and profoundly guilty. Despite being dangerous enemies of the church, they merit charity and attempts at conversion. They must be punished for their spiritual offenses but not persecuted for political or nationalistic reasons."[46] This is dangerous and unlikable sentiment, but although Catholics may dispute parts of it, this interpretation of the traditional Catholic position seems fair. However, Catholics can rightfully point to Vatican II, particulary the document *Nostra Aetate*, as an important turning point in Jewish-Catholic relations. Although it does not explicitly say that Jews can get to heaven without becoming Christians first, it is implied in the text. Noting that the salvation of the church is mystically prefigured in the exodus of the Jews from "the land of bondage," the text states that Jesus reconciled Jews and Christians on the cross and "made them one in himself." *Nostra Aetate* goes on to declare anti-Semitism a repugnant sin and to denounce all discrimination against Jews. Although Hindus and Muslims also gain support in the document, Jews stand in the spotlight.

The scapegoating that Jews have long endured continues, and some Christians would still exclude them from salvation. This is not really so surprising, for any claim to truth will necessarily involve denials of competing claims. So long as they remain Christians of any stripe, followers of Jesus presumably doubt that salvation can be as readily obtained outside their own religious society. This is a bracing fact of life in a pluralistic society—some of the people around us think we're headed for hell. It is difficult to say that Jews exclude Christians in a similar way, for Jewish heaven appears much less punitive.

It is surely impossible to summarize two millennia of Christian anti-Semitism, yet the dispute over heaven comes as close to explaining it as anything. It may well be that Christians genuinely wanted to "save" Jews (not all Christians, though—not those Protestants who see the full return of Jews to Israel as a prerequisite for the second coming of Christ). It may also be that Christians resented what they took to be Jewish scorn for an ill-conceived heaven.

The extravagantly abstract gesture of excluding Jews from heaven played itself out in terribly real ways—pogroms, exile, ghettoes, and mass executions. Remarkably, Catholics are now explicitly forbidden from holding Jews corporately responsible for the death of Christ, as a direct result of *Lumen Gentium* and *Nostra Aetate*. In 1964, then, the Vatican began what amounts to an extraordinary *volte face* in its relationship to Judaism. In 1969 the first man landed on the moon, some five years after the first Jews had made it to heaven. In chapter 4 we will see more evidence of rapprochement, when Pope John Paul II explicitly exhorts Jews to embrace and celebrate their Jewishness.

WRESTLING FOR THE KINGDOM

I have said that getting into heaven requires following certain rules and meeting certain criteria. The devil is in the details.

Speculation about heaven lifts us out of ourselves and drops us in confusion. Logical reasoning helps us make sense of the place: heaven, for which the heroic saints struggled, is being in the presence of God, is sharing his life. And since God is love, heaven must be love. Like the dancer who becomes the dance, God becomes his home. Were God to leave heaven, paradise would be an empty name. Where God went, we would want to follow. The everlasting life of the party, God could make a heaven of hell.

We find far-reaching disagreement between accounts of the afterlife. What any of those will look like and who will rule it may strike atheists as ridiculous questions, akin to arguing over how tall a unicorn is or how many angels can dance on the head of a pin. One reason for exploring any version of paradise is to see whether the underlying religion makes sense on its own terms. Given the enormity of the comparisons involved, I have limited myself considerably. I do not come close to exhausting critical sources in Catholicism, my focal point.

At the center of Catholicism stood the belief that you get to heaven through grace, which can be exercised through good works. In the sixteenth century Luther threw over this notion in favor of another—the individual as a sinner cannot merit heaven, but those who embrace Jesus as their savior will receive heaven as a gift. Later, John Calvin articulated his belief in predestination—each of us is already slated for heaven or hell, and there's no way of changing our fate. Again, disagreement over heaven greets us around every corner.

Zeal for heaven reasonably compels those the Spirit has moved to spread the good news. Proselytizing has long been front and center on the agenda of various Christian churches. It has been no stranger to Roman Catholicism. This problem can sometimes get in the way of good faith efforts to build bridges to other, unwilling communities. In June of 2001, for example, Pope John Paul II traveled to the Ukraine in the hope of mending the rift between Roman Catholicism and Eastern Orthodoxy which dates to the schism of 1054. Before his arrival, Orthodox priests held vigils to pray that the pope would not visit Orthodox holy places. Russian nationalists openly deplored the pope's visit as an affront to Orthodox religious sensibilities. Referring to Orthodox church leaders who did not especially want to see him, during a formal airport arrival ceremony that no Orthodox religious leaders attended the pontiff said, "I wish to assure them that I have not come here with the intention of proselytizing."[47] This affirmation seemed entirely appropriate from a man whose business is, after all, to lead and nurture an opposing religion. In Lvov, the regional capital of western Ukraine, the pope beatified thirty Catholics, twenty eight of them Greek Catholics, in two separate ceremonies. Most of them are revered as martyrs of the Soviet era. As always, naming saints, recognizing them as living in heaven, sends a political message.

On some level, the faithful are expected to exemplify the church and what the church stands for. They set the stage and spell out the vision. The missionary relies on being able to point to a payoff. Anyone advocating a new religion needs to enforce the appeal of the reward— hardly easy work. The missionary will be battling the doubters, drawing out the curious, gathering intelligence, sifting out substantive theological objections from routine whining, bucking up the lonely and the demoralized, and exuding a sense of community. A Catholic missionary might be forgiven for making the pope look more tolerant than he actually is. Part of managing the hunger for heaven comes down to opposing sin; there has to be a sacrifice (of wicked pleasures) if the payoff is going to mean anything. And so in addition to promising solace, relief from the pain of getting through another year, Catholicism, like other religions, has to point to rules in order to maintain an aura of seriousness, of legitimacy. How convenient that those rules fall into place around sex, an urge people may feel even more immediately than the need for heaven. One urgency may imaginatively reinforce the other in a zealot's mind, for fear of lust finds in sexual prohibitions a peaceful resting place, however temporary.

In conclusion: a church, a temple, or a mosque, when used as a place of worship, unites a group of people who agree in some important way about heaven and what it takes to get there. Over details they may argue endlessly, but there is something crucial binding them to something much larger than any of them. Death hangs over the gathering like a shadow, a grimly determined enemy. Sex is there, too, for it is sex, in the sense of regeneration, that allows people to cheat death for yet another generation. In the midst of the profound feeling of solidarity between worshipers, differences remain. Status, gender, race, energy level, personal warmth, sexual orientation, and depth of commitment set one individual off from another. We'll see that these differences tell a story about heaven, the moral of which is "on earth as it is in heaven."

Heaven's
Junior Varsity

American high schools, with acne caste systems and adolescent tests of social fitness, teach the virtue of long suffering. In sports, as in dating, reality crashes down on tender hopes. Every high school athlete is a winner, parents energetically affirm, yet some winners are more special than others. The better team members send manicured cheerleaders into a rehearsed frenzy and enjoy brief stints as local heroes. Varsity players understand no less than those relegated to the junior varsity that there would be no winners without losers.

Heaven, too, would appear to field a varsity team. And why shouldn't it? Jews, Christians, and Muslims all revere the memory of those who came before and championed the faith in the face of worldly obstacles. Forebears have talked to God, walked with God, argued with God, killed for God. They have battled for God and suffered for God and sacrificed for God. Surely, they've done more than we. So why shouldn't they enjoy a prize greater than ours? As I flesh out the uncanny similarity between paradise and American high school, I will again focus on Catholicism.

CATHOLIC CASTES

In a familiar passage from the New Testament, Jesus warns that it is easier for a camel to pass through the eye of a needle than for a rich man to enter heaven (Luke 18:25). What resting place awaits the rich man who does manage to squeeze or inveigle himself into paradise? It seems unlikely that he to whom a place has begrudgingly been granted will sit cheek-by-jowl with a chaste saint or a fearless martyr.

We sometimes say about money, "You can't take it with you." We say this to anchor money in this world and emphasize its uselessness in the next (in this mindset, we differ dramatically from, say, ancient Egyptians). However, we can take social status with us to heaven. Augustine says in *The City of God* that Christianity does not abolish social distinctions. Why, we might ask, should heaven? In the same work he explains that the expulsion of the evil angels from heaven created a heavenly hierarchy, one that supremely privileges or elevates the Blessed Virgin and the Holy Trinity. Each saint in heaven will receive a reward commensurate with his merit. The more important a saint you are, the closer you will stand to the Blessed Virgin and the Holy Trinity throughout eternity. The most influential Catholic theologian of all would have us believe that hierarchy pervades both this life and the next.[1]

Some seven centuries afterward, Saint Thomas Aquinas affirmed Augustine's account. Those who had behaved well on earth graduated to a position of honor, close to the Virgin and the Trinity.[2] Reading Aquinas, we almost get the impression that life on earth is comparable to the qualifying rounds in a modern swimming meet or track competition. Your performance in the morning rounds determines not only whether you will proceed to the finals later that day, but where you will stand if you do. The fastest qualifiers take the middle lanes. The most accomplished saints, whose merits are judged on the basis of earthly conduct, lock in their privileged lanes for eternity.

This idea confounded Protestant reformers, who allowed gender in heaven, but no social hierarchy. Luther (1483-1546) and Calvin (1509-

1564) denied the existence of what I am referring to as "heaven's junior varsity." They agreed that everyone in heaven will be equal, and they emphasized that our attention will focus on God, not other saints. These early Protestants couldn't abide the idea that God shares the spotlight or his authority with anyone else (including the Blessed Virgin). I interpret the very Catholic enterprise of canonizing saints to reinforce a varsity / junior varsity system (which is perhaps a gentler distinction than that between a higher and a lower class). The champions of the faith will enjoy the privilege of standing closer to the center of heaven, and the other souls in heaven will perceive the exalted status of the elite.

And so Catholics must balance hope for heaven against realism. Like the hunted priest in Graham Greene's classic novel *The Power and the Glory,* many Catholics have sensed "there was only one thing that counted—to be a saint." And yet, as Saint Jerome wrote, "If all are equal in heaven, our humility in this life is in vain."[3] Ultimately, we will have to settle for whatever modest room we can get in heaven, for the competition is pretty stiff. Although a station as one of the beautiful people in heaven sounds exhilarating, it is, alas, unlikely. But the other alternative to a lowly rank—hell—will prevent us from complaining.

WHAT WERE THEY THINKING?
A PSYCHOLOGY OF HEAVEN

Augustine reasons in chapters 15 and 16 of *The City of God* that just as sin is an unpleasant aspect of life, so too is slavery. It is because of our sinfulness that there is such a thing as slavery. Slaves must accept their lot in life and serve their masters cheerfully. It is harder to be a master than a slave, Augustine exhorts us to remember, for the authority masters wield comes as a greater burden than the service slaves must render.

In both Europe and the United States, Catholic monasteries and convents replicated distinctions between class and race that divided the societies against which these religious communities defined themselves. Serfs were not uncommon in medieval monasteries; such lowly laborers enabled monks to attend to the business of copying sacred manuscripts and studying theology. Monasteries long profited from popular piety, and the wealthy sometimes donated large sums to monastic orders. Worldly people who had advanced through the rat race might earn favor in the eyes of God by benefiting monks or nuns who had chosen a more contemplative path.

Monks and priests sometimes described themselves metaphorically as slaves of Christ, all the while overseeing literal slaves. In her history of Catholic nuns, *Sisters in Arms,* Jo Ann Kay McNamara details how sisters in the antebellum American South became enmeshed in slave systems they knew to be evil:

> It is a weary tale, well-known to American historians. Sisters coming from Europe learned to adapt to southern slavery and Americans were already accustomed to it. Novices often brought slaves as part of their dowry, and well-meaning patrons donated them to the sisters. Philippine Duchesne praised the honesty of a planter who gave her a slave to pay arrears on his daughter's tuition. Arriving in Louisiana from France, Hyacinth Le Coniat was shocked and horrified by the realities of American slavery: "They receive no attention or care. They are treated like beasts with little pity. And yet they are children of God!" Within months, however, she was complaining about the cost of hiring slave labor and asking for servants from France. When at last the community bought a slave, she stanched her tears at having paid for human flesh with the thought that she could instruct him in religion. The war came and the slave ran away. His ingratitude dismayed Hyacinth.

Avoiding moralistic finger-pointing, McNamara explores territory that will surprise many Catholics:

> Even in enclosed convents, the culture wars went on as ancient rules bent before modern demands and sheltered women confronted the mysteries of otherness. In Old Regime Europe, most convents were stratified socially so that the inhabitants were spared the unpleasantness of cross-class

accommodations. . . . Class distinctions carried over from Europe proved especially trying in the United States. With the decline of the dowry system and the rise of the active vocations that commanded regular, though pitifully small, salaries, religious vocations became steadily more accessible to working-class and peasant women. In Europe, most communities still made the distinction between lay and choir sisters, often modified by the insertion of a "middle class" of teaching nuns, but in the liberal atmosphere of the nineteenth century the practice caused discontent and guilt.

Sometimes parishioners would thwart the best intentions of a nun committed to social service:

> Philippine Duchesne originally came to America in 1818 to evangelize the Indians. From New Orleans she and her companions set out for Saint Louis and then to Saint Charles, where they opened a school for poor children but found themselves cut off from the near-by Indians. Each new school she founded was soon filled with white pupils whose parents objected to her efforts to include Indian and black girls.[4]

I do not accuse these nuns of simple hypocrisy. On the contrary, I emphasize that these nuns abided by reigning social conventions (even if the very idea of living chastely in an all-female enclave itself seemed unconventional). True, Christians often claim as their responsibility challenging unjust social frameworks, but it was perhaps to be expected that nuns would privately replicate some of them. Progress takes time, and what may seem obvious to us in hindsight puzzled them. The point to be taken is that the convent, like the monastery, amounted to an earthly model of heaven in Catholic imagination. If benevolent monks and nuns allowed racial prejudice and class snobbery to slip into their orders, it seems likely that many Catholics would have thought of heaven in similar terms. Besides, the Vatican had permitted slavery for many centuries. It seems reasonable that good Catholics expected, consciously or subconsciously, discrimination in heaven. After all, Augustine and Aquinas had both indicated as much. Even though lay Catholics may never have read either of these lynchpins of the Roman tradition, mothers and fathers likely heard sermons in church explaining the beatific vision in Augustine's or Aquinas's terms. And those mothers and fathers would have explained the cosmos to their children in roughly the same manner.

McNamara's nuns were conforming to a secular culture already in place. Catholic culture meshed easily with that other heritage. In 1593, the Fifth General Congregation of the Jesuit Order had strictly forbidden men of Jewish or Muslim descent from becoming Jesuits (the Society of Jesus being one of the more liberal Catholic orders); although the prohibition was mitigated in 1608 and again in 1923, it was not fully rescinded until 1946. What were priests and nuns thinking when they deliberately discriminated against persons of certain religious backgrounds? What were priests and nuns thinking about the slaves they held?[5]

Maybe these religious followers were taking cues from ambiguous references in the New Testament, where it does sometimes seem that a hierarchy will organize heaven. As we've seen, when asked what it takes to get into heaven, Jesus responded with a neat summary: honor God and love your neighbor. Immediately thereafter, Jesus offered instruction to those "who wish to be perfect": "go, sell your possessions, and give the money to the poor, and you will have treasure in heaven; then, come, follow me" (Matthew 19:21). What should we make of the idea that some people have treasure in heaven? Apparently others do not. In fact, most would not—only the virtuous would have it, or maybe they would just have more.

What use will treasure be in heaven? What should we make of the fact that its possession will set one group of people off from another? Maybe there will be an infinite number of gradations or castes in heaven. Catholic nuns, for example, are "brides of Christ." Doesn't it stand to reason that, in eternity, Christ will favor his many wives over other women? We need a hierarchy, or something very similar to a hierarchy, in order to make sense of Christ's revelation that, "Indeed, some are last who will be first, and some are first who will be last" (Luke 13:30). In order to come out a winner in eternity, you really ought to be a loser in the here and now (this, despite a conflicting parable in the New

Testament [Matthew 20:1-16] in which Jesus explains that all workers in a vineyard should receive the same wage, regardless of how much each had worked).

There seems something odd about lowering yourself in order to triumph. The idea conjures up a curious scenario—in contradistinction to the Olympics, where athletes compete to come out on top, so in a monastery or convent, the religious compete in a race to the bottom. Even if someone were to object that Christ was only speaking in parables, that we shouldn't take him literally, still it remains true that many saints have taken him at his word. Saint Thérèse Martin, to take a prominent example, never won a battle, stopped a plague, endured mutilation, or risked personal safety to help the poor. Yet she became a saint in world-record time (in 1925, when she would have only been fifty-two years old), simply on the strength of having humbled herself. The power of weakness can command awe in Catholic thinking.

As if to reinforce the difficulty of getting to heaven, Catholics have divided the canonization process into distinct phases since 1624, when the church's rules were established. After diocesan review, a promising candidate is declared "venerable." Then, after working a demonstrable miracle (confirmed by Rome) and further investigation, a would-be saint is beatified, or recognized as a model of holiness. After still another miracle and even more investigation, a candidate is canonized a saint. This process can stretch over many centuries, and some people have been languishing in the blessed (or "beatified") category for what seems like an eternity (for example, the fifteenth-century painter Fra Angelico). Pope John XXIII, who died only in 1963, is also there, but not expected to tarry much longer (this much-loved pope was beatified the same day as Pius IX, a sometimes-slurred pope). Pope Pius XII, head of the Vatican during World War II, is there, too. Controversy swirls around his promotion, given the allegations of his complicity with the Nazis. This is not the place to speculate on the integrity of any would-be saint or Catholic theology, only to suggest that Catholic culture reinforces the notion of hierarchy in heaven. Just as applicants to Yale hope for immediate admission, as opposed to placement on the waiting list, so too do the supporters of would-be saints hope their candidates can avoid lengthy delays. Meanwhile, the traffic jam on the path to heaven grows— by the turn of the millennium, John Paul II had created almost one thousand blesseds and saints.

It turns out, finally, that Dante's *Divine Comedy* was not just wild literary speculation—Catholics can expect distinct echelons in heaven. Dante the pilgrim receives several explanations of the balance between hierarchy and unity in the heavens. And yet a sublime pecking order strains through the cracks of his cautious qualifications. Although it might not have represented Catholic theology with unfailing accuracy, Dante's enduring text offers the same useful formula by which modern real estate agents guide clients: location, location, location.

INFERIORS IN HEAVEN WON'T MIND IT A BIT

Getting into heaven is hard, quite hard. Medieval patrons of the arts, no matter how wealthy, could not pay legitimate artists to paint themselves or their families into heaven.[6] Monied families could and often did have themselves painted into sacred scenes (looking skyward at the Assumption of the Virgin was a favorite), but heaven seems to have been strictly off limits. Only bona fide saints figured in God's town limits. Looking forward to the joy of heaven, meditating on the seriousness of the selection process, will only enhance the elation of arrival. Anticipation is the purest form of happiness, according to a popular German saying (*"Die schönste Freude ist die Vorfreude"*). So what if you find yourself socially inferior in the next world—shouldn't you be glad just to be there? Well, yes; but given how energetically some Westerners fight against social discrimination here on earth, some blessed souls might balk at the stratification of eternity. (Of course, many Westerners benefit from and covertly support such discrimination.)

It is not hard to guess which groups may find themselves at a disadvantage in the next world. Women top the list of likely suspects. Christianity didn't always subjugate women, nor did Islam. According to the Koran, women and men share the same moral duties: pilgrimage to Mecca, prayer, fasting during Ramadan, and almsgiving. The Koran granted women rights that Western women would not enjoy until the nineteenth century—divorce and inheritance. Contemporary scholar, feminist, and committed Muslim Riffat Hassan argues that the Islamic world has been misled by slanted interpretations of the Koran.[7] Chapter 4, verse 34, perhaps the definitive verse about women, turns on the Arabic word *qawwamun,* long interpreted as "rulers," "masters," or "custodians." Hassan contends the correct interpretation is "those who provide support or livelihood." She sees Islam as a woman-friendly force, one hijacked by misguided men. Let's focus on Christian heaven here, and on what it holds in store for women.

Saint Paul wrote longingly of a realm in which there would be neither male nor female, Jew nor Greek, slave nor free man. Ancient Christian men and women traveled together in chaste devotion to an apostolic vision and forged a new religion, one initially open to gender equality. Through virginity, women proved themselves as strong as men. Anyone rugged enough to lead an ascetic life deserved social privilege, and Christianity offered women the freedom to study and dispose of property. However, things gradually changed. The institutional church refused to admit women to the priesthood. Even though the church has long taught that the character of priests cannot mar the virtue of their sacraments, the gender of women can. An atheist or a child molester can transform bread into the body of Christ, but a woman may not.

It seems indisputable that the Vatican still privileges men—witness its continuing refusal to recognize female vocations. This double standard would seem to betray the oldest part of Catholic tradition, for early Christian culture glorified self-control. Women as well as men were capable of mustering the discipline necessary to remain chaste. Virginity toppled gender differences; through it, women could demonstrate their equality with men. As more and more monks failed at chastity, the virtue gradually changed shape, eventually becoming feminine. But regardless of how heroic they were, women officially made it into heaven in much smaller numbers than men.[8]

If men get to heaven more often than women, they also enjoy special privileges once there. Of course, official canonizations only capture a tiny percentage of those who supposedly make it. Yet those demographics might nonetheless tell us something about paradise, where a special group will spend eternity in enhanced glory.

The point to be taken here is that earthly leaders smiled on a system of favoring men, on the idea that women didn't really—or perhaps *shouldn't* really—mind it. (Remember that Augustine taught that heaven is free of envy, despite an obvious hierarchy.) It stands to reason that such leaders could just as easily privilege one class or race over another. The organizing idea is that one should cheerfully embrace one's mediocrity—those on the junior varsity bench are glad just to be at the game. Women and other undesirables may have to stand far away from the Virgin Mother, but they won't begrudge those in the front of the line.

Of course the junior varsity bench includes more than just women. Add to the list of also-rans the souls in limbo, the beatified who have not yet been canonized, and reconciled prostitutes, and the enormity of the junior varsity bench boggles the mind. There is no chance of transfer to another paradise if Aquinas is right that there is only one true heaven. If there is no separate heaven for Jews or Muslims or anyone else, it stands to reason that those of opposing earthly faiths will find themselves at a disadvantage in the next life. Can we on earth be of any help?

AFFIRMATIVE ACTION IN HEAVEN

Ancient Roman leaders ruled as the *pontifex maximus*—the "supreme priest," the secular popes of the Roman empire. The health of the state depended on heaven explicitly. Until well into the eighteenth century, the kings and queens of France and other Western nations ruled according to a mandate of heaven—the "divine right" of kings. Heaven above stood as a model for earth below, despite the sometimes rampant corruption of secular leaders. The people overthrew some of these leaders.

Does it make any sense to challenge heaven on other points—say the organization of, and admission to, paradise? Yes, because theologians may have made mistakes. But how would we know if they had?

The politics of heaven cascade down onto earth. Surely God does not discriminate, at least not beyond separating the saved from the damned. Some will object that those in hell are damned for a valid moral reason. Of course, moral reasons evolve, just as our ideas about fairness do.

Why not think of getting to heaven in terms of acceptance into an exclusive club or university? Affirmative action, still a controversial social policy, now regulates university admissions, governmental postings, and corporate hirings in America. Affirmative action seeks to rectify demographic imbalances; in order to diversify a work force or student body along racial lines, institutions explicitly aim to attract individuals from under-represented backgrounds. Affirmative action differs from equal opportunity employment; this separate process guarantees that no job or university applicant will be discriminated against on the basis of race, religious creed, ethnic background, or age. It is interesting that nondiscrimination clauses in many school districts, places of business, and universities overlooked sexual orientation well into the 1990s. Opponents of affirmative action charge unfairness: instead of basing hiring or admissions decisions on merit, they claim, officials make decisions on extraneous grounds.

For decades, Americans relied on the Scholastic Aptitude Test (SAT) as an objective arbiter. Students who scored well on this national examination deserved admission to selective colleges and universities. Students who failed to score well would naturally be passed over, it was thought; although the results of this test have always been just one factor among several in the admissions process, the SAT was important. Today, some critics allege that the SAT is itself unfair, privileging as it supposedly does Caucasian students from affluent backgrounds.[9] Racism, some say, taints the SAT. Entrance requirements for universities have come under fire, then; perhaps the cut-off point for getting into heaven will as well.

What interests me here is not race as a category, but rather the broader goal of embracing under-represented groups, groups that have perhaps been unfairly excluded or mistreated in the past. Those same people who would balk at the idea of affirmative action in heaven sometimes use religion as a cloak for converting Jews to Christianity, for denying gays and lesbians the legal right to marry, or for withholding ordination from women. Although Americans can no longer voice personal objections to a neighbor's religion or sexual orientation without risking an altercation or perhaps even the accusation of a hate crime, they can nonetheless protest against women and gay people in the name of religion. Religion justifies social objections that have become otherwise unfashionable.

We can't responsibly reduce even a single faith to a simple description, let alone squeeze the three major religious traditions of the West into a tiny box. And yet a broad pattern emerges from Western newspapers: more so than adultery or blasphemy, homosexuality angers heaven. Perhaps this insight helps explain why anti-discrimination clauses long excluded sexual orientation. Apart from a few references in Leviticus and the writings of Saint Paul, male-male sex doesn't surface as a major sin (there is no explicit prohibition of female-female sex in that corpus). And yet various Christian nations have singled out homosexuality as particularly offensive. This puzzling tradition reaches back to the fourth century. "For the first time in history, in 390, the Roman people witnessed the public burning of male prostitutes, dragged from the homosexual brothels of Rome."[10] The eagerness with which Christians have rooted out certain transgressions bears no obvious correlation to the hierarchy of sins laid down in the Ten Commandments and the seven deadly sins.

Christians interpret God's will, using their best judgment to predict what God wants but hasn't explicitly articulated. These good souls may be wrong—they certainly have been before. Affirmative action may have a role to play for sexual minorities. Since the advent of affirmative action advocacy in the United States, many universities and corporations have added nondiscrimination clauses to their admissions literature and mission statements. And so sexual minorities have benefited from the sympathy generated by affirmative action.

We continue to shape heaven by our own preferences. We are not so unlike Queen Victoria who, while dying and contemplating the various dignitaries whom she might be expected to receive at her first levee in heaven, rejected the assurance of a clergyman that she would soon be in Abraham's bosom. "We will *not* meet Abraham," she pronounced solemnly. She disapproved of the patriarch's behavior in Genesis (chapter 12), when he pretended to the Pharaoh that Sara was his sister rather than his wife, thinking the sacrifice of her virtue to the Egyptian potentate preferable to the offering of his own life. One could not imagine Queen Victoria welcoming to her own home a man who behaved like that.[11]

I have said that black people will still be black in heaven, the tall will still be tall, and women will still be women. What about slaves—will they still be slaves? The spiritual "Swing Low, Sweet Chariot" misleads us into thinking that slaves will find a better world in the heaven they evocatively long for in the song. In fact, there is reason to argue that the heaven prepared for them will be as segregated as the society they inhabited.[12] Not until one hundred fifty years ago did the Vatican alter its controversial moral teaching about slavery (of course, native Africans are only one of many groups that have been forced into slavery).

Can we desegregate heaven? Who segregated it in the first place? What would it take to desegregate heaven—arguing with God? We would do better to argue with ourselves. Now is the time for Christians to colonize heaven, spreading the gospel of affirmative action. Getting to heaven, and being there, might then transcend gender, race, and social status. Throughout the first centuries of Christianity, it was believed and taught that martyrs occupied a special status in heaven. When persecution of Christians largely ceased, the privileged caste expanded to include holy monastics, both men and women. Women are now elbowing their way into heaven, as more religious orders of women put forward their foundresses as worthy of Catholic canonization. Other under-represented groups should follow.

In contemporary America, no one would dare sniff that affirmative action comes down to poor, untalented people envying wealthy, gifted people. And yet it is only natural that "have-nots" should yearn for access to much of what the "haves" enjoy. The lessons of economic reform have sensitized Westerners to the plight of those confined to eating the scraps from the table of the rich. We do occasionally hear that some people living in poverty are joyful. It is interesting, though, that wealthy people almost never abandon affluence in their ongoing effort to find happiness. And the poor will almost invariably tell us they envy the rich. Even though Augustine maintains at the end of *The City of God* that there will be no envy in heaven, we see that there is plenty of it on earth. The saying "on earth as it is in heaven," at least as it is used in the familiar prayer beginning "Our Father, who art in heaven," encourages believers to accept direction from above. Instead of accepting their poverty or subjugated social status, though, many believers reach for more than they have. Those who reach frequently refuse to believe that God actually wills them to live in substandard or unfair conditions. And privileged believers who fear a sudden loss of power or status will similarly fight the idea that God's will is about to leave them destitute or common.

In the same vein, students at elite universities will frequently confess they don't like where they are. Life is too competitive, too demanding for them to be happy. And yet they wouldn't go anywhere else—if ever they transfer, it is to an even more competitive school. And students at less distinguished institutions dream of the opportunities they would enjoy at the same schools whose students will complain of excessive stress. Providing access to opportunity, opening up closed universities, has become a burning political issue in the United States, for it has become increasingly apparent that cultural minefields prevent the poor and people of color from attaining the excellence required by the admissions offices of such schools.

Americans have challenged the way such admissions offices work. Who would think to rail against the admissions officers in heaven? And yet, as we will see, this battle has begun. Look at some of the petty sinners whom Dante assigns to hell and ask yourself if all of them still belong there. Then read a history of civil rights in the United States and ponder the battle against inequality. Far from blasphemous, the expectation that heaven and earth resemble one another makes perfect sense in religious terms. Comparing the SAT to minimum heavenly requirements is not like comparing apples to oranges, for we model earthly justice on what we expect in the world to come (indeed, many evangelical Christians claim to ask themselves "What would Jesus do?" in any tough situation).

Religious leaders may seem to challenge God when they question theological doctrine or church tradition. On closer inspection, though, such leaders are challenging believers, specifically by pointing out that thoughts about God's will have been misguided or terribly incomplete. In the encyclical *Pacem in Terris,* John XXIII spoke up on behalf of minorities (Nos. 95-7) and refugees (Nos. 103-8).[13] He argued in a section called "Order among human persons" (Nos. 8-38) that moral norms spring from respect for the dignity of the human person. Why did the pope need to speak up about something that may strike contemporary readers as patently obvious? Because previous generations disagreed. When we reform the earth, we are modeling changes on an idea of heaven. And when we reform heaven, we reform earth.

HEAVEN: THE FINAL FRONTIER

How is getting into heaven like getting into Yale? Into the 1950s, Yale University quietly monitored and limited the number of Jews in entering classes. An enlightened Yale now guarantees equal access to Jews.

We have seen that some Catholic theologians have foretold a new kind of segregation. Your status on earth will determine how close to God and the Virgin Mary you get to stand in heaven—the "beatific vision" will favor some saints over others (at least in the Roman Catholic tradition). Before even beginning to assess the fairness of one's standing in heaven, it will be worthwhile to make sure there is an equal opportunity to get into heaven in the first place.

An obvious place to look for evidence of access to heaven is the clergy. In any given religious community, who is eligible for ordination? Who is a candidate to lead a church, parish, or synagogue? The answer until quite recently in the United States has been heterosexual, Caucasian males. What does this say by implication about the standing in heaven of people who don't fall into that category?

The ordination of women and gay people rips Jewish and Christian congregations apart. In June of 2001, for example, the governing board of the largest Presbyterian body in the United States voted decisively to lift the church's ban on the ordination of gays and lesbians as ministers and other clergy. The *Washington Post* reported that Jerry Van Marter, the church's chief spokesman, lamented, "opponents of lifting the ban are warning that it could tear the church apart." Ted Mikels, an elder of the Salem Presbytery in North Carolina, said, "Twice in the last five years we've voted on this, and each time it tears at the fabric of our presbytery."[14]

Later that same month the *New York Times* reported that a Boy Scout troop in Stamford, Connecticut, had found itself kicked out of the local Jewish Community Center.[15] The Scouts openly discriminated against gay men, and the liberal leaders of the Jewish Community Center in Stamford objected. The Scouts simply moved across town to meeting space in an Orthodox synagogue. Orthodox Jews embraced the Scouts' ban on openly gay leaders.

Though the battle for civil rights is not yet won, there is evidence of progress. Those who came before us, who lived under more oppressive social customs, had to settle for less. Their ordinary stories of struggle pose the question about heaven's fairness more concretely. On June 16, 2001 the *Washington Post* published the following obituary:

> Alice Jackson Stuart, whose attempt to integrate the University of Virginia in 1935 helped start a program making education available for thousands of blacks, died in Brookline, Massachusetts. She was 88.
>
> Stuart was the first known black person to seek admission into a Virginia graduate or professional school. After her rejection, the state established a tuition supplement fund for black students to attend graduate school outside Virginia.

in the pool or on the track? How, then, will we compete with the saints of old, some of whom were boiled, burned, and mutilated, others of whom persevered while their breasts were cut off or teeth yanked out, all in the name of preserving their virginity for Christ? Various faiths will blur the distinction between minimum and maximum human goodness. The writings of disenfranchised groups arise from a strong sense of being left out of the conventional stories and myths of Western culture. As such, they question rather than affirm the notion of a universal type of saint. At the same time, they also aspire to change our understanding of the past and present in a manner that transcends the local. Rather than luxuriating in their specific identities, scholars from these groups make claims about the world that they hold to be generally true (not true just for them). They believe that paying careful attention to the diverse groups who helped to fashion the modern world makes for better inspiration, not the end of inspiration.

Because people can be forgiven their sins, it may well be that heaven is full of people who have committed adultery. Some of the saints may have had gay sex. That sins can be forgiven doesn't mean we should or can take them lightly. But it certainly seems that the Vatican finds it more difficult to countenance certain sins than others.

Is sex just another issue, or is it the burning issue of today? Certainly, Christianity has faced many challenges over the course of two thousand years (for example, Pelagianism, iconoclasm, and Islam). The Vatican has wrestled with various issues and lost (for example, the morality of slavery and the position of the earth in our galaxy). Are sexuality and gender simply the most recent in a long line of difficult scrapes, then? Or can they be accurately portrayed as more potent than preceding crises? In increasingly secular times, it seems the one issue really capable of rallying the troops is sex. That in itself is perhaps a sufficient answer.

As they struggle to make sense of a more overtly sexual culture, believers may wonder where this debate will lead. How will the contemporary strife over sex play itself out in the afterlife? Think here of Ivan's conversation with Alyosha in Dostoyevsky's *The Brothers Karamazov*. In the "Grand Inquisitor" episode, Ivan says that he'd really prefer

The tuition supplement program was declared unconstitutional in 1950, leading to the gradual integration of Virginia's public university graduate programs.

Born June 2, 1913, in Richmond, she earned an English degree from Virginia Union University. She was teaching there when she joined an NAACP lawsuit challenging segregation at public universities.[16]

An unwanted student, an unlikely church leader. Stuart's is no doubt just one of many such stories, although she perhaps showed more bravery than other faceless victims, whose biographies are lost. Who will challenge segregation in heaven? What would such a challenge look like? If this world were our model, we might expect to find separate but equal heavens.

It is interesting that, although Virginia denied blacks admission to higher education, the state was willing to ship them somewhere else for college. This strategy for avoiding problems while perpetuating them reflects a blueprint Catholics have used for certifying the arrival in heaven of people who are just like us, only a bit better. By shying away from canonizing holy men and women of other religions, the Vatican raises questions about precisely where it thinks these good souls will end up. The same holds true for morally upright yet sexually active Catholics, who struggle to find someone like themselves among the saints. It is one thing to bless those on the junior varsity bench and another to celebrate them.

Catholicism lends itself to analysis because of its formal canonization process. Rome does not presume to decide on the holiness or afterlife station of non-Catholics. An ecclesial act, canonization is for Catholics only. It is perhaps unfair to ask why the Vatican insists on canonizing only Catholics, even though "the Roman Catholic Church does appear to be groping for some kind of formula for acknowledging non-Catholic Christians who meet its standards, at least in the case of martyrs."[17]

Heaven, the final frontier for affirmative action, dangles above ordinary Catholics. The Vatican guards it closely and justifies an exclusive admissions policy as a manifestation of God's will.

THE STORIES WE TELL

Affirmative action is all about seeing an old problem in a new way. The stories we tell about other people prepare the way for the conclusions we subsequently draw. We can portray anyone in a negative light or a positive one; it doesn't take a psychiatrist to detect bias or a dazzling litigating attorney to establish a case for merit or shame.

Even nonbelievers may find the stories of saintly heroism enthralling. Atheists may dismiss as myths accounts of what spiritual warriors have done in the name of holiness, but that doesn't mean they will fail to find the stories absorbing. There is a political side to whose story gets told, and how. As Eugene Kennedy has written, "Spiritually, we all live east of Eden now, and memories of innocence and exile resonate just beneath the clutter of the everyday, deep within us. That is why story, rather than literal history, is the language of religion. . . ."[18] Stories resonate with believers and nonbelievers alike; having a story to tell isn't the problem these days, but rather it's getting a chance to tell it.

A religious community grimly determined to resist the idea that gay people can exhibit heroic goodness may try to silence anyone with a story that flatters gays and lesbians. Individuals may tell whatever stories they like in a democratic society, but hierarchical religions are not democratic societies. The Catholic Church dictates which stories get told publicly; its own skill at crafting biographical sketches accounts for an important source of its power. The church's dominion to make saints relies on carefully translating lives into stories, and the church dislikes certain stories. For example, the American media lionized the openly gay Catholic priest Mychal Judge, who volunteered with the New York Fire Department and died on September 11, 2001 while ministering at the scene of the World Trade Center attack. A recovering alcoholic and an openly gay man who struggled with his vow to live a chaste, celibate life, Father Judge has earned many fans—both Catholic and not. These fans are pressuring the Vatican to canonize Judge; they trumpet their cause from a website devoted to getting him into heaven, so to speak.[19]

What about, say, translating gay biographies into gay saints? (Y, social historian John Boswell has argued that the church canonized a g couple and then later suppressed the details of these saints' person lives.)[20] Here someone may object—this isn't a matter of racial or ethn discrimination, but a question of sin. Gay people have sinned, they hav broken the rules, and so they have forfeited their claim on heaven. Simpl look in the Bible, a critic may exhort us.

A few passages from the Bible certainly condemn homosexuality. However, it cannot be denied that, unlike homosexuality, much of what was formerly forbidden has now been accepted (for example, tattooing, wearing clothes of blended fibers, and lending money at interest). The stories the Vatican chooses to tell reflect a selective bias. This is hardly surprising, yet it bears repeating. In the stories Catholics hear, the faithful can detect some sign of where they can hope to stand in heaven. Gay Catholics try to maintain a sense of humor about the news that's fit to print.

HEAVEN AND HUMAN LOGIC

Belief in heaven isn't necessarily just a blind leap of faith—Immanuel Kant, the father of modern philosophy, argued that it is a postulate of pure practical reason. Even if heaven is the static, unchanging place that Saint Thomas Aquinas described, still it remains that our views of it continue to evolve. That evolution supposedly conforms with human logic, or something like Kantian reasoning.

The very entrance requirements for heaven may stir our emotions. We might think of heaven as the ultimate revenge: you debase me in this life, but I will see you debarred from heaven in the next. Anger and envy buzz around the judgment of others, the assignment of someone we dislike to an eternity of unspeakable torture.

Generally speaking, we believe that talented people who work hard deserve their success and personal fortunes. It is somehow appropriate that they enjoy greater wealth or status than we. Similarly, champion athletes deserve their fame. How could we possibly compete with them

to have nothing to do with God, if God is really as people say.[21] What if we were to ask a slightly different question: Where do we want to live for eternity? Could all this strife over sex be a clue of some sort, that perhaps heaven is terribly shallow? What if someone qualified for heaven—even the varsity bench—and politely demurred? Much as we find the protagonist doing in the Book of Job, we might question the wisdom of celestial organization.

Ultimately, God's wisdom may simply be inscrutable to us, as Job learned. Or it may be that some religious leaders are making entirely too much of sex.

ONWARD AND UPWARD

Catholics may be more inclined than others to think of a junior varsity bench in heaven, and European Catholics may be the most likely of all. Take a tour through the great churches of Europe (most of them Catholic), and you will find yourself in cemetery after cemetery. We see tombs and the holy relics of saints. The more important the church, the bigger the tombs and the more visible the relics. Not unlike the pharaohs in ancient Egypt, various popes and cardinals had built for themselves elaborate burial places. Marmoreal, imposing, and forbidding, these monuments can't fail to make us see that these were very important people, no doubt varsity players in heaven.

What will happen to ordinary Catholics? Taking a walk through church cemeteries, we see plots of various sizes and grandeur. These ordinary people, or those who bury them, seem to be jockeying for prominence as well. There is competition everywhere, apparently. Even non-Catholics sometimes join the game. In cities such as Paris and Venice, for example, everyone knows where the chic cemeteries lie—Père Lachaise (not to mention the Pantheon) and San Michele. And in Buenos Aires, social climbers and blue bloods alike fret over whether they will land in La Recoleta (the local elites still resent Eva Peron's burial plot there, which they insist she did not deserve).

In cemeteries as in the high school cafeteria, we want to land beside the stars. We want to end up with fashionable people in a desirable neighborhood. And why shouldn't we?

"Heaven is large and affords space for all modes of love and fortitude," wrote Ralph Waldo Emerson.[22] Emerson's vision of heaven may reject a hierarchy, but theologians such as Augustine and Aquinas have embraced it. Perhaps it's true that those of us who dislike it here will cheerfully tolerate stratification there, but we moderns feel terribly entitled.

The struggle for human rights has taken many shapes, only one of which is the policy of affirmative action (which can be traced to a heated legal case in the 1970s initiated against the University of California Board of Regents, and a subsequent opinion by United States Supreme Court Justice Lewis Powell). I have suggested an analogy between getting into heaven and getting into exclusive social institutions here on earth. It should not seem far-fetched to suggest parallels, even if one cannot pinpoint the moment at which they break down.

A vast subject, heaven defies generalization, even as it invites spiritual fervor. John Paul II certainly thinks about heaven a lot, having earned a reputation as a "saint-maker." He has canonized more saints than all his predecessors put together (so far, about eight hundred have made it past the canonization finish line). Other cases he has proposed will come to fruition after he has met his maker.

All Christians want to be saints. The logic of longevity strains explanation: If the point of a healthy diet and regular exercise is to live longer, isn't a believer simply prolonging the wait for what he really wants? The modern world, so full of octogenarians, may frustrate the zealous, who will need more patience than ever.

In any event, it seems that many Catholics hope for too much when they envision equality in paradise. In this optimism, believers resemble the legendary heroine Guinevere from *Camelot*. Her parting words to Lancelot reveal a certain ignorance of where the penitent adulteress would spend eternity: "Therefore, Sir Launcelot, with thou well I am set in such a plight to get my soul heal, and yet I trust through God's grace that after my death to have a sight of the blessed face of Christ and at Doomsday to sit on his right side, for as sinful as ever I was are saints in heaven." The real-life model for Guinevere may well have made it to heaven, but any view of Christ's face she enjoys will likely be from the back row, squinting.

The Sex
We Don't Have

I never miss a chance to have sex or appear on television.

—*Gore Vidal*

John F. Kennedy would get a headache if he didn't have sex at least once a day, he once confided to British Prime Minister Harold Macmillan.[1] Gore Vidal was more public about his own sexual athleticism. The sex that happens around us preoccupies gossip columnists, television evangelists, and Viagra stockholders, while the sex that doesn't happen goes largely unnoticed. In an erotic paradise only somewhat darkened by AIDS, modern Westerners rarely applaud the opposite of sex, known variously as celibacy, abstinence, incarceration, loneliness, or bad luck.

Like a photograph, we can detect details in the negative that elude us in the positive. Pondering the sex that doesn't happen can deepen our understanding of the sex that does.

The media natters on and on about the sumptuous sex life we could be having. Every year a new survey titillates our curiosity as it investigates who has more orgasms: Protestant housewives, Jewish Republicans, or Muslim postal workers (the answer is never what you think). At his twenty-fifth Yale college reunion, Calvin Trillin pondered why "the most outraged and venomous response to the turmoil of the late sixties" came not from older generations educated in New Haven but his own. The answer he proposed was missed sex. As he put it, "alumni from the mid-fifties classes suspected that the world of rebellious students included lewd and excessive sexual activity, and the thought of having missed such goings-on by only a few years was driving them to distraction."[2]

Calvin Trillin would have us believe that the sex we don't have can haunt us, even alter our voting patterns. If he is right, the sex we don't have obstructs the hallowed path to self-fulfillment. True, missed sex can indeed color our assessment of how good life has been and consequently mold the advice we give to young people whom we hope will prosper.

To consider sexual satisfaction a fundamental human need may vex those for whom such pleasure is simply not important. We can remain agnostic here while pondering certain complexities of human flourishing: How valuable is sex to us? Valuable enough to end a marriage in the hope of finding better? Valuable enough to exit a relationship when a partner has had repugnant sex? What is the moral worth of sex never had? Why does it still make sense to prize virginity or fidelity in the West? Difficult questions; a broad category, the sex we don't have defines, ennobles, saddens us.

What does God have to do with any of this? If the Vatican is right, the sex we don't have can propel us to heaven as few other sacrifices will.

DIFFERENT TYPES OF NONE

Is it really better to have loved and lost than never to have loved at all? If so, might the same counsel apply to sex? Perhaps. In any event, those who have never loved at all can teach us something. Many are the types of none:

> It is one thing to forgo sex for awhile (until we marry or until a spouse returns from war) and another thing to swear off it forever.
> It is one thing to swear off one kind of sex and another thing to swear off all sex.

It is one thing to abstain voluntarily and another thing to obey under duress.

Sexual sacrifice triggers the imagination, as we struggle to comprehend the dimensions of the challenge. As a child, the nuns and priests spoke to my classmates repeatedly of someone called "the Virgin Mary." I had no idea what a virgin was, so the honorific was lost on me. When I did finally add that word to my vocabulary, I understood that adults considered this woman a model overachiever.

Sticking to a vow of celibacy differs from serving a prison sentence. A nun freely gives up sex, but an inmate does not, which means that the inmate doesn't sacrifice sex. And so, we might think, the nun deserves more admiration or needs more therapy. You don't have to be a nun, however, to make this choice. Miss Havisham, the old maid in Dickens's *Great Expectations,* voluntarily renounces sex. Jilted, she returns home from church and sits in the parlor for decades, still wearing her wedding dress, refusing both forgiveness and sex. Balzac penned some of his best novels about old maids, both male (*Le père Goriot*) and female (*La cousine Bette*). By their diversity, other literary examples speak to the variety of circumstances under which people forgo sex. In Thomas Hardy's novel *Jude the Obscure,* young lovers Jude and Sue Bridehead proudly shun sex, which they associate with marriage, a "hopelessly vulgar institution." Jude and Sue eventually lose ground to sensual desire, despite their best efforts.

We prize voluntary abstention more than involuntary. The different kinds of regret a nun and a convict feel color our moral evaluation of them. A nun purposefully gives up sex (or tries to), whereas a convict who may love sex suddenly finds that he can no longer have any (at least not with anyone of the opposite sex). Central to understanding both kinds of abstinence is an appreciation for how much people generally crave good sex.

People disagree over what qualifies as good or disgusting sex, sometimes even within themselves. "Coming out" stories such as writer Andrew Holleran's often showcase painful ambivalence on this point:

By the time I got to college, I was already skeptical; reading Nietzsche in the basement of the Catholic Club deepened that; and by the time I went to bed with another man, at the ripe age of twenty-six (surely a consequence of my Catholic upbringing), it was no longer an issue of Sin and perdition.

Or so I thought; till I found myself the next morning in a shower washing my mouth out with soap—not my mother, me—to clean the orifice which till then had been used for the "innocent" purposes of speech and nourishment: my first glimpse of the fact that we never really leave Catholicism behind.[3]

Sex and spirituality nourish us, and it is not so surprising that the experience of one should prompt anxiety about the other. Holleran, reflecting on early sexual forays, identified with the aggressor. He enlisted the church's help to fight against himself. Holleran later changed his mind, deciding to fight on his own side. He came to see the realms of the spiritual and the physical as overlapping. Consequently, giving up sex was more than just an instrumental sacrifice and, similarly, getting it was more than just a negligible luxury.

Well into the 1970s, being branded a homosexual landed a man in roughly the same sexual category as a pregnant but unmarried woman. Not so long ago, Western women understood that a single sexual encounter could ruin their entire future. Having sex before marriage led to the regret borne of forfeiting social standing. Nowadays, some Western women articulate a different kind of regret: not knowing how sex with different men feels. Financial independence and an urge to understand their own physical needs may compel contemporary young women to experiment as their male counterparts have.

Some artists and intellectuals, such as Leonardo da Vinci and Isaac Newton, have feared that indulging in sex would distract them from creative goals. Sigmund Freud, for whom sexual desire propelled the bulk of human actions, lamented that men who hoped for artistic or professional achievement would have to sacrifice lots of sex: "What he employs for cultural aims he to a great extent withdraws from women and sexual life."[4] Freud practiced what he preached. Obsessively devoted to psychoanalytical studies, he ceased having sex with his wife (who had already delivered six children) at the age of forty-one — the same year in which his career took off, with the publication of *The Interpretation of Dreams.*[5] The American artist Joseph Cornell, best known for his object-filled boxes, died a virgin in 1972, at the age of sixty-nine. He believed that he would lose his artistic abilities if he were to have sex.[6]

From ancient Greece to the modern West, soldiers and male athletes of various sorts have feared that an ejaculation would impair their performance and so have carefully avoided sex before competitions. The ancient Greek physician Galen allowed men one safe ejaculation per month. With soldiers, athletes, and intellectuals, we see that fear and regret work in concert to highlight the cost of sex. The more seriously one took personal or professional goals, the more likely one would be after lovemaking to regret the energy consumed.

For countless couples marriage has also dulled the sexual urge. Fights and emotional trials can blunt the libido. Remaining faithful to a spouse over the course of a long marriage requires what sometimes seems to be superhuman strength. Like nuns and priests, traditional spouses take vows of sexual restraint; true, spouses enjoy the moral right to have sex with each other. But if what they really want is to be having sex with someone else, they might feel like a nun or a priest. Remaining faithful to one's spouse today seems as difficult as remaining a virgin in previous centuries (before the dizzying age of information, when stealth is as easy as travel, when myriad opportunities cascade over the Internet).

Pregnancy might temporarily curtail desire for sex, as might illness or depression. Religious observance plays a role as well; Muslims abstain from sex during the days of Ramadan. At night, they may make love. A pattern of feast and famine will govern most of our lives in bed, and the unpredictable catalysts from peak to nadir can be fascinating. Context and circumstance will dictate the significance of missed sex.

REGRET OVER MISSED SEX

Even prosperous, healthy, well-educated people are vulnerable to regret, one of the heaviest spiritual burdens. No doubt social underdogs—people of color, women, gays and lesbians—occasionally rue opportunities never really open to people like them, but even the disenfranchised can have sex. Regret, the mental mashing to which Auden masterfully gives voice in the poem "As I Walked Out One Evening" (I know of no better or more stirring description than that contained there), deserves all the attention it can get from philosophers, psychologists, and novelists.[7] And sexual regret might merit a book of its own.

Regret mingles with grief and anger. In the Hebrew Bible, Rachel weeps for slaughtered children, who are no more. In every Olympics, disappointed athletes weep over gold medals lost. Parents worry their children are growing up too fast, and child stars appear on television as adults, lamenting the childhood they never had. Divorcing couples lash out at one another in part over promises not kept and in part over regret for time badly invested. Regret may seem less important than either grief or anger, yet regret is liable to linger on, years after grief and anger have subsided. The endurance of regret often frightens those wrestling with a difficult decision.

Regret over missed sex likely transcends culture, time, and class. Despite living in what Westerners sometimes perceive to be a sexually repressive society, Muslim women in Iran interviewed about their sexuality sounded a lot like the rest of us. "One woman who had resisted the courting attempts of a stranger many years before often looked for him on the streets; 'I imagine what it would be like to be married to him,'" the Iranian woman confessed. Wistful thoughts dovetail with realistic ones; regret over a prize missed may well gain energy from the dreary realization that the sex one has now leaves much to be desired. Another Iranian woman in the same survey said of her marital relations, "The first year is best. After that, it is all very disappointing."[8] The conviction that better erotic fulfillment lies elsewhere can persist and ignite adulterous impulses, a distinctly active strain of sexual regret.

The entry under "Sex" in the *Encyclopedia Judaica* includes the following Talmudic commentary: "for most people there is nothing harder in the entire Torah than to abstain from sex and forbidden relations."[9] Scholars of the Roman Catholic penitentials, which guided confessors until the twelfth century, have noted a preponderance of rules governing sex.[10] And in the *Encyclopedia Iranica,* we read of Islamic culture under the entry "Gender Relations": "One of the most compelling justifications for sex-segregation has been the belief that sexual desire is easily stimulated in both sexes and, if unregulated, can cause social mayhem and disorder."[11] Although women will sometimes object that sex isn't really that important, men usually will insist it is.

It might seem natural to celebrate sex not had as a triumph over lust, yet the powerful desire to have sex suggests regret is just as likely to surround the deliberately missed opportunity. Sexual regret may be rationalized as either sociobiological evidence for man's procreative duty or dismissed as a promiscuous inclination. Analogous to greed, sexual regret may consume us as it obscures our life priorities and our moral sense of how much is enough.

Marriage, or romantic commitment in general, may scare us for many reasons, one of which is closing off opportunities for sex. We anticipate regret, and so we hesitate. Adultery aside, many spouses refuse to do without sex:

> Interestingly, the world's most intensive birth-control campaign ever, China's 1979 One-Child-Only Policy, did not endorse abstinence. Before the campaign, 5 to 10 percent of couples used contraceptives. By 1982, this figure had risen to 70 percent. Half chose IUDs, a quarter tubal ligations, one-tenth vasectomies. About 8 percent relied on steroid pills, 2 percent on condoms, and the remaining 4 percent on either diaphragms or coitus interruptus. Only an infinitesimal, unmeasured percent abstained.[12]

Of course, sex with a spouse differs from adultery; the point here is that keeping lust under wraps isn't easy. *Jeffrey,* Paul Rudnick's popular play from the 1990s, hilariously portrayed the resolve of a gay man to stop having sex. Even the fear of AIDS, the incentive for Jeffrey's abstinence, ultimately takes a back seat to his desire for sex.[13] Fidelity may tax the strength of even the most virtuous, yet it is hard to imagine a married couple propping one another up through mutual confessions of temptations withstood. More likely, these temptations and their defeat will smolder just beneath routine discussions of how the day at work went. Silently, regret blossoms.

We might regret many things, to be sure, and each life will record particular, perhaps idiosyncratic priorities. According to a recent study, the most common regret of elderly Americans comes down to missed education, not missed sex.[14] This finding might suggest that sex isn't in fact as crucial to emotional fulfillment as the media would have us believe. Or the finding may just suggest that people are reluctant to confess to something the media implicitly portrays as pathetically sad. As I have said, a regret to which we may be reluctant to confess publicly concerns me here. Not only do contemporary media consumers receive the message that they should be keeping up with the Joneses, they also figure out that their sexual opportunities dwindle with age.

The philosopher Ronald de Sousa has usefully compared our contemporary hunger for sex to harried tourists who scurry through Europe in order to feel they haven't missed something important. For results-oriented tourists, sightseeing is not so much a pleasure as an achievement. The tourist wants "not to see but to have seen."[15] Following Aristotle, de Sousa points out that the mistake of the driven tourist is to think that by viewing something, he or she is seeing something. That's to say that the problem comes down to the tourist assuming that by crossing must-see sights off his list, he is enjoying those sights. He is wrong in the same way that sexual athletes are. Convinced that a good life will come down to satisfaction in later life or on the death bed at having had lots of sex, the sexual athlete rushes through carnal intersections in order to ward off anxiety, not to relish physical union with another person.

In a culture that celebrates consumerism, it is hardly surprising that someone might worry about getting enough of any good broadly considered desirable. Given the prevalence of sex talk in the media, we may find ourselves wondering how much sex others have. What would we see if we spied on the private lives of our neighbors and colleagues? How much sex are they having?

According to her biographer Anton Gill, Peggy Guggenheim's maternal grandmother liked to corner others with the question, "When do you think my husband last slept with me?" In Lisa Zeidner's popular novel *Layover,* the main character Claire Newbold claims to possess the ability to discern whether anyone she gazes at has had sex recently. (She feels sorry for those who haven't.) One of the surest ways to jumpstart a flagging cocktail party would be to speculate on the most recent sexual encounter of various guests.[16]

In various works, Freud argued that our very civilization demands sacrifices of sexual satisfaction—not from religious celibates but from ordinary citizens. Instead of fearing sex as a pathway to sin and ruin, we might fear regret instead. Instead of focusing on sex as potentially sinful, we might think of its absence as a pity. The real sin would be to live without ever joining this peculiar dance with another human being, and from enjoying the relief from isolation it provides. We might also worry that, variety being the spice of life, we have not tasted sufficiently from the banquet table. This is what it would mean to turn sin on its head: to declare sinful the belief in carnal sin, to seek out precisely what sin would keep us from.

In sum: there are important moral and psychological differences between the regret born of self-recrimination (I should have chosen x instead of y) and the regret born of longing for something one purposely declined. Although we can never recover the past, we can hold on to the memory of missed opportunities. Having once consciously decided to seize the day and pry from life what we want, we can later relish the memory. The recollection of having failed to realize a goal, though, may pain us for years. It will be hard to enjoy our own company if we fixate upon pleasures forever lost.

When we hear the story of a former priest who has jettisoned celibacy in favor of having sex for hours every day, we may detect a deliberate effort to make up for lost time and wasted opportunities.[17] To take just one final example, the definitive biography of Isadora Duncan, considered the harbinger of modern dance and an artistic genius, depicts a woman who discovers sex at age twenty-five and then never stops.[18] Regret is a powerful, motivating force. Often coupled with fear, it can drive the course we chart through life. Personal decisions take shape around the aim to avoid regret.

SEXUAL EXPECTATIONS

Visit the Grand Canal in Venice and feel the romance. Bask in the sun from the deck of a moving *vaporetto,* then flit through night over arching footbridges: you'll see for yourself why crowds throng to the crumbling seaport. Next, imagine yourself an employee of one of the luxury hotels that dot the Canal: What do you think people are doing in their rooms? Working in such a hotel must make you nod in recognition while reading Rimbaud's poem "The Repopulation of Paris," in which the poet strolls through the French capital and viscerally feels a city going at it.[19] Young Americans may recognize the same energy in the sensual frenzy of spring break in Ft. Lauderdale.

Of course, not everyone hopes for sex. But sexual renunciation would mean little if sexual expression didn't mean so much to so many.

Sexual asceticism enjoys an exalted spiritual status in Hinduism and Buddhism. Various ancient Greeks, such as Pythagoras and Socrates, revered abstinence as well. Quite apart from religious devotion, celibacy seems to lend a sort of hard-wrought glamour to a serious person. Of those philosophers university students consistently enjoy reading, bachelors figure prominently on the list. This may be because great thinking seems to leave little time for a sex life—at least not for Kant (d. 1804) or Kierkegaard (d. 1855). Although Nietzsche (d. 1900) and Wittgenstein (d. 1951) never married, we can only guess about their austerity (Nietzsche seemed to suffer from untreated syphilis and Wittgenstein's biographies include stories of secret affairs with young men). We might add to the list fascinating women such as Saint Teresa of Avila or Emily Dickinson. In any event, Nietzsche mocked the very idea of a married philosopher, much in the way that Catholicism has resisted the idea of married priests. Western civilization has benefited enormously from the ascetic sublimation of sex, it must be said.

Quite apart from asceticism, physical limitations can thwart sexual expectations. Marie-Antoinette had to wait seven years before consummating her marriage to the timid, sixteen-year-old Dauphin of France, who was to become Louis XVI. Her husband suffered from an intractable foreskin, a problem he was apparently in no hurry to correct, despite what her biographers have called Marie-Antoinette's intense need for affection. Military service and a variety of injuries can impair the physical ability to have sex. Despite the admittedly serious problems they pose, physical limitations do not bear on the foregone sex that interests me here. Sex sacrificed in the name of a higher cause does.

Many religious authorities and governments have tried to regulate or constrict sexual practices. Works in the social history of a Christian or a Muslim country now seem incomplete without some mention of sexual expectations of the nation at large. If ecclesiastical struggles to regulate pleasure have always been difficult, they are only more so now, in the Information Age. For global travel and virtual communication would seem to abet illicit affairs.

Sexual expectations can lead to love triangles, if not outright harems. In several European countries, mistresses have long served as a largely accepted marital aid. As Oscar Wilde once quipped, the chains of marriage are heavy, and it takes two to carry them, sometimes three. Particularly after his wife had produced a satisfactory number of children, a husband in a "French marriage" would focus his sexual expectations on another woman, all the while remaining married.

Even beyond mistresses, other interesting *ménages* will occasionally circulate in gossip channels. Harold Nicolson and Vita Sackville-West, a socially well-connected British couple in demand at many parties in the early and mid-twentieth century, apparently mingled often enough to produce two children. Otherwise, he pursued affairs with men and she with women (including her most celebrated lover, Virginia Woolf). Both Sackville-West and Nicolson insisted that they derived profound happiness from their legal union, unorthodox though the marriage may have been. Some married couples maintain sexual expectations that have nothing to do with the marriage.

In the modern West, many believe that we deserve romance, that we are entitled to it simply by virtue of heightened consciousness of its desirability. There's someone for everyone, as the popular saying goes. Even after marriage, though, sexual expectations may compel otherwise good people to transgress a promise of fidelity in order to obtain what it is they feel they need or missed. Human creativity and dexterity parade their dazzling plumage in the realm of meeting sexual expectations. Where there is a will, there is a way—and the various ways can be endlessly entertaining.

SEX COMES OF AGE

Courtly love poetry, which emerged in Europe at the end of the eleventh century, transformed romantic expectations. Whereas arranged marriages had for centuries taken shape around economic and social considerations, enthusiasm for love raised the stakes of conjugal unions. As attractive as the idea of marrying for money might have been, the idea of marrying for passionate love gradually captured the popular European imagination. Many came to believe that, far from a tormenting temptation, sexual enjoyment elevated us into noble beings. It was at about this time that marriage became a sacrament in Roman Catholicism, as opposed to simply a legal or financial union.

The profile of romance rose and fell through the centuries following those rhapsodic eleventh-century knights and noble ladies. In the late 1920s, responding to a new spate of sex-related books, an output no doubt tied to the rising popularity of Sigmund Freud, Americans James Thurber and E. B. White published the witty send-up *Is Sex Necessary? or, Why You Feel the Way You Do* (1929). Among the book's chapters was one called "What Should Children Tell Parents?" Nervous parents may have failed to find humor in such musings, precisely because their teenagers appeared to be flirting with disaster.

Writing in the early 1950s, C. S. Lewis warned about the creeping ascendancy of sex in the cultural pecking-order of what really counts in life: "Poster after poster, film after film, novel after novel, associate the idea of sexual indulgence with the ideas of health, normality, youth, frankness, and good humor."[20] In insisting that "this association is a lie," Lewis rejected a sex-driven society, one then already on the horizon, even before a full-fledged sexual revolution began.

In the early 1960s, American adults increasingly worried that college students were instigating a new and dangerous attack on propriety. Accounts of teenagers suffering from venereal disease began to circulate in the media. *Time* and *Newsweek* both featured cover stories in 1964 on sexual awakenings at elite American colleges. It now became acceptable to discuss formerly taboo topics such as homosexuality, contraception, abortion, and masturbation. Racy newspaper and magazine articles proliferated, and an eager market rose up to greet them as sex came of age in America.

Difficult as it is to pinpoint moments of cultural metamorphosis, sex had surely nudged its way into social prominence when the influential French philosopher Michel Foucault, exasperated with sexual liberation, took up the increasingly public path of eroticism in the 1970s. Sex caused as much pain as pleasure, he agreed with Freud, for people who hoped to live in harmonious communities quickly understood that they must deny themselves much of the sex they craved. Although they might indulge their personal appetites, our forebears did so at considerable risk (even spouses lived under the weight of rules governing the occasion, context, kind, or frequency of sex). The modern world differed from previous ages in so far as sexual expectations had indeed escalated. According to Foucault, modern culture teaches us that sex "has become more important than our soul, more important almost than our life."[21] Written in irony, Foucault's point mocks the modern media, which saturate us with sexual images.

Small wonder that our teenagers come to think of their culture as one in which people should risk everything for sex.

We expect more sex from life than our grandparents did. Surely this is what the Vatican's Congregation for the Doctrine of the Faith recognized when, in 1975, it complained in the *Declaration on Sexual Ethics:* "According to contemporary scientific research, the human person is so profoundly affected by sexuality that it must be considered as one of the factors which gives to each individual's life the principal traits that distinguish it." This same document noticed, "Meanwhile a moral decline is becoming increasingly widespread and among its most serious symptoms is the boundless glorification of the sexual."[22] A variety of subsequent testimonials bear out these intuitions. In her bestselling book *Reviving Ophelia,* Mary Pipher concludes that "Girls are having more trouble now than they had thirty years ago, when I was a girl, and more trouble than even ten years ago." The problem, she said, was that: "Girls today are much more oppressed. They are coming of age in a more dangerous, sexualized and media-saturated culture." A New England college student complained in a 1999 book of the shame of being a virgin, and nearly unremitting social pressure to begin a sex life. Sex will become more important in the generations that follow, and the sex we don't have will assume even greater religious and social importance.[23]

THE SEX WE MUST HAVE:
CONJUGAL DEBT

In the short story "For the Relief of Unbearable Urges," a Hasidic Jew obtains dispensation from a rabbi in order to visit a prostitute. The man sought out the advice of a rabbi because his wife had refused him sex for "many months." Upon hearing this, the rabbi responded immediately, "And you don't want a divorce?"[24] Catholics and ascetics will understand the logic behind this sentiment, yet this is precisely what Catholics expect of their priests and nuns. The sex from which the Roman Catholic religious abstain elevates them and inspires the faithful.

Medieval penitentials evoke the sheer difficulty of avoiding sex: from roughly the seventh through the twelfth centuries, Catholic priests throughout Europe relied on these handy guidebooks to interrogate contrite souls and then mete out punishment in the confessional. Sex dominated the penitentials, just as it no doubt did the lives of the faithful. In order to remain in good standing in the church, early Christians had to avoid sex under lots of circumstances: during the forty days leading up to Lent; during Advent, the weeks leading up to Christmas; while a wife was menstruating, pregnant, or lactating; while naked; during daylight; and inexplicably, on Wednesdays, Fridays, and Saturdays. Assuming they followed these stringent rules, medieval Christians gave up a lot of sex, all in the name of showing love for God.

It would be inaccurate to portray Christianity as a simple foe of sexual release. Earlier Christians understood the ferocity of the libido and figured it into their vision of a moral life. Although Saint Paul, a celibate, wished others could live as he did (we can almost hear his voice in the Book of Revelations, where we read of the 144,000 who have not "defiled themselves" with women [Rev. 14:4; see also 1 Cor. 7:7]), he urged those who could not withstand sexual temptation to marry, so that they would not sin.

Christian marriage sought to contain lust, as well as to engender heirs. Once married, the couple owed sex to each other. Saint Paul himself affirmed such a debt: "The husband must give the wife what is due to her, and the wife must give the husband his due. . . . Do not deny yourselves to one another, except when you agree upon a temporary abstinence in order to devote yourselves to prayer . . ." (1 Cor. 7:1-5). Paul was conforming to Jewish tradition here: "within ancient Jewish law, a woman had the right to sexual intercourse, in order that she might have pleasure and bear children, upon whose financial support she depended in her old age."[25] Paul worries that, once denied sex, a spouse might become irascible. Spotting an opportunity, the devil may then profit from marital discord and turn husband and wife against one another.

Although Saint Paul appreciated that women may desire sex, subsequent thinkers have, for the most part, surmised that it is principally women who owe sex to men.[26] About fifteen hundred years ago, the Byzantine theologian Saint John of Damascus (ca. 675-749), exhorted Christians:

> Let every man enjoy his wife. . . . Nor should he blush, but let him go in and settle down in bed, day and night. Let them make love, keeping one another as man and wife, exclaiming: "Do not deny one another, save perhaps by mutual consent." [1 Cor. 7:5] Do you abstain from sexual relations? You don't wish to sleep with your husband? Then he to whom you deny your bounty will go out and do evil and his wickedness will be due to your abstinence.

For two thousand years, Christian sexual expectations have largely amounted to an emergency plan: because there will always be a wolf at the door, we must devise a way to defang it. Hence, marriage. Some novels refer to the idea of conjugal debt and, in so doing, usually indicate that this sense of obligation had filtered down into the lives of ordinary people. In Italo Svevo's modern classic *Zeno's Conscience* (1923), the protagonist fantasizes about marriage to the woman of his dreams:

> I dreamed of victory rather than of love. . . . She was in bridal attire and was coming with me to the altar, but when we were left alone, we didn't make love, not even then. I was her husband and I had gained the right to ask her: "How could you have allowed me to be treated like that?" No other rights mattered to me.[27]

The idea that a woman owes sex to a man as his right may offend contemporary Westerners, and yet the sense of entitlement no doubt endures, tucked away inside our silent expectations of married life.

From the idea that marriage legitimizes the sex people already want to have, Saint John of Damascus draws a reasonable inference: that an unwilling wife will drive her husband out into the streets, where he is likely to cavort with prostitutes, the wives of other men, or perhaps other men. Tennessee Williams's play *Cat on a Hot Tin Roof* illustrates the danger and the steamy frustration of one spouse denying another, although in this instance a gay husband denies his voluptuous wife.

Several decades later, an American television series of almost unprecedented popularity made the point more baldly. In one of the first episodes of the HBO hit series *The Sopranos*, the wife of a New Jersey Mafia boss confesses her sins to a dashing priest she knows well.[28] Yearning to clear her conscience, Carmela Soprano admits to Father Phil that she resents her husband's new psychiatrist, who happens to be a woman. Carmela reasons that the therapist can help her husband in a way none of his previous mistresses could have. Yes, Carmela freely reveals, there have been plenty of other mistresses, none of whom ever mattered to her. Keeping an uneducated mistress was just another form of masturbation for her husband, she explains. She herself had been too tired to meet her husband's needs; keeping a house and raising a family often exhausted her. But an attractive psychiatrist threatened Carmela's security: such a woman could nourish a man both physically and spiritually. Gently but firmly, Father Phil admonishes the penitent Carmela that she is as sinful as her wayward husband: in pulling back from her husband's sexual hunger, she had driven him to seek women who had sex for money. Television viewers learned with Carmela an old lesson, that spouses owe sex to each other.

The idea of marital debt, the sex one spouse owes to the other, makes no sense apart from an appreciation of the sex we never have. Perhaps the most natural occasion on which to ponder the ethical significance of missed sex is after being denied sex from someone to whose body we feel somehow entitled.

Or when comparing Christian ideals to Muslim. Geraldine Brooks has observed that Mohammed "loathed the kind of sexual repression required by Christianity's monastic traditions."[29] One night, when a woman came to Mohammed's house to complain that her husband, Othman, was too busy praying to have sex, Muhammad was so irritated that he didn't even wait to put on his shoes. He went straight to Othman's house, his shoes in his hand, and berated him: "O Othman! Allah didn't send me for monasticism, rather he sent me with a simple and straight law. I fast, pray and also have intimate relations with my wife." Compare Mohammed's ire with this passage from a letter from Saint Paul to the Corinthians: "It is good for a man not to touch a woman. . . . But if they cannot exercise self-control, let them marry: for it is better to marry than to burn" (1 Cor. 7:1). The Muslim attitude seems to smile on sexual intercourse, whereas the Christian one seems reluctantly to tolerate it. Many Muslims see the West's sexual revolution as an inevitable reaction to churches that tried to suppress and make shameful a God-given urge.

To Mohammed, sex within marriage was to be enjoyed by the husband and wife alike. He especially encouraged foreplay and even referred to intercourse without foreplay as a form of cruelty to women. Nor does Islam set limits on the kind of sex married couples can enjoy. "Your wives are your tillage," says the Koran. "Go in therefore unto your tillage in what manner soever ye will" (Sura 2:233). Most Islamic scholars interpret this to mean that all kinds of intercourse, including oral sex, are permissible. As for positions in intercourse, few taboos restrict enthusiastic lovers.

Islam is one of the few religions to include sex as one of the rewards of the afterlife—although only for male believers. The Koran's various descriptions of paradise drip with sensual appeal. In a fertile garden with fountains and shade, male believers will be entertained by gorgeous supernatural beings with "complexions like rubies and pearls," whose eyes will be incapable of noticing another man, and "whom no man will have deflowered before them."

If Muslim women aren't mentioned as partaking in this sexual afterlife, at least they are provided for on earth. In many Muslim countries, one of the few grounds on which a woman can initiate divorce under Islamic law is the failure of her husband to have sex with her at least once in four months. For a sexually frustrated wife is more easily tempted to commit adultery, which leads to the social chaos of civil war.

Canadian historian Elizabeth Abbott has declared Islam (and Judaism as well) a sex-positive religion.[30] Mullahs worldwide will beam with pride over the award; curiously, some Catholics will also smile with approval that Abbott, herself a Catholic, bars her own religion from the list. Here, Abbott clashes with the well-known sociologist Father Andrew Greeley, who has argued that Catholics enjoy sex more than others.[31] According to Greeley, Catholics owe their distinctive sexual playfulness to gracious images of God, images they find in their Roman faith.

Through the centuries, there has been plenty of speculation on who wants sex more—men or women. It stands to reason that the sexual initiator will set the pace in an erotic relationship. If the initiator is more powerful—physically or psychologically—then he or she is likely to have as much sex as he likes. We should not simply assume that the initiator will always be male, nor forget that a partner can rebuff advances. Indeed, a woman bent on reassuring a man of her fidelity might be well advised to deny any interest in sex. What better way to persuade a jealous husband that she is not sleeping with other men than to insist she doesn't even like sex?

In sum: conjugal debt sets the married apart from the celibate. True, a married couple might agree to abstain from sex, but various religious traditions discourage such thinking. Especially the broader, secular culture would seem to: In a book urging that twenty-first-century women return to a servile role vis-à-vis their husbands, bestselling writer Laura Doyle counsels wives to make themselves sexually available to their husbands once a week.[32] According to separate studies, "American married women copulate, on average, one to three times a week, depending on their age. In many cultures women reportedly make love either every day or every night, except when rituals of war, religion, or other local customs intercede."[33]

THE ALLURE OF ALLURE

Being desired by people we see everyday might stand as a popular fantasy, judging from the advertisements in popular magazines. Beauty and sexual desirability count for a lot today, just as they always have. We sometimes think of education as a substitute for sexual attractiveness, a way of compensating for a lack. Writing about public contempt for Marilyn Monroe's intellectual pursuits, Diana Trilling wrote, "The notion that someone with Marilyn Monroe's sexual advantages could have wanted anything except to make love robbed us of a prized illusion, that enough sexual possibility is enough everything."[34]

One reason we may miss sex is the loss of power to enchant others: we make ourselves available, but find no suitable takers. Anxiety swells as we contemplate unattractiveness, while reassuring ourselves that we can excite interest ramps up our self-esteem. In part because we dislike the thought of missed sex—even when we find ourselves settled down in a relationship—we work to maintain our allure, pedaling away in health clubs, churning in chlorinated pools, running up steep hills. It will not do to insist that we are trying to please ourselves by looking good; for genuine narcissists this is no doubt true, but for the majority of gym patrons, the explanation must be more social. The play's the thing.

Primping and preening indicate emotional health in Freud's world, where everyone is thinking about sex. Only when something goes wrong does our mind pull back from sensual fantasies. Sexual repression works as a red flag for Freud; not everyone who takes his hand off the plough of self-improvement is necessarily repressed sexually, but many suffer from anxiety, which creates sexual repression. Although he had long been persuaded that all neuroses originate in sexual disorders, Freud argued in *Inhibitions, Symptoms and Anxiety* (1926) that anxiety was more active than he had previously understood. Fear of danger ahead, a pervasive sense of helplessness, dulled the normally robust libido.

An infinite number of worries may beset us, but one fate looms over all healthy people: aging. Given that sexual desire tends to wane with age, adults of a certain age might comfortably pull back from sexual adventures. But a culture that scorns or pities those not having sex may frustrate a quiet exit from the erotic sphere. It would be misleading and no doubt wrong to attribute the success of Viagra to a highly sexualized culture, for men who want to remain alluring may naturally seek to respond physically to compliments. If someone were to ask how it can be that older men miss something they rarely want anyway (that is, sex), we might respond that the allure of allure prompts them. Men want to remain appealing, and they worry that impotence will tarnish their appeal.

Critics might object that Viagra presses impotent men to want something they perhaps don't, but this can only explain some of the success of the drug. On some level, much advertising seeks to persuade us that we want something we have been happily living without. But advertising is not brainwashing, and eventually we make fairly careful decisions about what we really do or don't want to buy. It is hard to know whether the television advertisements for Viagra create desire where there is none, or rather restore hope. It may be that something like sour grapes overtakes would-be Viagra users. They realized some time ago that they could no longer achieve an erection, and they began to tell themselves that they didn't want to anyway. Now that Viagra enables them, what will they tell themselves? That they still do not really wish to, or that they can at last return to something they missed? Even the popularity of the drug cannot tell us whether men are doing what they want or what they believe is expected of them.

Our hunger for desirability may even reach into the fantasy life of others. A telling scene in the Academy Award–winning film *American Beauty* showcases a teenage femme fatale who studiously cultivates her allure.[35] A high school cheerleader, she flirts widely. When her homely best friend informs her that many of their peers—even undesirable ones—must be masturbating to the thought of her, the budding sex object gushes. She reasons that service as a masturbation fantasy indicates a high probability that she will succeed in her quest to become a fashion model. Like so many of us, the cheerleader wants to be admired, envied. What she lacks is a sense of danger, the danger of being envied.

Would-be monogamous souls find themselves increasingly undercut by a culture that glorifies physical attractiveness and the sensual delights to which it can lead. Meanwhile health clubs welcome faithful spouses who make themselves more attractive to people with whom they can't have sex. And couples engaged to be married, like religious novices contemplating vows of chastity, try not to think about all the sex they're about to give up.

While Saint Paul advised that it was better to marry than to burn, and best of all to refrain from sex within a marriage or never marry at all, the Catholic Church later forbade impotent men to marry, so central had the act of sex become. This ecclesiastical linking of allure to physical ability may surprise us by its cold-heartedness, but we needn't worry. Pills can now solve a multitude of problems.

Today antidepressants can restore sad people to happiness but, in the process, often deprive the formerly depressed of sexual desire. People complain about this side effect and stop taking their medications, although they feel little or no sexual desire while depressed anyway. A pill that both reduced anxiety and increased sexual vigor would conquer the drug market.

What if there were a pill that extinguished lust in the way that birth control pills can prevent conception? How many of us would take it, and under what circumstances? What about an operation that would erase lust permanently? Presumably, Buddhist monks and Roman Catholic religious (nuns, brothers, and priests) would opt for such a procedure, but would they really? Asking a seminarian or postulant nun to uproot his or her libido permanently would separate the wheat from the chaff in a draconian way; as it now stands, priests and nuns can always back out of their vows of chastity later. Regret is tamed by the assurance that we can always change our minds. Stamping out the allure of allure will require real effort from anyone who, at base, likes being wanted.

THE THING I DON'T DO

We may object to various biases, personal ambitions, or political positions, but few of them will repulse us as rape, incest, homosexuality, or perhaps sadism / masochism can. Rape and incest are crimes, although homosexuality isn't anymore (in most places). The sex we don't have stretches to rape and incest, and this is as it should be. Sex that doesn't happen intersects with both the forbidden and the merely repulsive, and this overlap can clarify the importance of the sex we don't have.

Through sexual acts we would not engage in, we assure ourselves of our virtue. This exclusion from the mental menu serves as a rationalization for morality. It also explains the great difficulty in overthrowing homophobia. Gay people have served the very useful role of bête noire: promiscuous heterosexuals may engage in all sorts of sexual indiscretions, but as long as they could point to gay sex as something they would simply never do, straight people could console themselves with the thought that they really were moral after all. If gay sex no longer shocks mainstream citizens as immoral, then it becomes harder for naughty heterosexuals to tell themselves that they remain basically upstanding.

We can tie some of the sex we don't have to disgust. We probably wouldn't want to marry a person who wasn't disgusted by anything. Disgust can help us tell whether we are dating marriage material. Problems begin, however, when couples disagree over what counts as disgusting. We must make a distinction between kinds of sex we won't have and people we won't have sex with. "We would never have sex with whips and chains" differs from "We would never have sex with someone of the same sex, or in our immediate family, or over the age of fifty, or plainly overweight, or of a particular ethnic background." There's a parallel to be drawn with the foods we don't eat. Various groups distinguish themselves by saying "We're the people who won't eat shellfish," or "We're the people who won't eat meat on Fridays," or "We're the people who won't drink caffeine." Food taboos parallel sexual taboos.

This distinction can be nicely summed up by contrasting regret (sex we would like to have but can't or won't) with disgust (sex we do not want to have). This contrast helps us see how far we've come morally. Our cultural progress requires a third category here: indifference. Exclusively heterosexual people may not want or seek sex with someone of their own sex. Whereas our heterosexual forebears generally regarded homosexual romance with aversion, many exclusively heterosexual people now regard it with detachment and even lend it their political support. The emotional impediment to civil rights for sexual nonconformists loses fire with each successive decade.

You reveal quite a bit more of yourself in discussing the sex you *do* have than in discussing the sex you *don't* have. Thus, people feel safer, less vulnerable, discussing the sex they don't have. Apart from the Marquis de Sade, most of us feel the necessity of protecting a sexual category that could be called "the things I don't do." Sex we consciously avoid would make us feel regret if ever we had it. Nuns and celibates include all sex under the heading "the things I don't do," whereas the sexually active list only certain kinds of sex there. The motivations for constructing the set differ markedly: a nun might say that her sacrifice of sex is important precisely because the sacrifice is so difficult to make, whereas a sexually uninterested person might say that her sacrifice isn't difficult at all. In any event, we ourselves fill the category "What I Won't Do" (even though our filling of the category may seem nothing more than acquiescing to social expectations). We decide what we won't do: sexual opportunities declined out of a desire to remain faithful may lead to regret, whereas incidents avoided and perhaps rarely even thought about will, upon reflection, likely conjure up disgust.

THE SIN OF SEX HAD: INFIDELITY

As adults, sexual expectations may play a role in our deciding whom to marry and even date. Just as a prospective employer may negatively view the "job hopping" of a potential employee, so may a prospective partner frown over the knowledge that a love interest has "gotten around."

After we marry, we often want our partners to look great in public—their good looks flatter us, we think, because others will notice that we have landed someone beautiful. (Interesting exceptions are Orthodox Jewish women who shave their hair and Muslim women who wear the burkha.) However, we wince at the idea that our attractive spouses may indulge the attention they receive for being attractive: we want our rivals to admire our spouses, but from a distance. Anxiety thwarts ambition in this arena.

The monotony and sexual abeyance of some marriages transports spouses to a state of frustration they may find familiar, especially if they had wed as virgins determined to remain so until nuptials. After years of marriage, however, the illusion of eternal passion will have passed. After passionate love has dwindled into companionate love, we find more disturbing the sex our partner might have had with someone else than we do the sex we are not having with our partner. It is one thing to continue to notice and appreciate the physical beauty of others after we've married: just because we've ordered doesn't mean that we can't still look at the menu. But it is another thing entirely to betray a spouse through adultery.

Lapses in monogamy, like lapses in celibacy, highlight the messiness of human free will. Self-control ebbs away from us when hormones rage, but losing the battle against lust can feel a lot like winning. Our confidants may plead with us to turn back. Sounding much like Hamlet castigating his mother for her sex life, they reason with us that the struggle will get easier with each successive night we avoid sex.

What defines someone as married is sexual fidelity, we might think, not a wedding certificate. This new definition could help us understand some of the resistance of many Westerners to the idea of same-sex marriage. Gay men, unlike gay women, have long been considered promiscuous, incapable of fidelity even to a "perverse" relationship. If gay men were capable of sexual fidelity, then they would in some (obviously nonreligious) respect meet the signal criterion of marriage. The big problem with thinking about marriage in terms of sexual fidelity is adultery: many married men with mistresses will insist that they are properly married.

Infidelity begins in regret over missed sex, and marriage vows begin in confidence that missed sex will not amount to much. Infidelity and optimism reserve to themselves distinct pleasures: secretly managing to get what you want, in the first case, and privately pondering the joy of never being able even to look at another man (or woman), in the second.

The high adultery rate in the West testifies to the regret we feel over the sex we are not having. Whether adulterers divorce to get more sex or to get sex with someone else, they feel regret. One of the most common reasons people give for leaving a job is insufficient pay. Insufficient sex likely breaks up marriages as well, although not so often as infidelity. The sex we never had therefore stands as one of the highest gifts we extend to people we care about.

But the sex we don't have can also amount to a political statement, as many men and women define themselves through revulsion to certain physical acts. The acts we would simply never engage in or people we would never have sex with are more easily discussed than what we actually do in bed.

Tempted spouses struggling to remain faithful to one another will tell you the importance of sex not had, just as ordinary people will when questioned about physical acts they find repulsive. And so, despite the sexual revolution of the 1960s, the sex we don't have still matters more to us than the sex we do have.

TIME OUT

What can be said about regulating sexual abeyance, planning its beginning and end?

It has become fashionable to refer to a child's punishment as "time out." The child has misbehaved and so his parents send him to his room. They explain that he requires quiet time in order to reflect on his misdeed. In time, he may resume play with other children. This is punishment, to be sure; but when applied to marriage, a "time out" might appear more of a reward. What I have in mind here is not the arrangement called "separation" that prefigures many a Western divorce, but something more like a day off from work.

This creative solution has found application to various problems. At the end of the 1980s, the King of Belgium, a devout Roman Catholic, realized he was losing the battle over abortion reform. Rather than give up the throne or approve of softer abortion laws, he abdicated for a day, the day on which the Belgian parliament passed the revised abortion legislation. He resumed his rule over a changed country with a clean conscience. Sexually, a "time out" would correspond roughly to declaring that in certain parts of the world or perhaps on certain days of the year, your otherwise loyal spouse may commit adultery with impunity. "Time out" sounds like the sexual option branded "the third way" among Catholic clergy; neither marriage nor celibacy, it worked its way into discussions of priestly celibacy in the 1960s and 1970s. The general superior of the Jesuits eventually saw fit to forbid explicitly "the third way."[36]

I would not advise married couples, struggling to cope with lust for others, to experiment with time outs. Internet chat rooms, like old-fashioned pornography, may serve the same end. Far from straining fidelity, such creative outlets may strengthen it. Exercising self-control as we might our muscles makes sense. In his autobiography *The Story of My Experiments with Truth* (first published in English in 1927), Gandhi recounts his arranged marriage as a thirteen-year-old boy and the Hindu custom of separating newlywed couples for much of their first year together. Gandhi took this custom to reflect the wisdom of Hindu misgivings over the fire of adolescent passion. Western-style "commuter marriages," in which spouses live in different cities in order to pursue their respective careers, may inadvertently serve this same purpose. Absence may make the heart grow fonder—provided, of course, one can resist the call of sex not had.

The idea of a marital "time out" does not sit well with the ideal of integrity, or singleness of heart. A faithful spouse who muses wistfully over sex not had might not seem laudable but is still preferable to a philandering one. Plenty of women have allowed their husband a mistress, perhaps the most concrete form of a "time out," but it is hard to imagine more than a few of these wives liking the arrangement. Happy are they who never need a "time out" at all.

REPRODUCTIVE RECREATION

What would we say of someone who possessed a fortune but who chose to live modestly? He or she might frustrate others who dreamt of riches. What good is the fortune, others might wonder, if you acted as if it didn't exist? Attractive people who forego sex for God or out of fidelity to a spouse might point to the moral importance, perhaps even to the pleasure, of self-discipline. Sex not had, like money not spent, showcases our willpower and demonstrates our commitment.

The sex we don't have may well frustrate us, but it has long delighted religious authorities. Christian aversion to contraception redoubled the recommendation for abstinence; the point of both was to please God. Faithful couples point to deliberately missed sexual opportunities with interlopers as concrete proof of true love. Since the twelfth century, the Roman Catholic Church has demanded sexual sacrifice (that is, celibacy) from nuns, priests, and brothers. And at the end of the twentieth century, the church formally demanded that same sacrifice from all gay and lesbian followers.

The sex we don't have involves type, frequency, partner, and abstention. Of all the reasons to forego sex, getting along in society (that is, holding a job, avoiding attacks brought on by jealousy) must be one of the best. In 1905 Freud published *Three Essays on the Theory of Sexuality,* a work in which he argued that sexual drives must be and effectively are repressed so that people can maintain stable identities. Freud understood that we will miss opportunities gone by, so much so that regret over missed sex can bother us in a way that regret over missed food or missed vacations cannot. Freud saw it as the cost of civilization; 1960s Berkeley students viewed it as a crying shame; AIDS taught that it was the cost of survival; the post-AIDS era will see it more or less as Freud did. Despite a plethora of reasons to regret lost youth, missed sex will likely remain one of the most common.

Erotic expression surely defies easy generalization, as does erotic repression. And yet we can see that the sex we don't have says more about us than the sex we do have. An anonymous contiguity of available bodies beckons modern urbanites and others with access to transportation. The sexually ambitious will scour each new landscape for opportunities. The more vital our media makes sex out to be, the more curious is sex foregone. Vows of chastity, like vows of monogamy, will be harder for us to honor than they were for our grandparents. Man (and woman) has no greater love than to lay down his libido for his partner, it now seems.

Aquinas and other theologians have maintained that original sin perverted us so that we prefer sex, wealth, and power to the greatest good of all, God. If Aquinas is right, then it may be that the sex we forego is no more noteworthy than the wealth or power we decline. Most people will report that sex is easier to get than wealth or power, however, which means there is something particularly remarkable about the sex we don't have. If foregone sex did not call out to so many men and women, there would be little point to asceticism. Like a fabulous party to which we are not invited, the sex we don't have beckons us to wonder what we've missed.

FOUR

Better a
Straight Jew than a
Gay Catholic?

To great media acclaim, Pope John Paul II ushered in the new millennium by apologizing to the worldwide Jewish community for Roman Catholic silence in, and perhaps unwitting contribution to, the Holocaust. This contrition is all to the good. Several months later, on July 9, 2000, the Pope publicly expressed "bitterness" over a gay pride festival held in Rome that day.[1] The Vatican had labored to prevent World Pride Roma, a gay-pride parade, from taking place. After the papal denunciation, international newspapers quoted Franco Grillini, the honorary president of an Italian gay rights organization, as saying that the Vatican hierarchy detests gays and lesbians.

Several different questions present themselves here: What might be the relation between ongoing homophobia and the Vatican's position? Can an analogy be drawn to anti-Semitism and the representation of Jews in Catholic liturgy? What should intuitively matter more to a religious group—beliefs about God or kinds of sex? I will discuss Catholic-Jewish relations here as an example of a larger phenomenon:

not just Catholics, but more and more Jews, Protestants, and Muslims are thinking of religious ethics primarily in terms of sex.

Through the centuries, Roman Catholic thinkers have had a lot to say about both Jews and sex. College students interested in reading about sex could hardly do better than to study Catholic moral theology (which, of course, covers more ground than just sex). Whereas Jews and gays long shared the same boat in Roman Catholic theology, the Vatican now smiles on Jews. In his magisterial work *Christianity, Social Tolerance, and Homosexuality*, the noted Yale historian John Boswell wrote:

> the fate of Jews and gay people has been almost identical throughout European history, from early Christian hostility to extermination in concentration camps. These same laws which oppressed Jews oppressed gay people; the same groups bent on eliminating Jews tried to wipe out homosexuality; the same periods of European history which could not make room for Jewish distinctiveness reacted violently against sexual nonconformity; the same countries which insisted on religious uniformity imposed majority standards of sexual conduct; and even the same methods of propaganda were used against Jews and gay people—picturing them as animals bent on the destruction of the children of the majority.[2]

Roman Catholic morality and sensibility pervade the European culture and history of which Boswell writes. Boswell's sweeping generalization holds true in spite of periodic attempts on the part of Catholic leaders to stem an historically steady current of anti-Semitism. For example, Benedict XV condemned anti-Semitism in 1916; his public statement responded to a plea from the American Jewish Committee, worried about the persecution of Polish Jews in the First World War. Other popes, for instance Benedict XIV, Pius X, and Leo XIII, also spoke out against mistreatment of Jews.

Pius XII, pontiff during the Second World War, made the following statement on August 3, 1946: "We condemned on various occasions in the past the persecution that a fanatical anti-Semitism inflicted on the Hebrew people."[3] The American writer Garry Wills, himself a Catholic, has called Pius XII's self-exoneration "a deliberate falsehood."[4] The English historian John Cornwell, also a Catholic, has deemed Pius XII "Hitler's Pope." Even though historians still argue over the road blocks to Catholic-Jewish relations, it seems fair to side with those who criticize the Vatican for sins of omission (witness John Paul II's own apology to Jews).

Something remarkable has happened since 1980, when Boswell noted that the Vatican had extended an olive branch to Jews. The Vatican has not embraced gay people—even gay Catholics—with the same enthusiasm. Could it possibly be that sexuality now matters to the Vatican more than religious belief? Could the Vatican (or anyone for that matter) believe that the final judgment of God will come down to sexual acts, as opposed to religious devotion? Yes. Sexuality has trumped religious creed in Rome—it *is* better to be a straight Jew than a gay Catholic. This argument could highlight a broader, emerging tendency in the West to reduce religious ethics to sexual ethics. With few exceptions, believers no longer go to war or take to the streets in protest over theology (for example, transubstantiation or the divinity of Christ); believers now fight chiefly over issues of sex and gender. In the face of a historical crescendo of public talk about sex, religious ethics has become less a means of worshiping God and more of a social organizing force. Sex bothers believers as differences in dogma no longer can.

WHAT CATHOLICS THINK ABOUT JEWS

For a few reasons, it is hard to pinpoint what Catholics think about Jews. Not only does the vast number of Catholics make generalizations difficult, but liberal and conservative insiders disagree over just who counts as Catholic. Ordinary Catholics, "Catholics in the streets," may struggle over how to articulate what ties them to Rome. Several *New York Times* polls in the United States in the past fifteen years have revealed that nearly one-third of Americans who identify themselves as Roman Catholic do not believe that Christ is physically present in the Eucharist.[5]

Anyone familiar with the most basic facts about the Reformation may struggle to understand how a person who does not believe Christ is physically present in the Eucharist can consider himself Roman Catholic. Talking about what Catholics think or believe in the twenty- first century is a tricky matter indeed. As I see them, ordinary Catholics do not stray far from church teaching in their quest for spiritual sustenance. They cheerfully tolerate adherents of other religions, as opposed to celebrating them.

It would take another book to detail how the Vatican has effectively tackled the problem of social control of the faithful of many different nations. In ways too complex to cover here, the Vatican shapes the beliefs of Roman Catholics of varying degrees of piety. Perhaps most immediate of all, priests function as authority figures in Roman Catholic culture.[6] The disapproval of a priest means something to practicing Catholics; the disapproval of a bishop means even more. When the pope speaks, he represents God Almighty, according to church doctrine.

Catholic culture absorbs anxiety and anger generated by the Holy See (that is, the Vatican). This is not to say that Catholics in the street will generally turn out to be conversant with theology or church history; to the contrary, most of them know only the basic outlines of their ancient faith. Ask a Catholic when Constantinople split from Rome, where the Pope spends his summers, or why to avoid meat on Fridays during Lent and see what explanation you get. Ask a Catholic what the Holy See says about gays and lesbians and you will hear an answer.

What does the Vatican think of Jews? The answer to this question in any era will color and largely determine the quality of Jewish-Catholic relations. If you look to Christian Scriptures for an answer, you will find a clear message:

> Indeed, God did not send the Son into the world to condemn the world, but in order that the world might by saved through him. Those who believe in him are not condemned; but those who do not believe are condemned already . . . (John 3:17-19)

The passage goes on to say, somewhat cryptically, that those who do good have a special relationship to God. Since the 1950s, Catholic theologians have pressed on this ambiguity to admit Jews into heaven. Many Catholics have become more compassionate, and more vocal about their compassion, in the last fifty years. Ordinary Catholics have noticed this transformation and applauded it (cynics will argue with this point, I recognize). Catholics fearful that their church may bear some responsibility for the death of six million Jews under German National Socialism will be inclined to embrace the Vatican's 1998 report *We Remember: A Reflection on the Shoah,* which purportedly exonerates the church of complicity in the Holocaust.

For many centuries the Vatican has allowed and even encouraged anti-Semitism. Perhaps successful, happy Jews confused Christians harboring doubts about Jesus. Jewish conversions to Christianity naturally comforted and reassured those put off by Jewish piety. Saint Thomas Aquinas had thought of Jews as willfully subversive, defiant in the face of what they knew to be truth. Referring to circumstances surrounding the death of Christ, Aquinas accused Jewish elders of affected ignorance, "for they saw manifest signs of his Godhead; yet they perverted them out of hatred and envy of Christ."[7] Medieval Christians blamed Jews for virtually every famine, war, or epidemic that threatened Christian communities. Christians sometimes forced Jews to live in urban ghettos. David Kertzer's 1998 book *The Kidnapping of Edgardo Mortara* personalizes the vulnerability of Jewish enclaves.[8] Kertzer's research begins in the centuries-old Catholic practice of secretly baptizing and then arrogating Jewish children. One child, Edgardo Mortara, was not only separated from his Jewish-Italian parents, who begged for their child's return; he was eventually adopted by Pope Pius IX himself. The two lived together in the Vatican as father and son in the late nineteenth century. The boy eventually became a Catholic priest and never saw his parents again.

The Third Reich's conquest of European lands in the twentieth century exacerbated the division between Catholics and Jews. As National Socialism in Germany increased both in power and in antipathy toward Jews, Pope Pius XII allegedly did little to help them. His decision not to condemn unequivocally Nazism and anti-Semitism during World War II continues to impede the modern church's relations with Jews. Pius XII explained that he could not have done more for Jews because he risked provoking a Nazi backlash against both Jews and Catholics living in Nazi-occupied territories. Contemporary defenders of Pius XII point out that Roman Catholic moral theology forbids risking innocent lives through the provocation of political powers. As I have indicated, debate over Catholic responsibility for the Holocaust continues.

Roughly two decades after World War II another pope, John XXIII, took definitive steps to eradicate Christian anti-Semitism. In the documents of Vatican II we find evidence of his abiding revulsion to anti-Semitism. In the "Declaration on the Relation of the Church to Non-Christian Religions" we read, "Even though the Jewish authorities and those who followed their lead pressed for the death of Christ, neither all Jews indiscriminately at that time, nor Jews today, can be charged with the crimes committed during his passion." The statement continues, "Indeed, the Church reproves every form of persecution against whomsoever it may be directed. Remembering, then, her common heritage with the Jews and moved not by any political consideration, but solely by the religious motivation of Christian charity, she deplores all hatreds, persecutions, displays of antisemitism leveled at any time or from any source against the Jews."[9] This pivotal document, *Nostra Aetate* (1965), renounces the charge that all Jews are forever guilty of the murder of Christ and deepens the impact of *Lumen Gentium* (1964), which had admitted Jews into Catholic heaven.

What is important to note in *Nostra Aetate* is that John XXIII doesn't so much affirm the holiness of Jews as he condemns religious persecution in general and anti-Semitism in particular. His message is clear: that Jews refuse a Christocentric view of God does not constitute good reason for shunning them, let alone speaking of them as naturally condemned to hell.

In moving public displays, John Paul II has honored the spiritual relationship between Christians and Jews. On April 13, 1986 the pontiff visited the synagogue of Rome, in the first recorded appearance at a synagogue by a pope since Peter. While there the pope said, "With Judaism we have a relationship which we do not have with any other religion. You are our dearly beloved brothers and, in a certain way, it could be said you are our elder brothers." John Paul II later presided over another unprecedented moment in the history of the Roman Catholic Church when, on April 7, 1994, six candlesticks of the menorah were lit and the Kaddish prayer for the dead recited in his presence at the Vatican.[10]

Though Jewish suffering in the Holocaust may well have prompted John Paul II's actions, it would be possible for a Catholic pontiff to deplore the Holocaust while maintaining that Catholics had little or nothing to do with it. John Paul II did not choose that course. In December 1990 he received an international delegation from Jewish organizations urging endorsement of their "Prague Statement." This document, drawn up in September of that year, focused on the liturgy of Holy Week (which precedes Easter Sunday) and asserted that some aspects of Catholic teaching and practice had fostered anti-Semitism. Although most Nazis had grown up in Protestant churches, Catholicism contributed to a dramatic increase of anti-Semitism that may have ushered in the Holocaust. The Oberammergau Passion Play offers a prime example: this dramatic depiction of the death of Jesus draws thousands of tourists to the small German town in which it has been performed once a decade since 1634. Hostile references to Jews used to pepper the performance.[11] The Anti-Defamation League in New York and Jewish leaders from around the world had criticized earlier productions of the Passion play for the way it blamed Jews; the director of the performance in the year 2000 consequently altered the traditional script.

Others in the church hierarchy followed the example of John Paul II's compassion. In late September 1997 French newspapers reported that the French bishops had convened at Vichy in order formally to ask forgiveness from Jews for Catholic silence in the face of anti-Jewish laws some fifty years earlier. *Le Monde* reported that the bishops went so far as to declare that the Roman Catholic liturgy of the Eucharist may have encouraged anti-Semitism.[12] Six months later, in March 1998, Italian newspapers were the first to report on Joseph Cardinal Ratzinger's official apology to Jews. According to the *Corriere della Sera*, Ratzinger avowed that Catholic anti-Semitism played a role in the (Catholic) toleration of Nazi persecution of Jews.[13]

Lastly, in January 2002, the international media reported on a little book titled *The Jewish People and the Holy Scriptures in the Christian Bible*.[14] Endorsed by Ratzinger, the scholarly work effectively rejected the way some Christians have viewed the Old Testament. According to the new book, Jews and Christians together wait for the Messiah: Jews, for one that will make his first appearance on earth, and Christians, for one that will be returning. Some Jewish leaders praised what they perceived to be the Vatican's new stance (*Dominus Jesus*, released by the Vatican the year before, emphasized the redemptive role of Christ and had exacerbated tensions between Catholic and Jewish scholars). The point to be taken from these various examples of rapprochement is that Rome really does seem to be working hard to mend fences with Jews.

Too little, too late? Jews no doubt appreciate whatever goodwill non-Jews show them. Some Jews may be sufficiently independent or angry that they don't *care* what non-Jews think of them. Yet the Catholic Church, as one of the most powerful institutions in the West, affects the ebb and flow of anti-Semitism to some notable extent. Although Roman Catholic pontiffs have commanded less and less authority in Europe since the Reformation, Jews could hardly fail to recognize the usefulness of a pope as a highly visible ally in the struggle against Christian anti-Semitism. For Jews, concern about relations with Catholics is largely, if not exclusively, practical.

WHAT CATHOLICS THINK OF GAYS

Like Jews, gays have suffered in Christian communities. Although the current pontiff has courted Jewish forgiveness and goodwill, it seems difficult to imagine that the Vatican would apologize in the near future for having ruined gay lives. Nor does it seem likely that the Holy See will publicly examine its conscience to check whether it has condoned or contributed to homophobic currents in Europe or the United States. Although gay people died in Nazi concentration camps for being gay, it would be wrong to say that ruling Germans disliked them as much or as consistently as Jews. It might seem that the Holocaust finally earned Jews the social support they had long been denied by Catholics, who for the most part had ruled Europe for centuries. And yet it took roughly four decades for Catholics to respond to the Shoah; John XXIII pushed to soften the Holy See's stance on so-called infidels in the early 1960s, but it was still two decades later before a pontiff would visit the synagogue of Rome. No, the Holocaust in and of itself cannot account for the new Catholic embrace of Jews.

The modern Catholic view of gay persons evolved in the decades following World War II. The Sacred Congregation for the Doctrine of the Faith (CDF) issued an historic statement in 1975, entitled *Declaration on Certain Questions Concerning Sexual Ethics,* which asserted the reality of a homosexual orientation. It had long been thought that everyone everywhere was heterosexual; some heterosexual persons, for one bad reason or another, committed homosexual acts. Persons involved in homosexual contact were not acting true to their nature. All homosexual acts had been roundly condemned, in part because they violated natural law, and in part because they could never result in the conception of a child, which the Holy See still views as the moral justification for all sexual activity.

In 1975 the Vatican defended homosexuals as persons who did not choose sexual desire for members of their own sex; homosexual persons were acting according to their nature when they engaged in erotic activity with others of their own sex. The document claimed, "In the pastoral field, these homosexuals must certainly be treated with understanding and sustained in the hope of overcoming their personal difficulties and their inability to fit into society. Their culpability will be judged with prudence." Here stands a parallel with the approved Catholic view of Jews as expressed a decade earlier in the *Declaration on the Relation of the*

Church to Non-Christian Religions. The new document on gay people clearly stated, "The particular inclination of the homosexual person is not a sin." What was a sin was the physical expression of homoerotic desire.

A companion document to *Declaration on Certain Questions Concerning Sexual Ethics* followed a decade later. Cardinal Joseph Ratzinger's 1986 *A Letter to the Bishops of the Catholic Church on the Pastoral Care of Homosexual Persons* articulated at greater length some of the themes expressed in the 1975 document. This second piece took a much harsher view of a homosexual orientation, calling it "an objective disorder," as opposed to morally neutral. Gays and lesbians were forbidden any erotic expressions of love, even within the context of relationships aiming for permanency. Enforced celibacy thus pushed gay and lesbian Catholics into the same moral universe as priests and nuns, who freely choose that universe. This is not the place to oppose the logic of enforced celibacy, but to consider what kinds of messages the Holy See sends.

For my purposes here, what is most important about the 1986 letter is this statement: "It is deplorable that homosexual persons have been and are the object of violent malice in speech or in action. Such treatment deserves condemnation from the church's pastors wherever it occurs. It reveals a kind of disregard for others which endangers the most fundamental principles of a healthy society. The intrinsic dignity of each person must always be respected in word, in action and in law." The 1986 letter acknowledged and responded to widespread hatred of gay and lesbian persons, much in the way that the documents of Vatican II did to hatred of Jews. Various cynics have disputed the sincerity of the Holy See in condemning violence toward gay and lesbian people and take the CDF's document to imply that the Vatican believes gays have brought gay-bashing on themselves.[15] I am prepared to take the Vatican at its word, though, and to maintain that the Vatican now explicitly condemns both Jew-bashing and gay-bashing.

Nonetheless, the Holy See has yet to embrace gay people as warmly as it has Jews. The Vatican sends us mixed messages about lesbians and gays. The gay psychotherapist John McNeill, a former Jesuit, is one of many who have claimed that Catholic tradition contributes to hatred of gay people. In response to Cardinal Ratzinger's letter of 1986, he wrote,

> In my more than twenty years' experience of pastoral care with thousands of gay Catholics and other Christians, the gay men most likely to act out their sexual needs in an unsafe, compulsive way and, therefore, to expose themselves to the HIV virus, are precisely those *persons who have internalized the self-hatred that their religions impose on them* (my italics).[16]

McNeill has gay Catholics of a certain kind in mind here (that is, deeply religious individuals), even though he recognizes that other religions have condemned gay and lesbian sex. McNeill shows sensitivity to the possibility that external homophobia can lead to internal homophobia: gay people can come to loathe themselves.

Despite its tepid embrace of gay and lesbian Catholics, the Vatican continues to scrutinize gay-friendly theologians and bishops. Public debate over Father Charles Curran divided Catholics. In 1986 the Vatican formally withdrew Curran's tenure in the theology department at the Catholic University of America. In his writing, Curran urged Catholics against seeing traditional teachings on sexual ethics as "exceptionless norms." For Curran, homosexual acts were not necessarily sinful. At roughly the same time, the Vatican publicly reprimanded Archbishop Raymond Hunthausen of Seattle for endorsing a local ordinance outlawing discrimination against gays. Although it was Hunthausen's antinuclear stance that ultimately landed him in trouble with Rome, numerous liberal Catholics went on record saying that the Vatican would not have chastised so vigorously a bishop unsympathetic to integrating gay and lesbian Catholics into the mainstream church.

The Vatican continues to worry about the increasing toleration of gays and lesbians. A 1992 document, *Some Considerations Concerning the Response to Legislative Proposals on the Non-Discrimination of Homosexual Persons,* incurred resistance from many segments of the American church. While deploring acts of violence against homosexuals, the document defended such violence as understandable because of the way homosexuals conduct themselves. The document even went so far as to suggest barring gays and lesbians from certain areas of employment, such as teaching school and counseling youth: "There are areas in which it is not unjust discrimination to take sexual orientation into account, for example, in the placement of children for foster care, in employment of teachers or athletic coaches, and in military recruitment."

The Vatican later claimed that this document was not meant to be published and disseminated, only to generate discussion among bishops (at the time, the state of Colorado had recently repealed local gay and lesbian nondiscrimination ordinances). The incident naturally saddened many Catholic families struggling to embrace gay members. Then, in the summer of 1999, the Vatican reprimanded two Americans, Father Robert Nugent and Sister Jeannine Gramick, for their ministry to gay and lesbian Catholics. The Vatican reiterated and emphasized its stance that gay and lesbian persons are "intrinsically disordered" and that homogenital contact is "evil." The CDF formally silenced Sister Jeannine, who left the School Sisters of Notre Dame and joined the Sisters of Loretto.

Gay and lesbian Catholics have more at stake in what the Vatican says about them than do Jews. Gay Catholics committed to their faith find themselves caught in a double bind. In his 1997 study *American Catholic*, Charles Morris offers the following description of gays and lesbians at Most Holy Redeemer Church, one of San Francisco's "gay" churches:

> They believe that the Catholic Church is the true path to salvation. They
> believe in the sacraments, especially the Eucharist. They think that the
> worldwide identity of the Church through Rome and the Pope is very
> important. And they think that the Vatican and John Paul II are simply
> wrong when they stipulate what kind of sexual practices are necessary to
> get to heaven.[17]

Plenty of other Catholic churches attract same-sex couples: St. Matthew's in Washington, D.C.; St. Monica's in Los Angeles; and, in New York City, St. Joseph's, Saint Francis Xavier, and Saint Veronica's.

Some gay and lesbian Catholics find it as difficult to walk away from their faith as it would be to abandon their sexuality. The pain felt by practicing gay and lesbian Catholics is only exacerbated by views such as that of James P. McFadden, president of the National Committee of Catholic Laymen, who lamented in December 1986: "you don't need to be Catholic to be Catholic anymore. If you dissent, you don't get out. That's the problem. Martin Luther looks like a prince compared to these people because he knew when it was time to go."[18] For some conservatives, dissent and its resulting pluralism threatens the church more than outright defections from the faith. American Catholics, whether gay or not, may be unusually fierce in holding onto their ties to Rome. Despite disagreements with the pope over various sexual issues, then, romance does not replace religion. The two may conflict, but the easy way out (ceasing to go to Mass, ceasing to try to belong within the church) is unacceptable for gays and lesbians who subscribe to the rest of Catholic doctrine and tradition.

Lesbian and gay Catholics must puzzle over the protection extended to Jews but denied to them. Lesbian and gay Catholics may feel trapped, for it must surely be worse to desert the faith than never to join it at all. Presumably the idea that there is salvation outside the Catholic Church only helps non-Catholics, not lapsed Catholics (who, if anything, might seem likely to be punished more severely than the faithful of other religions). As James Carroll notes in *Constantine's Sword*:

Catholics had renounced the "No salvation outside the Church" in 1953, when Richard Cushing, the archbishop of Boston, at the direction of the Vatican, excommunicated the antisemitic priest Father Leonard Feeney for bludgeoning Jews with it. But Feeney had Saint Thomas Aquinas, logic, and exactly 650 years of Church history on his side. In the years since the close of Vatican II, Church reform has faltered, and the logical inconsistency in the Church's position—making universalist claims for Jesus as the "absolutely necessary way," but not for the institution that alone shows the way to Jesus—has not been fully dismantled. Non-Catholics, so far, have seemed grateful for this more limited absolutism, and have not pushed against its hollow part. Catholics who have done so, like Hans Küng, have been silenced as teachers of Catholic theology.[19]

Curiously, lesbian and gay Catholics who worship Jesus fail to qualify for Vatican encouragement (in the way the Vatican encourages Jews to celebrate their Jewishness), presumably because they appear to threaten or oppose the church itself.

Various critics of Roman Catholic sexual ethics (Andrew Sullivan, most notably) acknowledge the compassion underlying the Holy See's somewhat radical acknowledgment of a genuinely homosexual orientation. A balanced assessment of official Catholic attitudes toward gays and lesbians should mention the generosity of the church, most notably in the archdiocese of New York, to persons with AIDS. The Catholic Church, it must be said, cares deeply about persons with AIDS. This generosity illuminates the disconnect between doctrine and pastoral response on which so many priests and nuns have commented in the years since Vatican II. That said, my focus in this book rests on Catholic doctrine, according to which one's identification as a sexual minority overrides the rest of one's self-identity, despite the pains the Vatican takes to integrate sexuality into a larger human personality. Being gay sets you apart from other Catholics in a way that being French, black, or Jewish does not.

HOW JEWS LOOK AT GAYS

The deep division in Catholic culture over gay and lesbian relationships finds a parallel in Judaism because some Jews struggle over questions about sex just as much as Catholics do.

Comparing the two faiths is quite difficult, for there are no formal differences within Catholicism, as there are in Judaism. Strikingly absent from the Vatican documents about the Jews is any reference to the four branches of Judaism: Orthodox, Conservative, Reconstructionist, and Reform. When we compare the moral status of straight Jews to gay

Catholics from a Catholic perspective, we see an inevitable awkwardness in the Catholic embrace of Jews, for not all Jews are alike. If the Vatican specified precisely what kind of Jew it embraced, however, Catholics would appear terribly legalistic and judgmental.

Orthodox Jews morally oppose homosexuality as fully as the Vatican does.[20] The film *Trembling Before G-d* (2001) details the emotional difficulty of gays and lesbians in Orthodox Judaism, which shuns and repudiates them.[21] What is interesting is not so much that liberal Jews have embraced gays and lesbians in synagogues as their moral justification for that embrace. In order to accept gays and lesbians, it seems, you must let go of Jewish doctrine, or *halakhah*. That is precisely the problem, according to more conservative Jews.

Reform Jews have come close to formal approval of same-sex unions that aim at fidelity and permanence. Eugene Borowitz, a Reform Jewish scholar who opposes the idea of a gay rabbi, has summarized the critical detachment of many Reform Jews from the *halakhah* of their religion as follows,

> Two specific forms [of the argument that the *halakhah* says more about social setting than about religious intuition] occur in discussions about a Jewish ethics of homosexuality. The one comes from thinkers who know, if only as a regulative idea for constructing a rational Jewish ethics, that the *halakhah* ideally moves toward neo-Kantian, universal ethical determinations. Thus, they can negate the content of the *halakhah* because we can be more fully universalistic than could our forebears. The second position is taken by thinkers who reason from the motives they understand to be behind the old proscriptions. Again, since we have a better understanding of the genesis and operations of homosexuality, we can assert a different sense of Jewish duty.[22]

Jewish scriptures forbid same-sex genital contact. Jewish scriptures also forbid, among other things, tattooing, and wearing fabrics blended of wool and silk. Borowitz here opposes Jews who believe that interpretations of scriptures ought to evolve as the base of human knowledge expands.

Borowitz's essay urges rejection of various appeals to the Union of American Hebrew Congregations and the central Conference of American Rabbis to embrace gay people, gay Jews, and even gay rabbis. A Reform Jew, Borowitz spoke with some alarm about rumors that the Leo Baeck College in London might officially accept "avowed homosexuals" as candidates for the rabbinate. Borowitz urged looking upon gays with compassion, but not allowing gay congregations or gay rabbis.

Many Reform Jews in North America (there is no such branch of Judaism in Israel) equate Reform Judaism with rationality and refer to theirs as a "religion of reason." The ethics of this "religion of reason" aim at universality. Reform Jews claim to focus not on what is moral for Jews, but on what is moral for humans. This move is curious: for centuries, the Holy See has thought of its edicts as ones to which all humans should adhere in order to achieve salvation. Since Vatican II, however, Rome has made a fundamental shift with regard to what it sees itself doing and whom it sees itself guiding. Since Vatican II, the Holy See views its pronouncements as generally applicable to humans but properly binding on Roman Catholics only. The Holy See does not, for example, speak to how Jews or Muslims should think of gay people. The Vatican argues in such a way that it hopes persons of differing faiths will be led to assent to papal encyclicals and letters; the Holy See does not, however, explicitly address the sexual ethics of other religions.

Reform Jews, perhaps the very loose equivalent of liberal Catholics, have embraced gay and lesbian Jews. This step has not been easy. Writing in 2000, Samuel Freedman reported from the front: "The gay-rights issue is now rippling through Reform and Conservative circles the way the gender issue did twenty-five years ago, providing the battleground for the collision of religious practice and modern mores, and it promises similar results."[23] The Reform rabbinate voted to bestow formal, theological approval to same-sex unions in March 2000. It seems most unlikely that Orthodox Jews, in some very loose sense the equivalent of especially conservative Catholics, will follow suit in the near future.

Reconstructionism, the smallest of Judaism's four branches, maintains a very strong commitment to lesbian and gay issues.

Orthodox Jews might appear natural allies for the Vatican in the skirmish over sex and gender, but precisely the opposite proves true. In very real terms, the Vatican disagrees deeply with *halakhah* over the matter of homosexual activity. Though *halakhah* denies the very idea of a gay person, the Vatican and Reform Jews affirm the reality of gay orientation.

Jewish ethicist Robert Kirschner recognizes *halakhah* as the chief obstacle to any defense of homosexuality in Judaism and accordingly sets out to undermine a premise on which Orthodox and Reform Jewish scholars have long agreed, that the *halakhah* cannot and does not change. Since *halakhah* clearly condemns homosexuality, any defense of homosexuality in the Jewish faith would have to begin by breaking the backbone of Jewish law. Wrong, Kirschner argues.

Halakhah reflects the vitality of the Jewish people and consequently can change. Kirschner exploits the example of deaf-mutes, whom *halakhah* had declared incapable of reasoning, or of communication beyond that of a child. Later, techniques for teaching deaf and mute people evolved and, Kirschner concludes, proved traditional understanding of *halakhah* wrong. We can adjust our understanding of *halakhah* as new information becomes available. New psychoanalytic information about same-sex erotic activity—specifically that there is an intrinsically homosexual orientation (as opposed to a single, heterosexual orientation from which troubled persons may deviate)—has made *halakhah* obsolete:

> What emerges from modern research of human sexuality is a far different picture than the ancient rabbis imagined. Halakhah assumes that sexual orientation is dichotomous and permanent. But modern research has shown that sexual reality is variable. It changes, with individuals, genders, and societies. Neither homosexuality nor heterosexuality is a monolithic category.[24]

Sex researchers from Freud to Kinsey to Simon LeVay have viewed sexual inclinations as utterly complicated. Insisting that *halakhah* has the capacity to recognize and to reckon with advances in empirical knowledge, Kirschner pleads for a reexamination that will reverberate throughout Judaism, even the conservative quarters.

Reform Jews tend to consider *halakhah* as a general set of guidelines, unlike Orthodox Jews, for whom *halakhah* stands as binding law. That fundamental difference notwithstanding, the question of what to do with gays and lesbians troubles conservative Jews just as much as it does conservative Catholics. It must be pointed out that Reform rabbis voted in March 2000 to allow the blessing of same-sex relationships. Because there is no "reformed" branch of Catholicism (of course, various Protestant faiths see themselves as just that), the official party line in the church opposes gay marriages.

SOME PROTESTANTS TOO

The world's Anglican bishops convene the Lambeth conference once every ten years in England. In the summer of 1998, angry disputes over what to do with gays and lesbians consumed much of these meetings at Lambeth Palace, which denied church blessings for same-sex unions and ruled that homosexuals should not be ordained priests. Three years earlier, Walter Righter, a retired Episcopalian bishop in the United States, found himself accused of heresy by ten of his colleagues. Although the Episcopalian Church had already ordained some gay men, Righter's colleagues condemned him for having ordained Barry Stopfel, an openly gay man who was living in a monogamous relationship with his male partner. In his book *A Pilgrim's Way*, Righter surmises that a strong conservative faction of bishops were still smarting over an earlier decision to allow the ordination of women in the Episcopalian Church. Righter's was only the second heresy trial in the Episcopalian Church in the twentieth century.[25]

Anglicans represent the liberal end of Protestantism. More conservative Baptist and Methodist communities (among others) have reacted with similar vehemence to the question of how to treat gay and lesbian people. In May 2000, the United Methodist Church upheld its ban on gay ordination and same-sex ceremonies. In 2000, four churches were expelled ("disfellowshipped") by their regional American Baptist Church associations for welcoming gay clergy and same-sex unions. They were allowed to stay under the national denominational roof only if they could find another association to offer them a philosophical home. Thus, First Baptist Church of Berkeley, California, led by the Reverend Esther Hargis, a lesbian who welcomes all families, is now associated with the American Baptist Church in Wisconsin. In May 2001, Lutheran Bishop Paul Egertson, leader of the Southern California Synod, resigned under pressure. He had participated in ordaining an active lesbian in Minnesota in April (the national governing statement of the Evangelical Lutheran Church of America requires celibacy in unmarried clergy). The Evangelical Lutherans have no national prohibition—yet—on same-sex unions, although they do ban gay clergy.[26]

The rest of the world has noticed Anglican efforts to integrate gay people into mainstream religions. In the summer of 2001, Time magazine featured a religion story with an interesting twist. Whereas the term "missionary work" will virtually without fail make Americans think of a movement from their country to a poorer one, one of the developing countries had sent a missionary to the United States. Rwandan bishop Thaddeus Rockwell Barnum set out to transform the alleged laxity of Episcopal priests in America. The problem? The Episcopalian Church allows gay ordinations and gay "marriages."

The bishop joined three other newly elevated bishops in denouncing gay marriage. Meanwhile, the presiding American bishop Frank Griswold and the Archbishop of Canterbury George Carey both repudiated the move, comparing it to a schism. True, conservatives within the church had fiercely criticized church leaders three years earlier for failing to censure Bishop John Spong, who had publicly disputed Jesus's unique divinity. But it is sex and gender issues that seem most to enrage Episcopalians. As Time reported, "The exodus of disaffected traditionalists exacerbated the church's drop in baptized membership from 3.6 million in 1965 to 2.3 million today." Where do all those disaffected Episcopalians go, we might wonder.

Bishops in Asia and Africa apparently worry about the moral decay in America. Bishops from developing countries assembled in 1998 and concurred in a 526 to 70 vote that "homosexual acts are incompatible with Scripture."[27] The *Time* article did not indicate whether these conservative bishops took a vote on whether doubt about the divinity of Jesus is compatible with Scripture.

Later that same summer, the *New York Times* reported that a dispute among Episcopalian priests in the state of Maryland had spilled over into federal court.[28] The Reverend Samuel L. Edwards, a conservative priest, refused to accept the ordination of women. The problem in question stemmed from his bishop, Jane Holmes Dixon, whom he resolutely refused to acknowledge. She took the unusual step of filing suit in federal court in order to remove Edwards from a position of leadership within his church. Technically, he required approval to move into her parish, as he had done several months previous to the suit. He failed to do so. Before moving to Maryland, Edwards headed an organization called "Forward in Faith North America," which opposed the ordination of women, gay men, and lesbians.

When the female bishop traveled to the parish, eager to welcome Edwards, she found that the congregation had locked her out of the church. She resorted to talking to a few parishioners in the garden outside the church. Apparently some other parishioners informed the bishop that she was trespassing. The church's top lay officer, a woman, declared that the parish was particularly opposed to the idea of ordaining gay men or lesbians.

The *New York Times* article mentioned that "several conservative priests and congregations have quit the 2.4-million-member denomination to join a new organization, the Anglican Mission in America." Where other dissatisfied Episcopalians go after leaving their church deserves sociological study. One can only speculate how these Episcopalians—those who leave their church over gender and sexuality issues—regard the Roman pontiff, who has taken a hard line on these same questions. Disgruntled Episcopalians may take a lead from their conservative Anglican brethren in England. Assessing the road ahead of Rowan

Williams, the new Archbishop of Canterbury, *The Independent on Sunday*, a British newspaper, speculated:

> Although doctrinally orthodox, Dr Williams's sympathy for homosexual clergy has already angered conservative elements in the growing evangelical wing of the church. And despite his mystical leanings, Dr. Williams's support for women bishops has alarmed the Anglo-Catholics, who are threatening schism.[29]

Earlier in the summer of 2002, leading evangelicals in the Church of England had written an open letter to the Prime Minister warning him of a split in the Church of England if the Archbishop of Wales, Dr. Rowan Williams, were appointed the next Archbishop of Canterbury.[30] With the appointment of Williams, the stage was set for ever more gender drama in the United Kingdom.

Catholic examples blend into the Protestant ones offered above. Several hundred Roman Catholics took to the streets of Manhattan in 1998, incensed that Terrence McNally had portrayed Christ as a homosexual in a new Broadway play, *Corpus Christi*. Catholic protest shut down the play. In time, though, the theater staged the production, despite bomb threats. A more extensive treatment of the tendency to reduce religious ethics to sexual ethics might offer more examples than I have included here, such as Christian revulsion to the film *The Last Temptation of Christ*. Arch-conservative Catholics set fire to a Paris theatre in 1986, and several people, unable to escape, died in the flames. In this film (based on an earlier novel by Nikos Kazantzakis), Christ is depicted as sexually interested in, and available to, women. Fundamentalist Baptist preacher R. L. Hymers led outraged Los Angeles crowds in protest over the film. The mob slashed movie screens and threatened to deface all property of MCA, which owned Universal, the distributor of the film. Lew Wasserman, MCA's chairman, was publicly burned in effigy.

Roman Catholics are hardly alone in the struggle to keep their faith pure of gender and sex rebels. A *fatwa* kept Salman Rushdie in hiding for nearly a decade. Some conservative Muslim leaders deplored Rushdie's fictional work, *The Satanic Verses* (1988), deeming it blasphemous. In a pamphlet entitled "In Good Faith," published in 1990, Rushdie understood his alleged offense to center at least in part on having portrayed the prophet Mohammed as a homosexual.[31]

THE ROMAN
PECKING ORDER OF IMPERFECTIONS

Until quite recently, Catholic theologians prized celibacy over marriage. The ideal moral state, celibacy opposed sexual expression. Passionate marriage, while not ideal, was better than promiscuity. But, under this view, even a pattern of heterosexual promiscuity was better than a single (homosexual) sin against nature.

In principle, at least, the Catholic Church has long appeared happy to put itself out of business, for if all the faithful were to embrace the celibate life, there would be no more Catholics. An advantage to sanctifying marriage is that the church can increase its membership and preserve its power.

Marriage morally justifies sexual intercourse in Roman Catholicism, but only between spouses. Such sexual activity, which must always aim at procreation, serves the useful purpose of increasing the number of Catholics in the world. Procreative sex conforms to natural law and carries with it the incidental benefit of giving birth to more Catholics. Consider the exhortation of Pope Pius XI in his 1930 encyclical *Casti Connubii*:

> Christian parents should, besides, realize that they are not only called upon to propagate and sustain the human race on earth, they are not just intended to produce worshippers of the true God, but to give their sons to the Church to join the fellowship of the saints and the servants of God so that the number of those who worship God and our Saviour should increase daily.[32]

Gay couples are unlikely to help increase the number of Catholics in the world, as Pius XII directed Catholics to do. But neither, however, are Jewish couples. If anything, Jewish couples will thwart the stated goal of Pius XII, because Jewish couples will rear children who not only do not "worship God and our Saviour," but who openly deny that Jesus is the savior of the world. And yet, as was shown earlier, the church has softened its stand toward Jews, and even apologized to them.

To meet with approval in the Vatican, people would ideally adhere to canonical Roman Catholic beliefs, both theological and ethical. They would be celibate or, if married, faithful to a member of the opposite sex. The Vatican has understood that these categories—celibate and married-but-faithful—exclude most of the world's population. What the Vatican says about the resistant rest of the world tells us a good deal about the Vatican itself.

In *Lumen Gentium*, perhaps the most frequently cited document of the Second Vatican Council, the Vatican said explicitly that Jews could gain salvation, not by conversion to (Catholic) Christianity, *but by being Jews*:

> those who have not yet received the Gospel are related to the People of God in various ways. There is, first, that people to which the covenants and promises were made, and from which Christ was born according to the flesh (cf. Romans 9:4-5): in view of the divine choice, they are a people most dear for the sake of the fathers, for the gifts of God are without repentance (cf. Romans 11:29-29). [33]

The Roman Catholic Church stunningly reverses itself in the Second Vatican Council. Accounting for the relationship between theologians in the Vatican and Catholics in the streets presents a great challenge, to be sure. That said, the Holy See sends Catholics in the street a clear message here in *Lumen Gentium*: Jews (and Muslims too) can get to heaven:

> Those who, through no fault of their own, do not know the Gospel of Christ or his Church, but who nevertheless seek God with a sincere heart,

and, moved by grace, try in their actions to do his will as they know it through the dictates of their conscience—those too may achieve eternal salvation.[34]

Never mind that Jews do not consistently endorse the idea of heaven. Although Jews of various sorts may view *Lumen Gentium* with a curious chuckle, religiously committed gay and lesbian Catholics may well marvel at the document.

To be a Jew is to identify with some defining aspects of Judaism (principal among which must be to deny Jesus Christ as the Messiah). Living as observant Jews involves some kind of defiance of Roman Catholic doctrine. And yet the Holy See has acknowledged a place for Jews in heaven. Will there ever come a day when the Holy See will affirm a place in heaven for gay people who do not simply identify themselves as gay but *who do gay things?*

To be a gay or lesbian person is in one sense to recognize predominant sexual desire for members of one's own sex, and in a narrower sense to engage in sexual activity with members of one's own sex. Living fully as a gay or lesbian person involves some kind of defiance of Roman Catholic doctrine. The Holy See has condemned and continues to condemn in harsh terms sexual activity between members of the same sex, even if two people of the same sex form a monogamous union that aims at permanence.

Anyone will tell you it is more socially advantageous to be straight than gay; could this advantage find religious justification? If so, then could Catholics pull the rug out from underneath this justification? They might well, particularly if they mustered as much objection to homophobia as they have done to anti-Semitism.

Is it conceivable that one day Catholic bishops will convene in order to question whether Roman Catholic teachings or moral stances have abetted homophobia? In all fairness, it must be said that the American bishops tried to do something like this two years ago. The letter they jointly issued, *Always Our Children,* aimed to stem the destruction of Catholic families by parents who rejected children who self-identified as gay or lesbian. Conservative backlash in the church forced the bishops to revise their original statement and to take a somewhat harsher view of gay and lesbian Catholics. Catholic reaction to the bishops' letter saddened many gay and lesbian Catholics, who found it inconceivable that French bishops or Cardinal Ratzinger might be chastised for taking too soft a stance on the question of what to think of Jews.

Jean-Marie Lustiger, the Jewish cardinal of Paris, celebrates his dual identity as a Jew and a Catholic. Having converted to Catholicism against his mother's wishes as a young boy, he claims to take pride in being the first Jewish cardinal. Lustiger does not practice Judaism but maintains a Jewish identity. It seems unthinkable that a (celibate) cardinal would openly celebrate being a gay cardinal. In any event, he could hardly be the first gay cardinal.

Catholics and Jews alike have good reason to celebrate the rapprochement of recent years. Committed Catholics who cheer for Jews, however, may feel confused when the topic turns to gays and lesbians within the Catholic Church. Exhorting Jews to be Jews while forbidding gays from being gay raises a question which threatens to undermine the centrality of theology in Catholic ethics: Morally speaking, is it better to be a straight Jew than a gay Catholic?

Yes, it would appear so. John Boswell, writing in 1980, was largely correct in asserting that Jews and gay people shared the same moral standing in Roman Catholicism. In 1980 things were already changing, but Boswell could only see through a glass darkly. From our vantage point today, it seems that Jews have left the moral category they long shared with gays. Invited to a higher table, Jews can now count on a Vatican enthusiastically committed to their well-being. Applauding the goodwill of their church toward Jews, gay and lesbian Catholics do so from their place at an outside table.

Gays have become the new Jews—in Catholicism, at least. Rome sacked the gay-positive Bishop Jacques Gaillot of Evreux in France early in 1995. This church official had advocated the use of condoms to stem the spread of HIV; he had also publicly sympathized with active homosexuals. After losing his job, he launched a Web site (www.parte-nia.com) from which to minister to marginalized Catholics. Gay Catholics who want to practice their religion today stand in a peculiar relation to Jews who do not want to practice Catholicism.

Why sex weighs so deeply may defy ready explanation, but it has long mattered to the Roman Curia. In her 1981 book *Understanding Catholicism*, Monika K. Hellwig provided a window onto how Catholics in the streets (as opposed to theologians) and non-Catholics view the Vatican: "What most puzzles many outsiders and most embarrasses many insiders about the Catholic faith today is the account that the Church gives of itself."[35] Hellwig, the executive director of the Association of Catholic Colleges and Universities, claimed that it is the Virgin Mary and the Pope who most confound people trying to make sense of Catholicism; some twenty years later, liberal Catholics might well add sexuality to that list.

SAME AS IT EVER WAS?

Cynics may argue that Christianity in particular, or perhaps religion in general, has always been about sex, death, and perhaps money. This view does not strike me as persuasive. It may be possible to argue that religious wars or religious debates hinge on preserving a particular way of life rather than a belief about God. Such an argument would slight the power and the prevalence of individual religious experience. There would be little incentive to make sacrifices (sexual, economic, or otherwise) if real people did not feel that they were pleasing God through such sacrifices.

It's not the same as it ever was—something important has changed for Jews, women, and gays. In Orthodox Judaism, for example, women are making important inroads toward gender equality. Increasingly, they are permitted to study the Talmud and have even been granted the right to divorce abusive husbands.[36] Reform Jews are voicing support for gay marriage.[37] Beyond that, Jews have gained institutional favor in Roman Catholicism, an institution long opposed to their quest for social equality. Vatican II allowed the possibility that God intended some Jews to remain Jews until the end of time—not as a negative example (as, for example, in Augustine's theology) but as a positive witness to the election of Israel. Of course, this election is in and through Christ in Catholic understanding, so the church in no way approves Jewish rejection of Christ. Nor does it raise any real possibility of canonizing a Jew who denies that Jesus was the Messiah. Nonetheless, in moving forward in the Vatican, Jews have gained a powerful ally.

Gay people have not fared so well. For centuries, Catholic theologians have thought of Jews and gays in similar terms. Whereas Jews and the various theological, moral, and social problems they pose appear repeatedly in early Christian documents, gay men or the sin by which they are known (that is, sodomy) first appear in the eleventh century.[38] Of course, the sinful possibility of what two men might do together had already occurred to anyone familiar with the book of Leviticus or the writings of Saint Paul. In the eleventh century, a new social category came to encircle a particular kind of sinner and this category resembled the theological and social caste into which Jews fell (or were pushed).

The cynical view that Catholicism has always focused on sex, death, and money can't readily account for Catholic anti-Semitism. For Catholic anti-Semitism or anti-Judaism involves God in some more immediate way. The skeptical argument that Catholics don't mean what they say—that in fact Catholics dislike Jews as much as ever—unfairly slights an institution that has in fact changed. A more persuasive but perhaps equally skeptical argument would be that Jews pose much less of a threat to the Vatican than do gay and lesbian Catholics. If the Vatican and other governing religious bodies in the West are in fact obsessed with sexuality at the dawn of a new millennium, then the most threatening adversaries stand within their own spiritual community. And so, this line of reasoning would have it, dissident Catholics of any sort worry the Vatican more than Jews, who are less threatening by virtue of their outsider status.

But even here a powerful objection emerges, for the new Roman pecking order of imperfections would appear to fly in the face of justification by faith, an ancient doctrine which means that God will exonerate sinners on the basis of their belief in Christ, not on the basis of their actions (see Rom. 1:18-3:20). Saint Paul, himself a Jewish convert to Christianity, was careful to emphasize that all people, both Jews and non-Jews, lived under sin. Therefore everyone needed to worry about redemption. According to Saint Paul, the works of creation invite everyone to recognize the one, true God—not just the followers of Jesus. To the extent that Jews resist belief in Jesus as the Messiah, they forgo justification by faith. But Jewish opposition no longer matters in the way it did for nearly two thousand years. And although gay and lesbian Catholics may claim an abiding devotion to Jesus Christ, their faith bears the stain of sexual disgrace. The disgrace, not the faith, defines them.

LEAVING GOD BEHIND

For many centuries, religious believers quite literally went to war over questions about what to think of God. I have not sought to assess the morality of wars over religion, only to suggest that religion no longer possesses that power in the West.

I have pointed to a few instances in which opposition to the social advancement of gay and lesbian persons has ignited religious protest. These few instances, some by now well known, illustrate a defining moment in particular religious faiths. I have not sought to define a religion beyond calling it a loosely organized way of linking sex to God.

I have taken the Vatican at its word. Skeptics will doubt that the revolutionary change with regard to the Jews only alters how the church looks, not how it works. I disagree with them.

I have confined my attention here to same-sex couplings, which can get you into real trouble in Judaism, Christianity, and Islam. Remarkably, denying Christ's divinity seems to cause less anguish in the Vatican than gay sex. This isn't so much an investigation of how Catholics and Jews get along as it is a meditation on what drives religious morality at the end of the twentieth century and beyond. I have not tried to indicate a strategy for achieving heaven, but rather have tried to point to and dramatize a puzzling conceptual conflict in contemporary Roman Catholic ethics. To bring this conceptual conflict into focus, I have chosen Catholics and Jews as examples of a broad tendency at work in other faiths.

I have not considered whether Christians might do better to think of their faith in terms of love instead of theology, or whether leaving Christ behind might benefit the Catholic Church. True, demoting Jesus would simplify relations with non-Christians enormously, as Catholic historian James Carroll has noted:

> Here is where the work of a Vatican III would begin, for it is impossible to reconcile this Christology, these cosmic claims for the accomplishment of Jesus Christ as the one source of salvation, with authentic respect for Judaism and every other "spiritual neighbor." The Church's fixation on the death of Jesus as the universal salvific act must end, and the place of the cross must be reimagined in the Christian faith."[39]

Sounding terribly conservative, I would urge Christians to embrace their Christianness, Jews their Jewishness, and Muslims their Muslimness. True, this tack has not worked very well historically, but it seems a great shame that we should have to give up who we are in order to get along with others. In theory at least, respect for others remains a viable way out of religious conflicts.

I have chosen a chapter title that turns on ambiguity: It is better to be a straight Jew than a gay Catholic, but better for what? It would be misleading to say that the Vatican condemns gay and lesbian Catholics to hell. When Cardinal Ratzinger, head of the Congregation for the Doctrine of the Faith, speaks against sexual failings, he stigmatizes them as sins. He does not assign the sinners to hell. When Ratzinger lays out his notion of church authority (as in the appendix to *Ad tuendam fidem*), he describes those who dissent as "not in full communion with the Catholic Church." He does not call them "damned." The Southern Baptist Convention is much more likely to damn sexual "deviants" than is the Vatican. Perhaps because, for the Vatican, the battles are waged, not over heaven, but over the boundaries of a very earthly church. That said, confusion remains. For Saint Paul did leave us with a list of people who will not possess the kingdom of heaven (1 Cor. 6:10), and both "the effeminate" and sodomites make his roster. Ratzinger does occasionally threaten to excommunicate dissident groups, such as pro-choice Catholics (for example, the German group "Donum Vitae," in 2000); he has also argued that we will not meet Nazis in heaven because of the "objective terribleness" of their crimes.

What are we to conclude about the crimes of gay people? Twenty-seven years after Rome declared a homosexual orientation morally neutral, the Vatican's chief spokesman revealed that gay men would no longer be allowed in the priesthood. The irony of a disproportionately gay priesthood will not be lost on Catholics who ponder how much teeters on the boundary between homosexual orientation and homosexual lovemaking. Ordinary Catholics should resist the impulse to link sexual failings with the loss of heaven.

Overall, it is better to be straight than gay: this persistent message beckons us from different religious creeds. Of course, the faith of ordinary believers may differ somewhat from the views of the reigning orthodoxy in their religion. The accepted beliefs proclaimed by religious authorities in any camp still count for something, however, and to some noteworthy extent will guide the assent or dissent of ordinary believers, who define themselves against the backdrop of ecclesiastical expectations. As the faithful and would-be believers sort through their own spiritual convictions, sex assumes ever greater importance in religious circles.[40]

FIVE

Sacred Public Relations

W hy on earth would Jews care if Catholics suddenly allowed them
into heaven? What difference does it make to Catholics if Protestants say
they are headed to hell? What does it matter whether our neighbors
approve of the sex we happen to be having, or not having?

The question of why Jews should care what Catholics say about them
is separate from, but related to, the question of why Catholics should
care what Jews say about them. Catholics can scarcely deny that they
begin the new century in a public relations crisis. Particularly in the wake
of the sex scandals of 2002, the problem has escalated far beyond just
what Jews say or think about Catholics.

Popular opinions may torture us, even compel us to change our
ways. What others think about our religion may sadden us, or sometimes
goad us to adopt a new one. Of course, some religious believers find it
impossible to imagine belonging to any other faith; for them, the
problem is only more pronounced. The self-loathing Jew, a familiar
figure in modern fiction, may give way to the self-loathing Catholic in
the West if international respect for the Vatican continues to sag.

Particularly in the United States, intellectual Catholics are taking
Rome to task in biting books that garner more attention than encyclicals.
The Vatican should take steps to improve its public image. Its bland Web

site does little to impress anyone struggling over what to think about the institution. Public apologies by bishops and even the pope himself will pack more of a punch than ad campaigns, which would seem ridiculous and inappropriate (although some American religious orders mounted campaigns in the late 1990s to recruit new members by improving the image of religious life, much as the military tries to attract enlistments). Hiring a public relations firm really isn't such a bad idea; the *Los Angeles Times* reported on June 4, 2002 that Roger Cardinal Mahony had hired the public relations firm of Sitrick and Company to help him through the sex scandal roiling America's largest archdiocese.[1]

Although "sorry" is for many people the hardest word to say, it can turn the tide. The world does still care about the Vatican's influence, and the Vatican does want to maintain its integrity. Attention to public relations nods to the importance of what others think of us and bespeaks the humility we ourselves show when admitting fault. Apologizing for mistakes and asking for forgiveness for institutional sins stands as the best public relations move of all. In 2000 John Paul II appointed an international commission of three Jewish and three Catholic scholars to examine the Vatican's culpability in the Holocaust, but the commission dissolved itself a year later. Two Jewish committee members claimed that the Vatican would not cooperate in the investigation. Moreover, the Catholic and Jewish scholars held competing historical perspectives and interpreted the Holocaust differently. The dissolution of this committee did little to improve the Vatican's public image. Committee member and Hebrew University professor Robert Wistrich proclaimed Jewish-Catholic relations at a post-war nadir.

The strategic worth of sacred public relations manifested itself again in the wake of the terrorist attacks of September 11, 2001 in the United States. The international media raced to portray radical Muslims as brutally cruel to women and dissenters. Then the media jostled for opportunities to portray Islam as utterly humanistic and the Taliban fighters as simply anomalous, indeed heretical. Religion, no stranger to the headlines, dominated television reports and office discussions. At stake was how Americans would treat Muslims in their midst and, importantly, how young Muslims would make sense of their own heritage.

WHAT OTHERS REALLY THINK OF US

The question of why we should care what others think of us strikes at the heart of religious morality, which seeps into social morality in a nation as religiously active as the United States. Often we really do care what others think about us. Sometimes the views of others are so compelling that we take them on as our own, converting from one set of beliefs to another. This is the goal of missionaries, politicians, teachers, and parents everywhere—to move those they care about from ignorance or error to supposed enlightenment. But religion safeguards and legitimizes prejudice these days. Many Westerners feel free to attack the racist, sexist, or homophobic views of others, but who dares to attack the religious views of a neighbor or fellow citizen? Very few. We do, however, see missionaries hard at work, trying to convince others to adopt a new set of spiritual beliefs. Such work must be done gently, quietly.

Of course others may decline our efforts to help them; indeed, people may resent us for even trying. Jews, to take an interesting example, have protested loudly the Mormon practice of converting Jews who died in the Holocaust to the Mormon faith (Mormons have also converted all the popes). After obtaining lists of names of Jews who died in various Nazi concentration camps, Mormons performed conversion rites on the deceased, whom they then proclaimed members of the Church of Latter Day Saints. Mormons have conceded and reversed the conversions that supposedly made Jews Mormons. Ambivalence about, or outright opposition to, religious missionaries, to continue along the same lines, reveals the motivating force of what others really think of us. Jews witnessed another expression of Catholic goodwill in August 2002, when a committee of the U.S. Conference of Catholic Bishops formally declared that campaigns that targeted Jews for conversion to Christianity "are no longer theologically acceptable in the Catholic Church."[2] Shortly thereafter, a spokesman for the Southern Baptist Convention accused Catholics of displaying "the most extreme form of anti-Semitism" by giving up the ancient struggle to convert Jews.[3]

Religious sensibilities differ, to be sure, but many college graduates will report that they endured a period of soul-searching while in school precisely because they had to defend a personal religious affiliation to others who may have criticized or simply questioned it. How, someone might ask a Catholic student, can you reconcile your Catholic identity with the birth control you use? At the end of the twentieth century, a survey of Italian Catholics living in Rome reported that "80 percent of Romans consider themselves Catholic but more than 70 percent of these Catholics condone birth control, divorce, cohabitation, and premarital sex. Fewer than half believe in an afterlife or believe that Christianity is the one true religion."[4] Is it simply hypocritical to identify oneself as Catholic and to use birth control, or is it rather a healthy sign of listening to one's conscience?

Can the negative opinion of others harm us? This comes to much the same question as whether we harm others by, say, holding a particular belief about the Virgin Mary or the morality of abortion. To take another example: Baptists oppose the very idea of infant baptism in principle, maintaining that only competent adults can make such a weighty decision for themselves. Clearly, Baptists care about the practice of baptism, but it is not clear that they would argue that an infant had been harmed by Catholic baptism. It's not clear either that Baptists would even consider a *Catholic* baptism a baptism at all. And yet Baptists do object to what Catholics do by submerging babies in supposedly holy water. Why do Baptists care? Because they want everyone to live according to God's will. Catholics may resent Baptist concern, but why should Catholics care? The answer involves our feelings, our ambitions, and our fears.

Sometimes we freely admit shame over our family or religious community, fully expecting that others will as well. In the wake of the terrorist attacks on the World Trade Center, in both 1993 and 2001,

Muslims around the world scrambled to denounce violence and clarify the tenets of their faith. In the 1980s and more recently, American Catholics beat their breasts publicly over revelations of priestly sexual abuse of children entrusted to their spiritual guidance. Catholics winced at news that African priests had secretly coerced nuns into providing sexual favors.[5] Out of fears of contracting HIV, these priests turned to their female colleagues for the sexual relief they had previously found in prostitutes. One priest forced a nun he had impregnated to undergo an abortion, which killed her. By admitting our shame, we hope to soften the blow of criticism issued by others. By beating others to the punch, as it were, we can protect ourselves.

Of course, the faithful within a given tradition may squabble. Family quarrels waged in public may embarrass conservatives, even while progressives take the soul-searching as a healthy sign of growing pains. When Orthodox Jews take to burning a Conservative Jewish establishment, though, arguments over how correctly to honor religious tradition have crossed a dangerous line. Conservative Catholics such as the Lutheran convert Richard John Neuhaus and the economist Michael Novak have lambasted the works of more liberal Catholics who have dared to raise questions about the morality of the church (for example, Garry Wills, John Cornwell, James Carroll, and Eugene Kennedy). In 2001 Cornwell declared in *Breaking Faith* that the remarkably energetic John Paul II will leave the Catholic Church in a worse state than he found it. In that same book he noted, "it has become increasingly difficult to write frankly of the flaws in the institutional Church without being accused of bad faith by an influential constituency of fellow Catholics."[6]

Whereas the Vatican used to excommunicate dissenters, it now seems to be the other way around. In 1949, for example, Pius XII excommunicated all Communists in the world, including millions who had never shed blood. Some five decades later, many Catholics are claiming that they do not want to be part of a church that subjugates women and resolutely refuses gay people marriage. In the spring of 2002, many American Catholics anguished over their relationship to a network of bishops and cardinals that had protected and hidden priests who sexually preyed on children of the faithful. The *New York Times* quoted the Reverend Jeff Thielen, the pastor of St. Lucy Catholic Church in Racine, Wisconsin, as saying: "I've been a priest since 1974. I almost wish I wasn't a priest. How can people stay Catholic in the face of this? It's unending."[7] Three months earlier, the *New York Times* had run a letter to the editor from one Wendy Cole of Las Vegas, who stated: "I am a lifelong liberal, unshakeable Catholic . . . I will never be ashamed for my faith, but I sure am ashamed for and embarrassed by these enablers [of pedophiles] running my church."[8]

A religious group in a pluralistic society risks much in failing to ponder its public image. We all want our churches, synagogues, and mosques to garner the respect of others. These religious spaces link the faithful to an enriching spirit. These spaces benefit those within, who in turn benefit those outside by virtue of an increased sense of integrity. It is not hard to imagine, then, the unpleasantness surrounding Rolf Hochhuth's 1963 play *The Deputy*, which first raised the charge of Vatican complicity in the Holocaust. Catholics throughout the world winced at the accusations that an institution they held sacred may have abetted, even encouraged, evil forces.

This artistic protest was far from the first time the Vatican had been accused of anti-Semitism. The sad story of Edgardo Mortara, to take just one example, circulated throughout Italy a century earlier. As already discussed, a Jewish family begged the Vatican for the return of their kidnapped son, who was living with the pope as an adopted son.

The Vatican no doubt wrestled with the matter of negative public relations, for while Christianity professes the virtues of love, the church seemed to act unkindly to Jews. Speculating on the motives of any given decree or speech is quite risky, but we can wonder about early Catholic attempts to express support of Jews. Take, for example, the following papal speech from 1928:

> the Catholic Church has always prayed for the Jewish people, depositories, until the coming of Jesus Christ, of the divine promise, regardless of their subsequent blindness, or rather, precisely because of it. Moved by that

spirit of charity, the Apostolic See has protected this same people against unjust vexations, and just as it reproves all hatreds and animosities between people, so it especially condemns hatred against the people elected by God, a hatred that today is vulgarly called "anti-Semitism."[9]

What prompted the statement was an official Vatican announcement that a Catholic society called the "Friends of Israel" was to be disbanded. That society united Catholics who aided Jews and prayed for their conversion. It seems the Vatican worried that these Catholics had allowed the spirit of charity to run away with them, for they had neglected to remember the historical crimes of Jews. In any event, this pronouncement shows public relations at work. On the one hand, the church wanted to reinforce the importance of Christian charity. On the other hand, the church wanted to assure those who heard the speech that it was a good institution, one of integrity. A condemnation of anti-Semitism, ambivalent though this one seems to have been, made the church look good.

Gradually in the twentieth century, the need for sacred public relations increased. The faithful of various traditions were held accountable for the very beliefs that set them apart from others. We still see evidence of proud separatists, to be sure, but fewer mainstream religious leaders will argue as baldly and boldly what Jonathan Edwards did in the classic American sermon "Sinners in the Hands of an Angry God: "*He that believeth not is condemned already.* So that every unconverted Man properly belongs to Hell; that is his Place; from thence he is."[10]

Many writers have explored hatred, violence, and social hostility. Living in Palestine or Israel, for example, you could hardly fail to appreciate the importance of what people on the other side think of you. Your very life depends on it. What I have in mind is much harder to pin down: the often unspoken, barely articulate beliefs strangers hold about you.

What people really think of us will likely affect where we want to work, whom we want to befriend, whom we want to avoid, and our own self-esteem. In a modern democracy, external sympathy or opposition will also indicate where we can hope to forge alliances. We want to be liked, generally, and we want others to help us get what we want out of life, or at least to stand out of our way. On another level, we may fear harm from someone who doesn't like people of our race, gender, sexual orientation, or tax bracket.

Minorities of any sort may fear harm based on their social identity (as a particular race, nationality, or political party, for example) and individuals may fear harm based on their personalities (as an arrogant or offensive or dishonest person, for example). Why would a rational individual fear the curse uttered by someone? Curses pulse through both the Hebrew Bible and the New Testament, but few educated souls today will admit to fearing them. Someone tells you that he has cursed you, and you dismiss it as a mere act of aggression, nothing to worry about. Even though you might take this as a sign of ignorance or weakness on their part, you might worry about practical consequences. This enemy may slander your name or mount a campaign to persuade others not to do business with you anymore. The very idea that someone might actively oppose us seems unsettling, however distantly.

Writing in 1959, just three years before the start of the Vatican council that would allow Jews into heaven, Rabbi Arthur Gilbert of the Anti-Defamation League balked at the idea that Catholics respected Jews. Gilbert reported having heard American social scientists insist that Catholics treated Jews better than Protestants did, a claim that struck him as preposterous. Gilbert wrote:

> Whenever I speak to Jewish audiences on Jewish-Christian relations, someone always inquires into the content of parochial school instruction. "Have the Catholics stopped teaching their children that the Jews killed Christ?" It is a widely held belief in the Jewish community that a significant aspect of whatever anti-Semitism exists in America derives from Christian

instruction concerning the violent commission of deicide by the Jewish people and their consequential rejection by God.[11]

Vatican II was officially to empty out this very source of Catholic ill will toward Jews (of course, whether Catholics honored the ruling of Vatican II is another question).

Catholics have turned away from the age-old practice of forcing baptism on Jews.[12] As I have said, Jews have protested Mormon reports of having "converted" those Jews who died in Nazi concentration camps. It could be that such displays of supposed goodwill remind Jews of the very real consequences of what other people think of us. Starting in 1096, popes and cardinals forbade the forcible baptism of Jews but insisted that any such baptisms were nonetheless valid. "These baptisms, it was said, even if conducted under the threat of death, were recognized by God. The souls of those baptized, whether they had assented or not, were indelibly marked with the seal of Christ."[13] David Kertzer writes that, "According to Church teachings, a person who helped save the soul of an unbeliever earned divine blessing, performing a deed that would be remembered at heaven's gate. As a result, noble families competed for the honor of acting as baptismal godparents for Jews, the trickle of converts being small compared with the robust ranks of the nobility."[14]

Nowadays, when there is no longer a fear of secretly baptized children being removed from their Jewish parents, why would Jews fear that Christians might secretly baptize a Jewish child? Secret baptisms may strike some as an act of aggression, to be sure. But why should this gesture affect Jews more viscerally than the knowledge that their Christian friends and colleagues are praying for their conversion?[15] The answer must involve history, offering up as it does a parade of sad examples of anti-Semitic humiliation. How would Christians feel about Jews praying for *their* conversion? Judaism for the most part has never been a religion bent on converting others, certainly not in the way Christianity or Islam has. In any event, Catholics would likely laugh off such prayers, although Catholics might appreciate the prayers of Jews when plagued by illness.

Other examples of why we care what others think strike closer to home. Vanity, like the survival instinct, may occasionally prompt us to evaluate our popularity. Do they really like me? If not, why not? What can I do to change their minds? Do I even care? Vanity may lead us to think about our funeral—what sort of eulogy may be given, how many people will attend. We read the biographies of famous people and, although we do not expect one ever to be written about us, we may imagine what ours would look like.

We have heard repeatedly about the therapeutic effect of diaries and journals: committing to paper reflections on our lot in life. We wonder whether our self-assessment conforms to the assessment of others. We understand that what others say about us after we're gone or even before may affect the way our children are treated and the fate of projects to which we devoted our energy. The Christians of Denmark and Norway today receive regular praise for having risked personal safety to denounce publicly Nazi deportation of Jews. Christians in Poland, Germany, Belgium, and Lithuania, on the other hand, tend to suffer blame in these same assessments of a national integrity.

Corporate moguls, if they are to succeed, must remain sensitive to public opinion. The longest court trial in British history, begun in September 1990, ended up a public relations disaster for the McDonald's corporation. The fast-food giant sued five members of London Greenpeace for libel. Although McDonald's more or less won the suit in 1997, several of the allegations prompting the legal action proved to be accurate. The world consequently learned of charges of low pay, cruelty to animals, and improper advertising. McDonald's then began to court public approval by dispelling ideas of deceit and corporate greed. To make it, McDonald's learned, they needed to show greater accountability to the world at large.

In April 2002, twelve American cardinals dramatically flew to Rome, at the pope's command. At issue was the burgeoning sex scandal in the American church, where the faithful cried out for transparency in hierarchical decisions. Infuriated and betrayed Americans learned that American bishops and cardinals had been working public relations as well, specifically by covering up cases of priestly sexual abuse. In an effort to protect the church's image behind the scenes, bishops put young children at dangerous risk of sexual abuse.

At a press meeting after the papal sessions, only two of twelve cardinals showed up to answer questions before the press. The other ten cited "previous obligations" and explained that late meetings prevented attendance at the press conference. Sacred "PR" comes down to maintaining public confidence or, if lost, restoring it. The representatives of American Catholics bumbled public relations, and the church now needs a larger public relations campaign to reverse the damage done by the cover-up brought to light in 2002.

Some people are better than others at screening out the opinions and beliefs of neighbors and colleagues. Some of us feel a need to be loved and accepted that borders on the pathological, whereas others simply can't be persuaded to care. It isn't so hard to think of a person who doesn't worry what others think about him. He refuses to recycle cans and bottles, for example, even though he knows he incurs the disrespect of his neighbors. To take an example more germane to the subject: Non-Christian Americans have protested the expenditure of public monies for Christmas decorations, and Christian neighbors have sometimes fumed with anger. When we're not invested in the opinions of others, we are not invested in *them*. On some level, disregarding the thoughts of others amounts to disregarding people. A little of this is necessary to get by in the world; too much of it suggests arrogance, selfishness, and even misanthropy.

In a modern democracy, the beliefs of others collide with ours. You may believe that every woman has a fundamental right to an abortion; however, those who disagree with you may work within the law in order to deprive you of access to an abortion. You are stuck with their rules: this is the downside of democracy. If a political faction sympathetic to your view changes the law, then your opponents are stuck with a law they consider intrinsically immoral. They may cry that life under corrupt laws makes existence sad and heavy.

Even before modern democracies, kings and queens generally cared what their subjects thought about them. And vice versa. So what others think about us has mattered and continues to matter, even when their opinions are not exactly likely to result in any specific action.

The passing of time separates us from groups of people whose judgment of us may turn out to be quite different from that of our peers. How many Christians in the year 2000 believed in the kind of sexual restraint that governed their forebears in 1950? The question has no definitive answer, but it is impossible not to notice a gaping change of opinion. Our own parents and grandparents might wince at our contemporary beliefs. But we think that if they could see things through our modern eyes, they would agree with us. This confidence has started many an argument.

Deep religious commitment only exacerbates this problem of what others think of us. In the pagan world of ancient Greece and Rome, there was always room for one more god. The gods of other families or states didn't threaten locals. With monotheism (first Judaism, then Christianity, and then Islam), all that changed. Foreign gods became profoundly threatening. Wars broke out over the discovery that someone worshiped a different god, or worshiped your god differently. Many contemporary believers still feel uncomfortable with the idea that otherwise esteemed neighbors and colleagues worship differently. Diversity in matters of race is perfectly reasonable, they may think, but diversity in matters of faith is not. This view makes some sense, as something very big is at stake— not just the salvation of the neighbor or colleague, but also the comforting certainty that assures us that we are leading good lives.

General preferences across opposing groups should not be taken as sociological facts, yet these preferences can usefully distinguish one group from another. Rural Protestant sects may value spiritual "fits," speaking in tongues, and perhaps snake handling in a way Roman Catholic groups rarely, if ever, do. For the latter, visions of the afterlife or apparitions of the Blessed Mother are more common examples of inspirational departures from the ordinary, although even those visions are frequently frowned upon institutionally. Even when what others think of us comes down to what they think of a group to which we belong, we may still feel personally insulted. Take marriage, for example. How would you feel if someone from another religious background told you that you weren't in fact married to your spouse, even though you thought you were?

As it turns out, Roman Catholics believe something potentially more offensive. Non-Catholics don't need a wedding at all in order to be married. According to canon law, non-Catholic couples are not subject to any formal obligation in contracting marriage. They don't need a religious or a civil ceremony—they just need a mutual desire to stay together forever as man and wife. The wish to be married, "the marital inclination," is enough.[16] Not for Catholics, though, who are held to a higher standard. Catholics must be married before a priest, a formal representative of God.

The Catholic position might offend Protestants, Jews, and Muslims, who are held to a lower standard. The marriage example reinforces the fairly obvious point that what other people think of us is often complicated. Opinions and motivations may not be so transparent as they appear. Still, our question remains unanswered: If Roman Catholics do in fact consider married Jews, Protestants, and Muslims married, why should non-Catholics care about Catholic standards? They don't. The truth is often that we really don't care what others think about us, and such indifference is surely healthy.

When we do care, we fear that we are what others think of us. And so we court the admiration of strangers, or people we really don't care about. Admiration from them may make it easier for us to believe that the people whom we know admire us as well but don't say anything, on the assumption we already know they do.

Anyone who would suffer at the disclosure of a potentially damaging secret knows the importance of what others think of us. In a world angry at and hateful of lesbians and gay men, motives for hiding are obvious. The great Spanish poet Lorca, for example, once lived in fear:

> Lorca knew the perils of homosexual love. He knew about Oscar Wilde's imprisonment, and he had read *De Profundis;* his copy of Wilde's book

was heavily marked. He could scarcely have been ignorant of his own country's attitude toward same-sex love. The Arabs who settled Andalusia had sanctioned it. But the Inquisition had persecuted homosexuals, and the Catholic Church continued to regard them as deviants of the worst sort. Lorca knew how people gossiped; as a teenager he had gone weeping to a friend's house after learning that someone was spreading a rumor that he, Lorca, was homosexual.[17]

After appearing on *Jenny Jones*, an American television talk show, in March 1995, a heterosexual man hunted down and killed a man who had confessed to having a crush on him on a national broadcast.[18] The killer lashed out against someone who had raised suspicion about his own sexuality. The heterosexual man did not want others to think he might be gay.

Given how many people seem to assume that Roman Catholic priests are gay, it is perhaps not so surprising that the Vatican too should become sensitive to public relations in the sexuality arena. An extensive survey undertaken by the *Kansas City Star* revealed that at least four hundred priests had already died of AIDS by 2000.[19] Public discussion of the number of priests struggling against the disease broke some of the taboo surrounding the sexual orientation of priests, who are, after all, still mortal. Such public awareness may well have another effect: the historian Garry Wills, himself a practicing Catholic, has predicted: "the admission of married men and women to the priesthood—which is bound to come anyway—may well come for the wrong reason, not because women and the community deserve this, but because of panic at the perception that the priesthood is becoming predominantly gay."[20]

The pope believes, along with hundreds of millions of Catholics, that he is God's representative on earth. Yet on some level, all obedient Catholics believe that their actions also represent God's will on earth, standing for something in the eyes of people of other faiths. There is a continuum here. At one end of the spectrum, you may care what others think because you are hoping to convert them. This is a form of "leading by example." By living a happy life of virtue, you can persuade them that your religious beliefs are proper. Even within a religion, we expect our rabbis, priests, nuns, ministers to inspire us, to reassure us that we are in the correct religion—perhaps even within the correct faction of a particular religion. At the other end of the spectrum, we care what others think for purely instrumental reasons. We want them to stand out of our way. Ideally, they will help us get what we want; at the very least, though, we don't want them to impede our goals. And so we care about them because we care about us, in a selfish way.

To some extent, the continued success of a religion depends on the integrity of its leaders. That explains why sex scandals (for example, the fury over Jimmy Swaggart's indiscretions with a prostitute, or Jim Bakker's with a church secretary) pack such a punch in religious circles. If preachers tell believers that God will punish immoral behavior but act immorally themselves, they lose their credibility. Nothing has threatened the future of the Roman Catholic Church in America more than the widespread revelations of priests sexually abusing children of the faithful. Others will be less likely to respect us, much less to convert to our way of believing, if they find our beliefs incoherent on their own terms or if we lack the courage of our convictions. Matthew Arnold denounced Henry VIII, who combined "the craving for forbidden fruit and the craving for legality."[21] This is what Nietzsche aimed to do—to show nineteenth-century Christians that they failed to live up to their own vile standards.

In the late twentieth century, an ex-president of the Southern Baptist Convention in the United States still felt justified in declaring publicly that God does not hear the prayers of the Jews. Various Protestant preachers, such as Jimmy Swaggart, have proclaimed that Roman Catholics are not Christians, but idol-worshiping pagans.

It's one thing to say, "You're going to heaven." It's another thing to say, "You're going to hell." In the latter assertion, you're likely insulting an entire group by association. Getting away with an assertion such as that makes it more likely that you will act in such a way as to harm the group. Even more likely still is the possibility that others will use your own suffering against you. Thus Bernard Häring, the most influential Roman Catholic moral theologian of the twentieth century, has written that God speaks through misfortune. While it is a terrible sin to take pleasure in the suffering of others generally, Häring writes, we can rejoice over the tears of "awful enemies of God" because such tears are proof to the whole world that God's enemies were on the wrong path.[22] It can be disconcerting to say the least to realize that our neighbors are withholding their sympathy just when we feel we need it most. And it can be devastating to learn that our neighbors are telling their children that our house burned down because God was trying to tell us that we have been going to the wrong church.

Well into the twentieth century, Catholics thought that Jews willfully, perversely sought to annoy them. Many Catholics believed that Jews really understood that Christ was the Savior—Jews just sought to persecute or undermine Catholics: "For it was an ancient and firmly held view of Catholic theologians that if the Jews would only listen with open hearts to the arguments for the Christian faith, they would instantly see the error of their ways and convert."[23] In recent years, much the same impasse has surfaced between gay people and conservative religious believers, who deny there is really such thing as a gay person. There are only heterosexuals and others who, for one bad reason or another, seek to undermine popular morality by having sex with others with the same genitalia. The idea that such unnatural couples might be "making love" deeply offends these heterosexual vigilantes. Here again, it is generally imprudent to conclude that those who disagree with us are only seeking to annoy us. This is a narcissistic pitfall.

There is something curiously comforting about discovering that people of other faiths applaud or tacitly support our actions. An amusing instance of this coincidence of support from strangers of what we were going to do anyway surfaces in Noël Coward's comedy *Private Lives.* An improbable reunion of a man and woman who had divorced five years earlier reveals that the two still love one another. The English divorcees discover one another on a honeymoon cruise, each having remarried that very day. They decide to run away with one another to her Paris apartment. There, ruminating on their most unusual predicament several days later, Elyot and Amanda grope for some way of making sense of their marital history:

AMANDA: Do you realise that we're living in sin?

ELYOT: Not according to the Catholics, Catholics don't recognize divorce. We're married as much as ever we were.

AMANDA: Yes, dear, but we're not Catholics.

ELYOT: Never mind, it's nice to think they'd sort of back us up. We were still married in the eyes of heaven, and we still are.

AMANDA: We may be alright in the eyes of Heaven, but we look like being in [a] hell of a mess socially.[24]

Audiences invariably laugh; we all grasp the shallowness of this clever couple's attempt to justify having left spouses hours after their respective second marriages. While hardly inclined to embrace a new religion in order to justify their actions to the spouses they had effectively jilted, Amanda and Elyot pause for just a moment to situate themselves in a foreign ethical frame. The temptation to remain there fades.

A similar, sure-fire laugh line surfaces in Stephen Sondheim's musical *Company* (1970); in the often imitated "I'm Not Getting Married Today" number, a terrified bride-to-be questions her betrothed about the point of their wedding. Thinking aloud, she gasps, "I'm so glad we're not having a big Catholic wedding! Because that would only make me feel like a big sinner when I got divorced a year later!" We find occasional examples beyond fiction. The Protestant writer Kathleen Norris achieved bestseller status in the late 1990s with *The Cloister Walk,* her meditative account of the joy she found in a Benedictine monastery.

Non-Catholics who try on the religion of Rome likely do so for the sake of convenience; such thought experiments can teach Catholics how they look to others as few other experiences can.

We care what others think about us for personal reasons—our integrity and our reputations matter to us. We also want others to think of us as sensible people, and that our lives make sense. We worry about the corrosive way in which others can scoff at our dreams and sabotage our self-confidence.

The question arises whether the importance of what others think of us boils down to purely pragmatic worries. Maybe it's the case that we really couldn't care less what people think about us—all that matters is what they do to us. As long as they are nice to us, on this view, they can think we are despicable. Fine.

This is emphatically not the Roman Catholic position, nor the Jewish. There is some philosophical support for this conviction, though. Kant wrote that actions are all-important. It is easy to show kindness and respect toward people we admire. That kindness and respect holds little moral worth. We demonstrate our moral fiber by helping people we do not enjoy helping. Morality should be hard, Kant thought.

People should behave kindly, Jews and Christians have agreed, and should cultivate fellow-feeling. Kant, a committed Protestant, valued the moral importance of character less than Jews and Christians traditionally have.

For the longest time, Jews couldn't get Christians to change. Christians thought Jews were headed to hell, and that was that. Jews may well have given up caring a long time ago about Christian respect they could not obtain. Now that Jews seem to have that respect at long last, shouldn't they be glad? Perhaps, but not for Catholic approval. Rather, survival and the freedom to live as they like might prompt some Jews to celebrate this signal advance.

We might expect improving relations between any two religions to alter conversion stories. Instead of trumpeting a change of heart, a convert might move quietly from one way of thinking to another. In early 1945, for example, the Chief Rabbi of Rome and his wife were baptized in the Basilica of St. Mary of the Angels. In his account of the conversion, former rabbi Israel Zolli waves the flag of Catholicism.[25] The preface to the memoir dwells on sharp condemnation Zolli received from the Jewish community he left; it prudently points out that the Catholic Church has historically excommunicated heretics with equally sharp invectives. Prospective converts from Judaism to Catholicism or vice versa could expect ostracism. Due in part to a general erosion of the force of the supernatural in religious imagination, the severity of a religious community's response to a potential convert may well have softened since the middle of the twentieth century. We know that people of other religions now permit themselves to evaluate how we react to converts who leave our faith for theirs: bystanders today may vocalize more freely criticism of a religious community that pummels a deserter. The lesson to be learned from this, for better or for worse, is that religious communities do well to squelch their opinion of someone who checks out of his spiritual heritage. And converts themselves will likely hesitate over singing loudly about having seen the light.

We care about our fragile reputations, which rest on what others think of us. We seek admiration and abhor humiliation. More importantly, we fear that what others think about us may spill over into the realm of actions. We abhor adults who terrify our children with talk about hellfire. We ignore those same adults as we flip past the television channels on which they appear, but we likely simmer when we pass them preaching on the street or at the mall. Our more civilized neighbors tend to keep their beliefs to themselves. They smile pleasantly and act the role of the good neighbor. They know better than to discuss such volatile subjects as politics or religion. But what they really think of us surfaces when they start to talk about heaven.

DISASTROUS PUBLIC RELATIONS

Buckingham Palace kicked its public relations machinery into high gear in the 1980s as problems erupted on multiple fronts. Princess Diana and Prince Charles misbehaved and then divorced; Prince Andrew and Sarah Ferguson followed suit. The queen stepped up public appearances and even began paying taxes. Then the queen faced stinging criticism for showing insufficient emotion upon the death of Princess Diana and publicly apologized, more or less. Next, Prince Edward and his wife Sophie suffered media contempt for having taken advantage of royal connections, despite having promised not to do so. All things considered, though, Buckingham Palace probably managed its public relations more effectively than the Vatican during the same period.

Sanctions prove useful to nations that oppose the policies or practices of another country. One country may refuse to trade with another, to furnish humanitarian aid, or to send a team of athletes to compete in the Olympic Games. Religions rarely behave in this way, at least not explicitly. But the public at large, it is fair to say, does withhold sympathy for religious groups or cults perceived to be cruel, unfair, or misguided.

Jews and Muslims compete for international sympathy as turmoil in the Middle East divides Westerners. Around the world Jews work tirelessly to educate us about the Holocaust in an effort to prevent another from happening. Assessing the historical progress of predominantly Muslim countries, Princeton professor Bernard Lewis wrote in 2002: "the long quest for freedom has left a string of shabby tyrannies, ranging from traditional autocracies to dictatorships that are modern only in their apparatus of repression and indoctrination."[26] Some report card. Although Lewis is no doubt correct, ask yourself how you would feel if intellectuals agreed that your culture amounted to a disappointment, an embarrassment. "By all the standards that matter in the modern world—economic development and job creation, literacy, educational and scientific achievement, political freedom and respect for human rights—what was once a mighty civilization [that is, Islam] has indeed fallen low."[27]

The convent at Auschwitz proved to be a public relations disaster for the Vatican. And the 1987 canonization of Edith Stein (a Jewish philosopher who converted to Catholicism, became a cloistered nun, and was later killed in a Nazi concentration camp) angered many. Now the proposed canonization of Pius XII has many deriding the Holy See as willfully self-deluded, secretly anti-Semitic. Loyal sons of the church are pummeling the Vatican. Nuns are taking the church to task as well: In October 1979, Sister Theresa Kane welcomed the Holy Father to the United States with an earnest plea (issued in public) to reconsider the ban on ordaining women. Six years later, a book entitled *Lesbian Nuns: Breaking Silence* challenged the church's rule of celibacy.[28] Other, sometimes prominent, Catholic gays and lesbians (John McNeill, Gianni Vattimo, Andrew Sullivan) continue to pound the church. With friends like these, who needs enemies? The painfully honest reflections of these Catholics join the books produced by non-Catholics (such as David Kertzer and Susan Zuccotti) and deepen the sense that the Vatican deserves blame.

Part of managing public relations involves minimizing disputes in-house, so that an organization can display a united front to the world. Bishops wield institutional power and enjoy a signal power to affirm or undermine the pope's ruling on a given issue. Not surprisingly, the Vatican thinks long and hard about appointing bishops. "A priest supporting the ordination of women, optional priestly celibacy, or birth control will not be made a bishop."[29] John Paul II has succeeded in finding bishops loyal to his views on these contentious subjects. Bishops are required to confer with the pontiff once every five years (in an "ad limina" visit). While praising John Paul II's genial openness to discussing any topic during informal exchanges, one American archbishop reported that the pope "pounded on the table for emphasis when the question of women's ordination came up at one lunch."[30] Jesuit priest Thomas Reese goes on to aver that the relationship between theologians and the papacy is worse today than at any time since the Reformation, and that if the papacy continues to lose its credibility in the intellectual community, schism could be the "disastrous consequence."

HARM TO SACRED PRESTIGE

Sometimes, when we see what others think of us, we cannot stand the sight. To the extent that we are free to undo our mistakes, we can reach out to others by correcting flaws and admitting them. Scoffing at their criticism carries risks. They may turn their backs on us and leave us to ourselves.

Why should Catholics care what others think about them? Because Catholics worry that they may be what others say they are; because Catholics genuinely want the respect of others; because Catholics hold themselves accountable for their own culture.

Even a moral institution must demonstrate sensitivity to the importance of self-presentation if it is going to wield any moral authority. An impressive array of theological texts and charitable gestures bolsters the institution's claim to high moral seriousness and, indeed, rectitude. Harm to sacred prestige carries untold costs, spilling over editorial glosses in secular newspapers to religious conversion rates and taunts on the local playground. Following the example of corporate CEOs or senators may not be such a bad idea: accountability and damage control do serve a purpose. Of course, damage control is rarely necessary when leaders have arranged for transparency of operation, when they have made sure that those beneath them can readily understand what the right hand and the left hand are doing.

SIX

Religious Conversion as Political Protest

W hat would we say of someone who converted to a new religion out of protest? What if an already religious person became so angry over a change in his church that he moved to a new church that denounced that same change? What if, hypothetically speaking, traditional Anglicans or Lutherans left their churches out of protest over the ordination of women or the loosening of strictures on lesbian and gay people? Where would they go? The Catholic Church might look appealing, given the uncompromising stance the Vatican has taken on these issues.

How would we ever know if someone were to convert to another religion out of protest? He might admit as much, as Malcolm X did in his autobiography. Christianity had not been good to black people, he believed. White Christians had deployed their religion as an insidious rationalization for the subjugation of African Americans, and so Malcolm X converted to Islam. He encouraged other black Americans to follow his lead.

More likely, however, a political convert would offer us another reason. The new religion, perhaps suspecting a questionable motive, could hardly be gratified, for the conversion would be less an embrace of a new faith than a refuge from the old. The new religion might congratulate itself on external confirmation of the soundness of a particular decision or stance, but acknowledging this narrow victory would demean the religion by reducing it to a burning political issue or two. The religion, like the convert, would both recognize an incentive for remaining silent about the protest and rejoice over someone's having seen the light spiritually.

Here I want to suggest the attractiveness of the Vatican to someone dissatisfied with liberal changes in his own church. Sometimes we can distinguish between a power play and a spiritual awakening, and once in a while converts will confirm our cynicism. What will become of a religion that devolves into a political sanctuary for spiritual protesters?

RELIGIOUS CONVERSION

The central Christian beliefs—the existence of God, the immortality of the soul, the punishment of sin—coexist with much more particular ones. Christians differ endlessly on such matters as transubstantiation, the virginity of Mary, the Trinity, and the source of religious authority. Of course Jews and Muslims disagree internally as well, and it is possible to "convert" from one relatively strict branch of Judaism or Islam to a more relaxed one (or vice versa).

Conversion by definition seems to entail humility: in moving to a new faith, we admit that we were mistaken. We rejoice that we have corrected an important spiritual error. William James has described this shift as a passion of willingness or acquiescence that can dissolve feelings of anxiety.[1] Conversions can occur suddenly and dramatically: Saul of Tarsus fell off his horse and heard God groan ("Saul, Saul, why are you persecuting me?"), Augustine writhed in a Milanese garden, pulling out his hair and hitting his face with his fists (as recounted in Book VIII of his *Confessions*). In 313 A.D. the Roman emperor Constantine converted to Christianity and literally transformed the Western world (in part by jump-starting a persecuting ecclesiastical machine). More often than not, though, conversions probably happen gradually and quietly. People convert in order to prepare for, indeed to make more likely, the occasion after death when they will meet God "face to face" (1 Cor 13:12-13).

True believers, motivated by ecstatic expectations of heaven's sweetness, might naturally wish to lasso neighbors who seem poor candidates for heaven. In theory, at least, such altruistic concern makes sense. Hoping to save Muslims worldwide from eternal damnation, the head of the Southern Baptist Convention exhorted his members to "pray and fast that God will miraculously reveal himself through Jesus Christ to Muslims" as the holy month of Ramadan drew to a close in 2001.[2] Calling Christianity "the only true religion," the Reverend James G. Merritt appealed to his flock of sixteen million members in the United States to help Muslims find "the true way to heaven, and this is through Jesus Christ." It is easy to dismiss such an appeal, along with similar ones made on behalf of Jews and Hindus, but no doubt Southern Baptists receive a steady stream of converts every year. These converts would likely praise the zeal of their new brethren.

Conversion stories can make for fascinating reading. Stephen Dubner recounts his spiritual journey from Catholicism to Judaism in *Turbulent Souls: A Catholic Son's Return to His Jewish Roots*. Born and raised in a devoutly Catholic family, Dubner discovered later in life that his parents were converts to the faith from Judaism. Slowly, he admitted to himself that he had never felt at home in Catholicism. Judaism exerted a spiritual pull, and he followed, much to his parents' chagrin. After converting, he felt for the first time that he had properly chosen his religion.[3] Eugene Pogany tells a similar story of conversion, but from the opposite direction, in *In My Brother's Image: Twin Brothers Separated by Faith After the Holocaust*. Pogany's father converted to Catholicism with his brother, who became a priest in an Italian monastery. After having lived as a devout Catholic, Pogany's father later returned to Judaism. That return profoundly troubled the relationship between the two brothers.[4]

Sometimes conversion stories come off sounding like propaganda. The trumpeting that resounds through *Bread from Heaven: The Stories of*

23 Jews Who Found the Messiah in the Catholic Church may rally the troops in Rome, but it will leave Jews cold.[5] Those who expect converts to dwell on the difficulty of the journey may forget the joy of epiphany; it is perhaps not surprising that converts tend to focus on the joy, not the struggle. In any event, testimonials of this sort stand as unscientific models of what most of us would consider genuine conversions. Common to these stories are details of agonizing over the decision, feeling powerless to resist the supernatural claim on one's identity, and being joyfully swept away. They essentially affirm what G. K. Chesterton, himself a convert to Rome, referred to as the three stages of conversion: detachment from the faith; skepticism about it; and then determination to resist what one really wants.[6] No doubt conversions in general make it difficult to sweep them into one tidy theory, a point not lost on Chesterton. Jaroslav Pelikan, a Lutheran theologian who teaches at Yale, has warned:

> Neither Protestants nor Roman Catholics are entitled to act as though conversions in their direction always proceeded from sincerely Christian motives, while conversions in the other direction always proceeded from selfish or ignoble motives. Motivation is a complex and subtle thing, especially in matters of religion and most especially in a decision for or against conversion. . . . Pilgrims in both directions are motivated by a mixture of desires and convictions. . . .[7]

With this caveat in mind, I will nonetheless proceed to raise the matter of questionable motives in religious conversions, but only in relation to Catholicism.

QUESTIONABLE MOTIVES

All sorts of people have converted to another religion for all sorts of reasons. Henri IV, the first Bourbon king of France, is famous for allegedly saying of his conversion to Catholicism at the end of the sixteenth century *"Paris vaut une messe"* ("Paris is worth a Mass"). A

Huguenot, Henri de Navarre could become king of France only if he converted from Calvinism to Catholicism. He converted for a reason decidedly nonspiritual. Several decades earlier, Henry VIII of England had grown frustrated that he could not fight heaven (that is, the pope) on its own terms. And so he changed the terms of heaven, declaring the old rules null and void. Moving swiftly from Roman Catholicism to the new Church of England so that he could legitimize the kind of sex he wanted to have, Henry VIII converted out of Rome for what has struck many subsequent Catholics as a bad reason.

Graham Greene confessed to a questionable motive as he recounted the anxiety surrounding his own conversion, which he considered bogus. He feared initially that his bad motive would be exposed—he was converting to Catholicism not because he believed in its truth, but because the woman he wished to marry had laid it down as a condition. In the course of taking the required instruction classes prior to acceptance in the church, he underwent a genuine conversion he feared others would not subsequently believe:

> I had cheated him [Father Trollope, Greene's instructor] from the first, not telling him of my motive in receiving instruction or that I was engaged to marry a Roman Catholic. At the beginning I thought that if I disclosed the truth he would consider me too easy game, and later I began to fear that he would distrust the genuineness of my conversion if it so happened that I chose to be received. . . . [8]

Greene, who went on to become a devout Catholic, judged his own initial conversion purely instrumental. That wasn't really a conversion at all, Greene tells us from the posture of a true believer. Today, marriage must stand as the most common of all questionable motives. In order to marry a beloved, one has to convert into his or her religion. Sometimes, love prompts us to view heaven from a different angle.

Power can seduce every bit as irresistibly as love, and yet various politicians have managed to withstand the lure. In 1928 Alfred Smith faced the same battle John F. Kennedy did in 1960: Americans did not want to elect a Roman Catholic to the presidency, regardless of how effectively a candidate campaigned. Neither Smith nor JFK thought of converting; this may have been out of sincere devotion to their religion, out of fear of what the public would say about the conversion, or perhaps both. In any event, the political climate seemed to have changed by the time of the 2000 presidential campaign. Running as Al Gore's pick for vice president, Senator Joseph Lieberman, an Orthodox Jew, fielded far fewer questions about his religion than either Smith or Kennedy had. Unlike Henri IV, modern politicians don't have to convert to acquire the power they seek.

Although discerning legitimate from illegitimate conversions vastly exceeds my abilities as a researcher, I do wonder about them. How would a judge decide? What sets the limits of the "spiritual"? Is it the process, the intensity, the persistence? Catholic theology denies that a person can know whether she or he is in a state of grace. Few would deny, however, the possibility for insincerity. Describing the efforts of French Jesuits to convert Native Americans in the eighteenth and nineteenth centuries, John Cornwell has written: "After some twenty years of supreme effort, living among the people in their long houses, the Jesuits realized that they were making little headway: the Hurons found Christianity obnoxious and were cooperating for material rather than spiritual gain. Food was often traded for baptism."[9] Converting into a religion for material or political gain may not differ so much from exiting religious life for personal enrichment or satisfaction. Writing in 1995, Thomas Fox suggested that the church had been giving a cold shoulder to priests who had left religious life in order to marry. According to him, those priests have banded together in order to protest the official church, whose initial reaction was "to deny their existence, to put them out of mind" and to forbid them from doing sacramental work.[10] If the church can feel betrayed by former priests, why not by new converts?

Eugene Gallagher has pointed out the shortcoming of William James's influential account of conversion, which distinguishes between "institutional" and "personal" religion. Gallagher regrets that James confines himself to the latter.[11] James focuses on the converts' immediate experience but misses or perhaps deliberately refrains from examining the ongoing, largely institutional dimension of conversion. The way in which converts tell the story of what has happened to them, how they died and came back to life, binds them to their new communities. Gallagher underscores the power of those stories to bolster a religion's institutional success.[12] Like Gallagher and the scholars he credits for similar insights, I focus on the sociological dimension of conversion rather than the personal. If it could be proven that a church, synagogue, or mosque tolerated the bad motive of a convert, we might think less of a supposedly spiritual group (spirituality is itself political on some level). It also seems likely that the faithful in that church, synagogue, or mosque would think less of their own spiritual community. This insight raises the question of what the faithful make of zealous converts, or any converts for that matter. What, for example, will liberal "cradle Catholics" make of new, conservative members who applaud an aspect of Catholicism the old-timers lament, even protest? This leads us back to the question of why we should care about what others think of us.

Some older Catholics will understandably resent the conversions of some newer Catholics, for the new song of the convert may interfere with the prayers of veterans. Lamenting the Vatican's refusal to soften its stance on sexual matters, Mark Jordan has taken to praying for the conversion of the Vatican itself:

> Since gay Catholics believe that God does try to guide even the Vatican bureaucracy, and since most of them also believe that the Vatican's present teachings on homosexuality are not inspired by God, they must trust God to offer during each night and during each day the grace to change the Vatican. Every morning in Rome is a morning on which the pope or his curia could be converted. If they don't convert today, that needn't imply some lack of divine will. It may imply something about human stubbornness. It may also suggest the magnitude of the changes required.[13]

New Catholics who favor conservative sexual politics may threaten their more liberal brothers and sisters in the faith. This sort of conflict may initially resemble the resentment of a small child who suddenly learns he has a sibling. The small child may resent the newcomer, who receives precious attention he or she thinks really should go to him or herself. But the conflict over converts goes much deeper, because it involves taking a religion on its own terms and asking whether it is being true to itself.

What should a religion do with converts whose motives are suspect? Those who convert to a religion in order to assume political power over an entire country must be rare, but those who convert in order to join a family of another religion are not. The risk to a religion is that it will debase itself, appear shallow to the faithful, if it admits people for reasons other than spiritual.[14] Whether we expect converts to report a single, mesmerizing epiphany that continues to hold them in its ethereal grip, or a gradual process of spiritual deepening and reorienting, we will likely find a distinctly social reception to envelop the new believer. The convert will find himself embraced by a new community that affirms and celebrates his modification.

Potential converts are people who think just like us. They haven't yet realized it, though. With a little help, they can find their way.

HUNGER FOR CONVERTS

What prompts missionaries? Are they on a quest to increase the power of an institution they proudly represent? Are they piously striving to spread the good news to people whose lives will supposedly be enriched by it? Perhaps hoping to save others from hell?

Novelist Louise Erdrich focuses on these difficult questions in *The Last Report on the Miracles at Little No Horse* (2001), a fictional story of a priest who travels to North Dakota early in the twentieth century to convert Native Americans to the Catholic faith. At one point, one very elderly priest says to a much younger one: "It all goes back to conversion, Father, a most ticklish concept and a most loving form of destruction. I've not come to terms with the notion even now, in my age, when I should be peacefully moldering up there on the hillside with the bones of my friends." In this passage, Father Damien, now an old man, explains that after seven decades of living among the Ojibwe Indians, he remains undecided as to which way of living is more to be recommended—the Roman or the Native American. In a flashback to Father Damien's past, we learn of the day he first reached the reservation. Entering the town in a wagon driven by his Indian parishioner, he is asked, "Why do you black gowns care if we pray to your God?" Shortly afterward, a nun who has lived on the reservation for some years counsels the young priest about the rituals of the Ojibwe. Pointing out that they often become drunk at ritual dances, Sister Hildegaard suggests to Father Damien, "You could easily baptize them while they're tranced." Upon seeing the new priest for the first time, Fleur, a young Indian girl, wonders:

> What was it that made the black robes desperate to gather up the spirit of the Anishinaabeg for their god? Fleur decided that the chimookoman god was greedy, which made sense as all the people she had seen of their kind certainly were . . . hunting down every last animal . . . and swiping all they could.[15]

Not surprisingly, those to be converted may question the motives of their would-be converters. Today, the very idea of missionaries makes many of the faithful squirm. Certainty of one's beliefs does not sit well with respect for the opinions of others in increasingly diverse societies. In Erdrich's novel, the Indians who received visits from Catholic missionaries felt somehow condescended to. Today, many people feel insulted when a religious missionary tries to save their soul.

As always, counterexamples can help us understand the topic under consideration. In *Catholic Converts: British and American Intellectuals Turn to Rome,* Patrick Allitt details the conversions of John Henry Newman, Orestes Brownson, G. K. Chesterton, Graham Greene, Evelyn Waugh, Dorothy Day, Thomas Merton, and Marshall McLuhan.[16] These conversions all seem valid, as tinny as that may sound. In each

case, the person converting was quite well-educated and came of his or
her own accord. Allitt views these Protestant conversions as yeast that
leavened a dulling and anti-intellectual religion.

The reasons any convert offers for his change of faith should not
surprise us by their variety. Any religion may offer diverse attractions;
Catholicism certainly does. David J. O'Brien believes most conversions
to Catholicism are proper and genuine:

> perhaps the majority of Catholics who think of the work of the Church as
> specifically "religious," by which they mean prayer, worship, catechetical
> instruction, efforts to win conversions, and charity toward the poor and
> suffering. These acts take precedence over the Church's efforts to trans-
> form society, important as those efforts may be.[17]

Here O'Brien sets out the two central motivations I have in mind—the
spiritual and the practical (or the genuine and the expedient)—and
expresses confidence in the primacy of the former.

Tricky as it certainly is, we can indeed talk about proper and
improper conversions. Can we hold a religion responsible for its
converts? It would seem perfectly reasonable to do so. To be true to itself,
a religion that admits newcomers by the narrow gate should care deeply
about the primacy of spiritual motives.

RELIGIOUS CONVERSION AS ESCAPE

If you belonged to a religion that held red hair to be immoral, you might
well come to hate your own red hair. If you found yourself born into a
religion that condemned your sexual attraction to members of your own
sex, you might well come to hate yourself.

What would you do? You might try to stifle your verboten attraction.
You might try to deny it. You might convert into another religion that
blessed or at least accepted your forbidden urges. Or you might just leave
religion altogether.

Ellis Hanson has written an engaging account of the attraction of Catholicism to homosexual aesthetes in the late nineteenth and early twentieth centuries. He argues persuasively that "decadent" writers individually and collectively found in Catholicism a romantic cult of the imagination and a spiritualization of eros. The very label "decadent" conjures up self-indulgent escapades and willful perversion, but Hanson shows us the passion underneath the showiness. He portrays decadent writing as a literature of ongoing Christian conversion, a continual flow of religious sensations and insights alternating with pangs of profanity and doubt. The mystical faith of decadents such as Paul Verlaine, Oscar Wilde, Walter Pater, and Evelyn Waugh seemed to find in Catholicism not just an aristocratic attitude and ceremonial pomp, but also a genuine spiritual striving. Shallow, yes, but genuine nonetheless. About J.-K. Huysmans's conversion to Catholicism Hanson writes, "What Huysmans sought in art and in Catholicism were the visionary flights of imagination and inspiration that he found in early modern mystics and satanists. He sought respite from mediocrity and atheism."[18]

What is striking about Hanson's path-breaking account is how it reveals the appeal to homosexuals of an institution that condemns them. Hanson sets out artfully the extent to which Roman Catholicism also celebrated and validated esthetes seized by the grace and beauty of the world beyond. Ordinary plebeians may fail to unlock the symbolism of rituals and symbols, but they too seek an escape from the suffering of the workaday world. Whether from suffering or from drudgery, churches offer an escape. That is not such a bad thing.

RELIGIOUS CONVERSION BY CREATIVE LOGIC

One of the more ingenious, and no doubt more offensive, modes of conversion has been to assume that someone else agrees with you, even though he insists he does not. This amounts to saying, "that person over there seems so compassionate, so moral—he must be more like me than he has grasped."

In a contribution to the *HarperCollins Encyclopedia of Catholicism,* Father Richard P. McBrien insists that there are people who would join the Catholic Church if only they knew the truth of its claims; hence the idea that a Torah-revering Jew might worship Jesus without knowing it. According to the Second Vatican Council's Decree on Ecumenism, the Catholic Church includes some non-Catholics. These other Christians "who believe in Christ and have been properly baptized are brought into a certain, though imperfect, communion with the Catholic Church."[19] Consequently, the worldwide, or universal, church is at once identical with the Catholic Church and larger than the Catholic Church. The church still teaches, however, that its traditions are normative for other Christian churches. Only those who "accept her entire system and all the means of salvation given to her" are "fully incorporated into the society of the Church."[20] Observant Jews are, in a sense, junior varsity Catholics.

What I am calling religious conversion by creative logic (the "inchoate desire" loophole, through which religious others can be considered Catholics) differs subtly but importantly from religious conversion by force. Conquest and invasion of a foreign land long entailed coercing the defeated to convert to the religion of the victors. It hardly seems likely that these conversions were genuine, if by genuine we mean inner reorientation to the truth of a faith.

We shouldn't be too quick to accuse the Catholic Church of presumptuousness here. Bestowing honorary membership on a Jew or a Protestant can be taken as a sympathetic act. So too can the recommendations of Jews or Protestants that a particular Catholic be considered a saint. Take Mother Teresa, for example, or Pope John XXIII, regularly referred to by Italians as "il pappa buono" or "the good pope." At least one Jewish group has petitioned the Vatican to canonize John XXIII, who, as an Apostolic Delegate to Turkey, sent thousands of blank birth certificates to Budapest so that Jews there could claim Christian birth and thereby escape Nazi territories.[21] And in a eulogy for his friend Richard M. Clurman, the former editor of *Time* magazine, William F. Buckley, Jr., said, "It came to me last Thursday, when the news [of Clurman's death] reached me just after midnight, that I have always subconsciously looked out for the total Christian, and when I found him he turned out to be a nonpracticing Jew."[22] The American social activist Dorothy Day also comes to mind: some souls seem so transparently and thoroughly good that even those outside the confines of the believing community sense their saintliness. There is even some precedent for non-Catholics to petition the Vatican to canonize a good person who lived as a Protestant. Lutherans urged the Vatican to canonize Dietrich Bonhoeffer, who protested the rule of Hitler and consequently died in a Nazi concentration camp.

Creative logic of the sort I have described here sits on top of a generous impulse—to think of strangers as familiars. Political overtones emerge from efforts to persuade others that they in fact agree with us, even when they insist they do not. What Catholic, fighting a serious illness, would reproach a Jewish or Protestant friend for praying for his speedy recovery? It would be uncharitable in the extreme to respond that the prayers of foreign believers will do no good. We accept those prayers in the same spirit of charity that prompts creative affiliations among the religiously different.

RELIGIOUS CONVERSION BY EROSION

Sometimes believers feel that they are standing in the same place but the earth beneath them is shifting. Catholicism itself is changing now, from within. Like a coral reef, the religion evolves with time, growing in certain areas and shrinking in others. Change within a church may produce conversions to another faith. Protests, typically informed and passionate, lead to the same negative result as attrition.

Attrition, a powerful enemy, stems from skepticism or indifference. From within a particular religion, it looks a lot like conversion—people leave. That they don't leave you for someone else softens the disappointment somewhat, but not entirely. Rejection is rejection.

Religious conversion by erosion may stem from ignorance or apathy. Sometimes a flock fails to grasp the essence of its faith and so ends up wandering out in left field. Perhaps if the faithful really cared about their spiritual identity, they would seek out someone in the know and have a talk. They might also go to a library or scan the Internet for answers to questions. If they feel largely comfortable in their beliefs, they may nonetheless cast about for verification that what they've held all along conforms with the party line.

Religious conversion by erosion threatens to call off the dance. Imagine a sign on an elaborate old church: "Catholicism cancelled due to lack of interest." Historians have written at great length about pagan conversions to Christianity, but we read less about converted Christians who relapsed back into paganism, which seemed more exciting. Still other pagans found that Christianity smacked of cannibalism and licentiousness and, after having embraced it, rejected the religion as downright repellent.[23]

Many Catholics over the age of fifty continue to talk about Vatican II and the genuinely extraordinary changes it wrought. Arguably just as significant are the changes happening within Catholicism—not the changes decreed from on high which trickle down to the masses, but the silent, gradual way in which the masses ebb away from doctrine long enforced from above.

To the extent that there exists a genuinely scientific method of measuring changes in the beliefs of successive generations, modern day polls must be it. According to a 1994 poll by the *New York Times,* a high percentage of Americans who self-identify as practicing Catholics do not believe that the priest changes the bread and wine into the body of Christ at Mass (the doctrine of transubstantiation).[24] What becomes of a religion whose own adherents fail to endorse or outwardly oppose what are supposedly its central tenets? Christ's physical presence in the Eucharist differs substantially from the morality of same-sex acts, to be sure. Not just believers in the street but ecclesiastical leaders as well seem now to have shifted focus from beliefs to behaviors. And so improper sex registers more clearly on the radar screen than other unorthodox views, such as the supreme authority of the pope or the moral unacceptability of remarriage after divorce.

Catholic theologian and professor Mark Jordan gives voice to the strong pull of erosion in *The Silence of Sodom:*

> Other homosexual Catholics who remain in regular parishes fall back on the claim so commonly heard from gay priests and religious: Staying is the best way to change things.
>
> The familiarity of this claim doesn't guarantee its truth. It may simply be mistaken. Remaining within officially Catholic structures may not be in fact the most efficient way to change them. We might effect reforms much more quickly by shaking the dust of Catholic parishes from our feet and leaving them behind.[25]

This "conversion" away from Catholicism toward sexual liberation might not seem to be religious, although many such "converts" think of the turn in just those terms: gay writer Andrew Holleran, a "cradle Catholic," has confessed to switching from the God of Abraham to the God of Priapus.

JEWISH AND CATHOLIC
BARRIERS TO CONVERSION

Unlike Protestants, Jews and Catholics find themselves locked into their faiths: Jews through blood and Catholics through baptism. According to traditional Jewish belief, identity travels through the blood of a mother. A Jewish woman will always give birth to a Jewish child. That child will always be a Jew, come what may. And according to Roman Catholic theology, the sacrament of baptism is indelible. This means that once a person (an infant, a child, or an adult) has been baptized Catholic, he will always be Catholic, come what may. This means that Jews and Catholics can never leave their respective faiths. Hence Jean-Marie Lustiger, the cardinal of Paris, calls himself a Jewish Catholic. Born a Jew, Lustiger converted to Catholicism all by himself at the age of twelve. He has collected competing identities, neither of which he can shrug off.

Religious identity defies ready explanation. Being part of a minority—be it a religion, a race, or a sexual group—no doubt increases the odds that a person within that sociological subset will take the relevant part of his identity seriously. Freud, for example, grew up in a family devoid of religious devotion, yet he believed something indefinable made him a Jew:

> What tied him to Judaism, he wrote to the brethren at B'nai B'rith in 1926, was not faith, "for I was always an unbeliever, was brought up without religion though not without respect for the demands, called 'ethics,' of human culture." Nor was it national pride, which he thought pernicious and unjust. "But enough else remained to make the attraction of Judaism and of Jews so irresistible, many dark emotional powers, all the mightier the less they let themselves be grasped in words, as well as the clear consciousness of inner identity, the secrecy of the same mental construction."[26]

A pull that could hardly be described as rational magnetized Freud. Religious identity anchors individuals in a rolling sea of ebb and flux, providing an orientation from which to judge other experiences.

Other identities compete and combine with the religious inclination, sometimes overwhelming it. But many believers will report that the religious inclination claims pride of place in their multifaceted personalities. In some instances, a religion will dictate to those who have taken its path that they have no choice but to remain. There is no escape. Individuals will ultimately decide for themselves whether to accept this belief, but an unfriendly culture may lock an unwilling Jew or disenchanted Catholic in a permanent stranglehold.

Sexual desire, like Freud's religious identity, may seem permanent, unchosen. And yet many heterosexuals have called for homosexual reform, psychiatric or religious interventions that will convert a sexual deviant into a sexual conformist. Such critics deny the stability of sexual orientation, much as the Catholic Church denies the stability of Jewish identity when it courts Jewish converts.

The Catholic Church welcomes Jewish converts. But what about gay and lesbian converts?

RELIGIOUS HANGERS-ON

When you break one of the big rules in Catholicism, you can find yourself either excommunicated or sent to what I'll call the "penalty box." Excommunication happens much less in the modern world than it used to. But the penalty box continues to take in regular waves of Catholics whose offenses, while not significant enough to merit excommunication, prevent them from receiving Holy Communion. The guiding rule of the penalty box is that anyone in it must forego the Eucharist. Time spent in the penalty box does not, however, relieve the faithful of the obligation to attend Mass weekly and on holy days (for example, the feasts of the Assumption, the Immaculate Conception, or the Ascension).[27]

What can land you in this metaphorical holding cell, the penalty box of Catholicism? Remarriage after divorce can, as can the use of birth control,[28] premarital, extramarital, or gay sex. Any mortal sin makes Holy Communion off-limits until you have properly confessed the sin to a priest.

What, then, do we make of people in the penalty box who challenge the rules?[29] What should we think of someone in the penalty box who insists she will not admit to wrongdoing but wants to remain a bona fide Catholic?[30] Such is the predicament of one Martha Sahagun de Fox, who became the first lady of Mexico in the summer of 2001. A divorcee, like her husband, she tied the knot in a civil ceremony. As the *Washington Post* reported, "The two conservative Catholics defied church law by remarrying—and can no longer take Communion at Mass—thereby becoming an emblem of the practical struggles of modern Mexicans." A cynic might think that the couple wishes to remain Catholic for political reasons, but that does not seem fair. True, they continued to endure the wrath of church conservatives, but journalists concurred that Mexicans generally had already accepted the divorcees as a couple. They appealed for an annulment of their previous marriages through influential Mexican cardinal Norberto Rivera, and they arranged an October 2000 meeting at the Vatican to plead their case directly to Pope John Paul II. Each can claim a past of unbroken personal devotion to the church. Of her disqualification to take the Eucharist at Mass, the first lady said, "I am not in any way downplaying the great value of Communion for Catholics. But I am absolutely certain that communion with God can be achieved in many ways other than bread and wine."[31]

Why those in the penalty box don't simply check out of the game can be difficult to understand. Religious motivations are often a mystery that makes the gap between us and them seem larger. Religious hangers-on, those who hold to a faith that has in some sense rejected them, become political protesters, whether they mean to or not. The logic of "the personal is political" guarantees that rule-breakers who refuse to leave politely will ruffle ecclesiastical feathers.

Religious hangers-on can be just like political hangers-on. Just because a party you oppose gains control of the government of your land doesn't mean that you are going to abandon your party. You stay, hope for the best, and focus on the next round of elections, when you hope your party will return to power.

Churches also swing between liberal and conservative leaders. With its rigid hierarchical structure, the Catholic Church keenly feels pendulum shifts. Think for example of the papacy of John XXIII. Pius IX had condemned the proposition that "the Roman Pontiff can and should reconcile and accommodate himself to progress, liberalism, and recent civilization."[32] The Second Vatican Council set the stage for political conflict several years later. Loosening the conservative stranglehold on Roman Catholicism, Pope John Paul XXIII opened the Second Vatican Council with a speech that has become famous. In that speech, he criticized doomsday naysayers who nostalgically saw the past as uniformly favorable to the growth of the church and the present as uniformly disadvantageous. In scolding these "prophets of doom," as he called them, the pope celebrated the exciting possibilities of the future and, indeed, the present. In mounting what could hardly fail to be seen as a political attack, and in subsequently allowing Jews and Muslims into heaven, John XXIII deepened the divide between conservatives and liberals within the church and inadvertently compelled both conservatives and liberals to seek allies in other religions. John, with his insistence on "reading the signs of the times," moved the church forward at the expense of aggravating divisions that had been festering for decades.

To be sure, many religions have hangers-on. In Catholicism, religious hangers-on almost always qualify as sexual outlaws: divorced Catholics who have remarried, Catholic couples who use birth control, or gay/lesbian Catholics. In his study of the effect of the gay issue on American churches, Keith Hartman asked several gay and lesbian Catholics in Durham, North Carolina, whose Dignity group had recently been expelled from their parish, why they stayed in a church that didn't seem to want them. Here is one of the answers:

> I think there are basically two ways to view the Catholic church. One is to look at the letter of the law of the church, which to my mind is ignorant and destructive. The other way is to look at the individuals in the church, and to realize that those individuals are in fact the church. I have personally experienced profoundly knowledgeable, compassionate, and politically powerful people in the church—priests, nuns, monks, not to mention a multitude of lay people, who have made my path as a gay man in the world immeasurably easier.

And another:

> The reason I stay in the Catholic church is because of its tradition of prayer and sacrament. I ultimately came to the Catholic church because of its emphasis on how prayer deepens one's experience of the world. I don't find that in other Christian traditions, except perhaps in Quakerism. And although the Quakers have a fine tradition of prayer, they don't have a

tradition of sacrament. Sacrament is an affirmation of the sacredness of the world. It serves as a focusing device that allows me to deepen my experience of the presence of God, and to do that in community.[33]

Gay and lesbian Catholics, like divorced Catholics, will often explain that they neither can nor wish to move away from their spiritual heritage. Rooted deeply in their identity, many disenfranchised Catholics will insist they are as Catholic as they are gay (or divorced). This presents a problem to mainstream believers.

Hangers-on will often find themselves on the defensive as the old guard ushers them to the door. The faith of the unwanted defies easy explanation, for such marginal believers sometimes see their defiance as an act of faith. Indeed, Father Bernard Häring practically recommended resistance in the wake of the birth control encyclical *Humanae Vitae* in the late 1960s. Just when it seemed that the Holy See would formally allow married Catholics to use birth control, Pope Paul VI refused to budge. Häring, a member of the Papal Birth Control Commission, described the effect of this ruling on the faithful as "traumatic" and encouraged dissenting Catholics to follow their consciences:

> If the pope deserves admiration for the courage to follow his conscience and to do the most unpopular thing, all responsible men and women must show forth similar honesty and courage of conscience. I am convinced that the subjective and conscious motive of the pope was love for the church. Those who contradict him must do it also out of love for the whole church, out of love for those whose faith is endangered. This also can and must be a service of love for the successor of Saint Peter.[34]

Opposition, then, can rightfully claim to be a proper way of showing love for the pope, at least according to the most influential Roman Catholic moral theologian of the twentieth century.

No doubt to most gay and lesbian Catholics who choose to stay in the church, hope seems reasonable. They hang this hope on the supposed sacredness of conscience. If Catholics who violate the Holy See's ruling on birth control do not need to confess the fact and may still take communion, so may Catholic gays and lesbians whose erotic relationships strive for permanence take communion as well. Gradually, Catholic gays and lesbians hope, their chosen faith will come to agree with them.

CATHOLICISM AS THE
LAST RESORT OF CHRISTIAN MISOGYNISTS

A few converts to Catholicism have baldly stated their attraction to a church that keeps women and gay people "in their proper place."[35] Early in 1995, for example, the Most Reverend Graham Leonard, the Anglican bishop of London, "swam the Tiber." Cardinal Basil Hume of Westminster, England's Catholic primate, received Leonard into the faith. A married man, Father Leonard granted England's *National Catholic Register* an interview, one in which he called the vote over the ordination of women "the trigger" of his conversion.

Brian Brindley's obituary, which reads like a story line for a situation comedy, peppered the March 8, 2001 edition of Britain's *The Daily Telegraph*.[36] Other British newspapers captioned the mediaworthy story of an Anglo-Catholic canon who converted to Roman Catholicism after the Church of England voted to allow women priests. At his conversion, he took the confirmation name of "Leo," after the pope who had declared Anglican orders null and void. Although something of a showman, Brindley seems genuinely to have objected to the ordination of women and to have taken his conversion to Catholicism seriously.

An Oxford graduate who was ordained a priest in 1963, Brindley dressed flamboyantly, preferring the dramatic style of nineteenth-century Roman Catholic prelates. Upon his death, *The Times* of London pegged him a "larger-than-life *bon viveur*." His career ended suddenly in 1985, after an undercover journalist betrayed his fast friendship with Brindley and published an account of the priest's sexual fantasies, all of which involved young men.

It seems reasonable to conclude that Brindley converted to Catholicism out of protest over gender trouble in the Anglican Church. Brindley may or may not have objected to married Catholic priests, but he surely knew of them. American Catholics do not always understand that Eastern-rite priests may marry. Almost twenty percent of Catholic priests—those in Romania, the Czech Republic, and the Ukraine, for instance—may legally take wives. Brindley indicated no interest in himself taking a wife; the point to be taken here is that he converted into a religion that does allow married priests in certain instances. Debates over the desirability of allowing Catholic priests to marry can become nearly as heated as arguments over whether to ordain women as Catholic priests.

Other, more sober conversion stories indicate support for the Vatican's gender stance. Mrs. Linda Poindexter, wife of Rear Admiral John Poindexter, was an Episcopalian priest from 1986 until her conversion to Catholicism in 1999. For this American woman, there was no question as to whether she could keep both her spouse and collar. She relinquished her status as a priest. In an interview with the *National Catholic Register* in August 2001, she defended the all-male, celibate priesthood of her new religion (which is not to imply that she converted expressly for this reason).[37] Upon her conversion, she was quoted by the *Episcopal New Service* as saying, "I believe that the church should not encourage people in a morally and physically dangerous sexual expression."[38] Poindexter objected to Episcopalian support for the ordination and blessing of those in same-sex relationships. She also stressed her aversion to abortion.

Poindexter stands as a curious case, but the Anglican priests make for an even more interesting point. Few people seem to realize that there are in fact some married Catholic priests, almost all of whom have converted from the Anglican church and after marriage. The Vatican does allow such men to keep their wives (the same is true of married priests who convert from the Greek Orthodox Church). Canadian historian Elizabeth Abbott has gone so far as to call Anglican men who convert to Catholicism over the issue of women "egregious misogynists, united in their rage over female ordination."[39] She does not estimate the size of this subgroup, although she is surely not making a mountain out of a molehill. That the Roman Catholic Church would allow such conversions isn't really so surprising: it must be flattering to hear the competition tell you that you were right all along.

These requests for ordinations of married priests came to the attention of the Vatican. Abbott comments wryly on "an alacrity astounding in such a sluggish institution" and reports that the pope duly approved the requests. She quotes from a letter in which the United Kingdom's five Roman Catholic archbishops broached the conversions to their own priests, who naturally were celibate and would have to remain that way:

> At the present time the Catholic Church is welcoming into full commun-
> ion a number of married clergymen of the Church of England, often
> together with their wives and in some cases their children. . . . Many of
> these clergy wish to be ordained priests in the Catholic Church   We
> are convinced that their ministry will enrich the church. . . . The Holy
> Father has asked us to be generous. We are confident that you also will
> welcome and appreciate these new priests when, in due course, they . . .
> take their place in the presbyterate of many of our dioceses.[40]

If the wives of any of these priests converting to Catholicism ever worried about holding on to their men, they likely breathed a long sigh of relief. For the Vatican specified that none of the converting priests would be free to marry again. Beyond that, the Vatican opened a four-year window in which Anglican priests could decide to "swim the Tiber," as they say. Haste was in order.

Yet those Roman Catholics who had left the priesthood in order to marry a woman would not be allowed to return to the priesthood with their wives in tow. Abbott judged this incongruity unfair, a penalty that burdens Catholics and privileges converts. She concluded that the Vatican consciously allowed what I am calling conversions of political protest:

> Certainly, after years of indifference to them, the Church did not have a
> *crise de conscience* about its unmanned pastorates, nor a *moment de panique*

about the relentless flight of conflicted religious from their cloisters back into the uncelibate world. No, what motivated the Church was the strength of the Anglican rebels' conviction about the fundamental unsuitability of women as priests, a conviction today's Church Fathers share and are committed to sustaining.[41]

It would be a mistake to draw an analogy between the Episcopalian priests Abbott has in mind and Henri de Navarre, whom I mentioned earlier in this chapter. Whereas it seems to have been greed or ambition that motivated Henri IV, Abbott says misogyny prompted the angry priests.

If Abbott is correct, then we should also examine the reasons of those who convert out of the Anglican Church for evidence of resentment toward lesbian and gay people as well. Any dissenting Protestant minister whose home team votes to allow the ordination of lesbians or gay men might find the Vatican suddenly appealing.

Sadly, no doubt, those Catholic priests who have left their orders in order to marry (or, when gay, to set up house with a man) must feel like political protesters as well. As quietly as they may try to exit their jobs, their departures brim with political overtones. Informed Catholics know that their tradition of priestly celibacy dates back not to Saint Peter but only to the twelfth century. In fact, Saint Peter had a wife, as did Saint Paul. It wasn't until 1139 that priestly celibacy became mandatory, at the Second Lateran Council. Toward the end of the twentieth century, some bishops asked the Vatican to explore the wisdom of priestly celibacy. In a letter delivered on October 11, 1965, Pope Paul VI explicitly forbade the Second Vatican Council from discussing the subject. John Paul II subsequently showed the same intransigence.

FAKING RAPTURE

Spiritual upheaval can flare up in multiple dimensions, any two of which should caution us against reducing religious experience to a single vector. And speculation on conversions is hardly irrefutable. That said, we can reasonably venture explanations for why people make the decisions they do.

Converting from one religion to another provokes the question of why one bothers. Put positively, rapture beckons us: put negatively, eternal punishment frightens us. It might be thought that there are many heavens—Hindu, Buddhist, Jewish, Muslim, Presbyterian. But this intuition might qualify as blasphemous in the West—because there is only one God, there will only be one heaven. We might legitimately wonder if Jews, Catholics, Muslims, and Protestants really worship the same God.[42] I have sidestepped this important question, focusing instead on the kind of joy converts might feel.

There are at least two distinct ways of examining religion—official church doctrine tells one story, and popular practice another. My interest in religion stems more from psychology than from doctrine. To be sure, I care about official pronouncements—how religions explain to the world what they are and what they stand for. More interesting to me is how doctrine trickles down to ordinary believers and molds what they eat, where they take their vacations, how they bury their dead, why they return to the fold after lapses of various sorts, and how they have sex. Religious converts likely consider the popular aspects of the religion they're moving into just as much, if not more, than they think about the doctrines undergirding and defining that faith.

Faking rapture, like faking orgasm, highlights the peril of saying too much. When we fear rejection from a person or institution we want to keep around, it behooves us to signal a certain appreciation. A new convert can appreciate the church through various dimensions—social, psychological, aesthetic, historical, mystical, and political—which means that satisfaction in any one of those areas may compensate for inadequacy in another. At base, new converts may be picking and choosing from the smorgasbord of their religion no more than those who were born into it. We seem to hold converts to a higher standard, which may not be fair.

As it stands now, the Vatican appears a magnet for conservative men wary of their increasingly liberal Protestant churches. What if the Holy See were to soften? Where would those gender-based dissidents and converts to Catholicism go?

SEVEN

Fertility Cults
and Sex Scandals

Judaism continues to deny, as it has for some two thousand years, that Jesus is the Messiah. But that distinction between Jews and Christians may no longer point to the core of Christianity. Whereas Catholics previously constructed their cosmology around the defining tenet that Jesus is more important than anything else, they no longer do. The center of Catholicism has shifted toward the sex question. I have suggested that what is happening in Catholicism represents a general shift in other Christian denominations as well.

To the extent that sex moves to the center of religious experience, at least in the social expression of that experience, a curious parallel with ancient fertility cults emerges. Primitive pagans of various sorts organized themselves into fertility cults, which aimed to enhance agricultural abundance and human fecundity. Such cults demanded considerable investments of time and energy from their adherents, who worried about the volatile, invisible powers peering down on humanity from the sky. These powers supposedly governed the harvest, and it seemed only natural to propitiate them.

Well into the twentieth century, parents in agricultural communities needed ever more hands to man the farm. Even parents in urban centers worried about frightening infant mortality rates, and so almost everyone hoped for a large family. It cannot be said that mainstream believers in the modern West still exhibit an overriding desire to reap reproductive riches. Despite reliance on artificial forms of birth control, though, many believers in the modern West do pine for offspring. The contemporary focus on regulating fertility bears a certain resemblance to the old fixation with coaxing fertility, a resemblance worth noting.

Another resemblance comes into focus as sex moves to the center of Catholicism: some organized religions increasingly seek to govern social proprieties, much in the way country clubs do. Sexual nonconformists have been as unwelcome in most churches as in most country clubs, and the two organizations coincidentally reinforce each other's goals to some important extent. Instead of focusing on battles one might expect the Vatican to pursue vigorously, the Holy See instead enforces policies important to country-club boards.

Since 1950, a variety of debates has ignited the Catholic hierarchy, both in Rome and in the United States: nuclear disarmament and capital punishment, for example (in contrast to the ordination of women and gay people, the church falls in with the Left on these matters). But sex now tops them all. With each step the Vatican takes away from a longstanding focus on the necessity of Christ for salvation, the church approaches the profile of a social club. While allowing people of other faiths into Catholic heaven is all to the good, the move increases the peculiarity of an outmoded investment in heterosexuality. The link between heterosexuality and fertility cults shines brighter in the current light, when sexual and gender nonconformists emerge as the principal threat to the psychic security of conservative Catholics. And the idea of Catholic bishops protecting priests who prey on children upsets everyone. The solution to the problem will be sniffing out gay men from the seminaries and sacrificing them for the good of all.

FERTILITY CULTS

By the term "fertility" I intend the straightforward meaning of fecundity. Fertility anxiety arises in both agricultural and reproductive arenas. Hunters, gatherers, and would-be parents naturally hope for regeneration. Traditional farm labor neatly represents an archetypal fertility cult; everyone works in concert to coax riches from the land. Doctors and nurses working in new reproductive technologies typify an even bolder model of fertility cults today. Both men and women can suffer from reproductive dysfunction (that is, infertility) and reprotechnology offers hope to them both. The medical professionals who facilitate conception achieve feats previously only imagined in science fiction.

It is hardly surprising that our ancestors worried about bringing forth large numbers of children, for they knew next to nothing about human reproduction. Indeed, the fertilization of human eggs remained a mystery to scientists until the end of the nineteenth century. Especially today, when we understand a great deal more about the technical aspects of making babies, conceiving and bearing children preoccupies many traditional couples and those single, professional women who fear that they cannot or will not become pregnant. The progress of human civilization does not seem to diminish the desire for offspring; to the extent that such progress can overcome longstanding reproductive obstacles, it only increases expectations that those who want biological progeny will succeed. Contemporary sociobiologists proffer theories and data to persuade us that young lovers choose mates in significant part by subconsciously predicting the likelihood of healthy, vigorous offspring, a probability which can supposedly be discerned through the face and body of a prospective mate.

James Frazer renewed popular interest in fertility cults with the publication of the influential and voluminous study *The Golden Bough: A Study in Magic and Religion* (1890), which specifically pondered how killing figured into fertility rites. Several decades later, Mircea Eliade frequently touched on fertility rituals in *Patterns in Comparative Religion* (1958), a work long regarded as canonical.[1] Eliade's treatise unfolds in many directions; one representative thread examines an age-old belief that certain stones can make infertile women conceive; such stones were thought to harbor the spirits of ancestors. Such a "theory" evolves over time, Eliade explained, such that people may not realize what they're doing today when they unreflectively cringe before certain stones or perhaps actively seek them out. Emphasizing the significance of the rhythm of the seasons in the religious experience of agricultural societies, Eliade locates the origin of primitive religious practice in the reproductive fears of people who lived in farming communities. Even now, Eliade suggests, we harbor plenty of unrecognized instincts, psychic reactions that connect us to the harvests of our ancestors.

The link between bringing forth new life from the land and from humans requires little time to understand: just as spring eventually overtakes winter, so does the birth of a child offset the death of an elder. The earth, like the human species, regularly yields new creations. Rebirth, whether purely symbolic or literal, has been seen to link women to the earth. Eliade notes, for example, that Finnish peasant women used to sprinkle the furrows of fields to be plowed in the spring with a few drops of milk from their own breasts. Eliade also remarks on a practice he describes as common: sprinkling the plough with water before its first use of the year. Noting the symbolic link to baptism, Eliade suggests that the water also symbolized semen, perhaps not so unconsciously.

Crop abundance preoccupied people whose existence depended on what the earth could bring forth—this much is not hard to see. Once again, a certain natural link was seen to extend to women, who were expected to produce more labor for the maintenance of farms (not just in primitive societies, but throughout Europe well after the Middle Ages):

> This solidarity of all forms and actions of life was one of the most essential concepts of primitive man, and he turned it to magical advantage by following the principle that whatever is done in common will have the

most favourable results. The fertility of women influences the fertility of the fields, but the rich growth of plants in turn assists women towards conceiving.[2]

Women, fields, fertility: in Hellenic, Muslim, and Christian societies, marriages often took place in the fields, particularly in the spring. Because death naturally leads to thoughts about life, the hope of fertility also blossomed in the minds of earlier people attending funerals.[3]

Drawing on a work ethic according to which people get out of life what they put into it, fertility cults called for concrete proof of one's devotion. A good harvest, the dramatic culmination of months of hard labor, deserved sacrifices of live animals. Among the Aztecs and the Khonds, human sacrifice eventually became common in order to ensure a strong yield. Offering up human life, the very commodity most highly prized, seemed a good way of proving seriousness about the task at hand. It seemed instinctive to many of our forebears that some sort of higher power oversaw the harvest; appeasing or flattering this power would increase the likelihood of a good result. Primitive people lived in constant fear that the power in question would lose its force or turn its back on them.

What works such as Eliade's and Frazer's demonstrate is that reverence for fertility gods runs throughout much of Western history. Where such reverence began is hard to say. We certainly find it in the Hebrew Bible. In the fourteenth or fifteenth century B.C., Canaanites worshiped Baal, their chief god, because they believed he controlled the rain. "Even among the Israelites, Baal had his high places (Jer. 19.5; 32:35), his altars (Jgs. 6.25-30), his sacred stones (4 Kgs. 11.18; 2 Chr. 23.17) and his prophets (3 Kgs. 18.19, 22)."[4] Devotion to Yahweh, the God of Abraham, drowned out praise of Baal. The prophet Elijah challenges the prophets of Baal to a contest in the First Book of Kings, Chapter 18. Following the rules set out by Elijah, four hundred prophets of Baal place a bull upon an altar and then call upon Baal to ignite it for them. As the pagan prophets writhe in frustration, Elijah jeers and then summons Yahweh to set the bull on fire. Elijah slaughters all four hundred of his rivals and, as the Hebrew narrative would have us believe, the cult of Baal as well. It should not seem farfetched to suppose that ancient Hebrews transferred to their God much of the faith previously held in Baal's ability to bring forth abundance.

The enormously popular celebration of Lupercalia in ancient Rome conveniently combined the hunger for a rich harvest with the demands of libido. Celebrated on the fifteenth of February well into the third century of the Christian era, the festival unleashed the licentiousness of the young men who cavorted nearly naked around the city. The scions of better families would don bloody goatskins, using them as loincloths, and whip anyone in their path. Whipping enhanced conception, according to Roman legend. After the pagan competition, parties held throughout the city would celebrate the young men who had impersonated wild goats, the embodiment of sexuality. Enhancing fertility was hard work, but somebody had to do it.

Witchcraft overlapped with and perhaps even grew out of early European fertility cults. The persecution of witches attests to popular investment in the dark power held out by fertility cults (a rational response to witches would have been indifference). Persecution of witches would seem a mark of ignorance or bigotry, and yet witches were taken dreadfully seriously; considered a bona fide threat to mainstream religion, suspected witches suffered drastic trials. A skeptic would call the witch trials of previous centuries a kind of showdown between rival fertility cults. Although the theory is impossible to prove, social opposition to witches may have sprung from fear that they might just manage to interfere with the reproductive cycles of the earth or the brethren. Witch trials make sense when we ponder the depth of fertility anxiety.

Christianity has long revered fertility. For centuries the sprawling world religion has pulsated with disapproval of birth control and, more vocally, interference with pregnancy. The Catholic Church flexed its still considerable muscle in 1960s America and claimed victory in a legal case that reached the Supreme Court (*Griswold v. Connecticut* [1965]), the result of which was the legal prohibition of prescribing any means of birth control. Physicians lost licenses if they prescribed diaphragms, for example (the pill had not been invented at the time); condoms were permitted, allegedly to prevent the spread of disease. I am not trying to collapse Christianity into the fertility cults that preceded it. Rather, I am trying to highlight what the two admittedly vast categories have in common.

The juxtaposition of fertility cults with an established religion such as Roman Catholicism needn't seem antagonistic or offensive. According to *The New Catholic Encyclopedia*, "Since religion is intimately connected with the existential situation of man in the cosmos, the central place of fertility and vegetation cults ought not to cause surprise, for they deal with the mystery of life itself: mortality and regeneration, the solidarity between all levels of existence, the necessity to kill in order to live or preserve life, etc."[5] Just when you would expect the Vatican to endorse new reproductive technologies, though, it forbids them. Tampering with nature, such as *in vitro* fertilization, violates the rules. Infertile couples must accept God's will and resign themselves to a childless marriage or adoption. Catholic opposition to new reproductive technologies not-withstanding, regeneration drives Rome's thinking about affective alliances. But what long set off Christianity, Judaism, or Islam from ancient fertility cults was the subordination of regeneration goals to ones regarding worship. Beyond that, it should be noted that we can interpret regeneration figuratively as well as literally. These religions can regenerate themselves by winning new converts, which means bringing forth new children is not the only path to abundance.

Reproductive duties, of course, do not extend to Roman Catholic priests and nuns, who must swear off sex. Catholicism opposes fertility cults, then, in a way Judaism and Islam do not (that is, by virtue of a celibate clergy).[6] And yet Catholicism holds onto the fascination with new life in a way that almost suggests fear, the same fear that animated the fertility cults in Frazer's and Eliade's pages. In a world preoccupied with the challenges wrought by overpopulation and the allocation of scarce resources, this fear looks increasingly like the worry of social elites that the wrong sort of people may ruin things for the rest of us.

COUNTRY CLUBS

Anywhere people gather, social interaction follows. We call "culture" the shifting combination of invisible forces that mold this interaction. Any culture will be at its best, arguably, when peace prevails and the economy churns briskly. Poverty, war, and desperation dissolve manners and the expectation that others will behave honorably. In particularly bad times, it seems that anything goes. In especially good times, by contrast, the finer points of social interaction can take on almost ridiculous importance, every gesture and intonation holding the power to offend or alienate others. In good times and bad, the leisure class enjoys its free time, while much of the working class dreams of grasping some for itself.

It is hardly surprising that organized religion also includes a social aspect. Given the absence of computers, phones, and coffee machines, religious spaces contrast with the modern office and thereby with white-collar work (the kind of employment that generates capital). And with the absence of physical labor, religious services resemble leisure more than blue-collar work (the kind of employment that generates goods). Whereas the work place focuses on the bottom line, the religious space culminates in higher bliss.

Social niceties hover over many organized leisure activities. Roman baths, which legitimized a culture of civilized nudity much in the way ancient Greek gymnasia had done, preceded European spas and the kind of luxury vacation memorialized in the 1988 film *Dark Eyes* with Marcello Mastroianni. Membership in a proper club is not always a criterion for rarefied relaxation—think of the hotel in Thomas Mann's *Death in Venice* (1913) or the tuberculosis hospital in his much longer work, *The Magic Mountain* (1924). In these milieus, hefty price tags keep out undesirables.

Restaurants have always done that; they became vibrant public spaces in the eighteenth century and widened the domain of leisure.[7] It was about this time that public spaces in general began to hit their stride. We might expect the need for socially exclusive clubs to rise in proportion to the availability of attractive public spaces. Crowds annoy elitists who may wish to be admired and applauded, but only from a distance. A thorough study of country clubs would offer a broader taxonomy than I have room for here. Suffice it to say that country clubs combine a bit of cuisine with a panoply of sports facilities and even a flicker of political activism. As such, country clubs stand as a fusion of leisure activities, any one of which may invite social exclusivity.

In the late nineteenth century America formalized an exclusive form of public frivolity in the country club. James Murray Forbes established this American interpretation of class division in Brookline, Massachusetts. There, in 1882, he established an association called, appropriately, The Country Club. By 1930 there were at least 4,000 such organizations in the United States.[8] A discussion of country clubs is curiously absent from Veblen's stinging satire *The Theory of the Leisure Class* (1899), particularly from his analysis of conspicuous leisure in Chapter 3.[9] This oversight may be due to the relative newness of country clubs at the time of Veblen's writing. In any event, a great deal of what he says in this influential treatise applies to the culture of country clubs. Unlike, say, the YMCA, which began in 1851 in the United States, country clubs accepted only posh Christians.

Country clubs did not really start a new social trend (toward exclusion), but only formalized an ancient one. Nonetheless, country clubs gradually took on a distinctive ethos of their own in American culture. In the short stories of John Cheever, for example, the American country club epitomizes marital fidelity, decorum, and chastity.[10] Walker Percy's *The Second Coming* (1980) and Philip Roth's *Goodbye, Columbus* (1959) likewise make central use of the country club as a plot device: it's not easy being rich or socially superior, we learn. These stories concern country club culture, rather than offer up descriptive accounts or sociological analyses of country clubs per se. These stories implicitly convey the preposterousness of an unwed mother hanging out by the pool or a gay rights activist pamphleting the dining room.

Religious affiliation often went hand-in-hand with the country club, although this pairing largely remained unspoken. Catholics and Jews knew better than even to apply to Protestant clubs and tended to found their own instead. Initially, though, Jews had enjoyed some success, at least in Manhattan:

> Prominent German Jews eventually gained some access into New York City's elite city schools, but anti-Semitism among gentile members began to stifle the entry of Jews. Jesse, Joseph, and William Seligman were among the upper elite of New York's Jewish society, and they were among the earliest members of the Union League. Both Jesse and Joseph had been club vice presidents, but in 1883 the club's membership committee rejected Jesse Seligman's son, Theodore, for membership, stating that the decision was "not a personal matter in any way, either as to father or son. The objection is purely racial."[11]

So much for trying to soften the blow of rejection. They might as well have said: "we'd like you if only you weren't Jewish, honest." As country clubs escalated in wealth and prestige, the need for limiting membership mounted.

According to Daniel Oren's study of elite American universities, *Joining the Club: A History of Jews and Yale*, quotas regulated admission during the first half of the twentieth century. Jews and Catholics applied to Ivy League schools that did not want them; although certain country-club memberships could arguably boost one's career even more than a particular university pedigree, education was at least in theory more important.[12] And so it is not so surprising that Jews and Catholics sought out influential schools that didn't really like them. Oren argues plausibly that everyone knew what was going on in university admissions offices, just as country-club boards made no secret of how they were operating. Some of those passed over managed to keep a sense of humor nonetheless: "Groucho Marx supposedly said that he would not belong to any club that was willing to have him as a member. One country club offered to waive its no-Jews rule if Groucho did not use the swimming pool, and he replied: 'My daughter's only half Jewish, can she wade in up to her knees?'"[13] Although Groucho likely exaggerated the actual interchange with the membership committee, the joke worked precisely because it played off very real discrimination.

WASPish sensibility dominated the archetypal American country club. Opposed to Dionysian wantonness, country club devotees only whispered about sexuality, as though it were a beast to be contained. Apollonian in profile, country clubs constricted the forces of nature and smoothed the rough edges of old fertility cults. Norms of propriety do not shift noticeably in these enclaves; for this reason the 1960s were not a good time for golf and country clubs. Counter-cultural young people denounced them as representative of America's evils, particularly racism, but also contempt for the lower classes.

Country clubs civilized fertility by projecting confidence in the face of the raw, frightening mystery of uncontrollable forces of nature. County clubs were not just American; a pivotal scene in Buñuel's 1967 cinematic masterpiece *Belle de jour* (in which Séverine encounters a prostitute) takes place in the Parisian equivalent of an American country club (these clubs, which continue to thrive, are largely clustered in Paris's Bois de Boulogne). Liberal-leaning Americans generally agree with the thesis of Oren's book, *Joining the Club,* that in order to develop a proper sympathy for African Americans and Jews, we must appreciate their exclusion from social institutions such as country clubs and elite universities. Of course, American institutions of higher learning are hardly unique in this regard: posh English secondary schools such as Eton, Harrow, and Winchester prepared young men for the kind of social exclusiveness they would encounter at Oxford and Cambridge. The 1982 film *Another Country* certainly made Cambridge look like a country club, much as *Chariots of Fire* (1981) had done a year earlier. On these shores, Exeter and Andover appear like country clubs with organized work goals. Princeton dropout F. Scott Fitzgerald makes his alma mater seem like quite a country club in *This Side of Paradise* (1920). The list goes on.

In the mid-nineteenth century, Nietzsche argued that Christian churches had come to serve the same function as stages in the ancient Greek world. According to the author of *The Birth of Tragedy* (1872), an ecclesiastical service resembles a tragedy, with its gripping death drama and cathartic aftereffect. Today, many Christian churches serve another substitutive role—that of leisure center devoted to regulating and enforcing social mores.[14] The church isn't just four walls and an altar, of course—it's the people who make up the church. These people sometimes seem to care less about theology than about keeping their distance from social undesirables.

It would be unfair to call the Roman Curia a men's club, and yet that is precisely how it has seemed to generations of Catholic women, particularly those interested in ordination. Professional opportunities for men abound within the ecclesiastical ranks of conservative and Orthodox Judaism, Anglicanism, and Islam. Despite some distinctively liberal policies (for example, on economics and capital punishment), the Catholic Church maintains a rigidly conservative stance on the place of women in church life. Desire to join the priesthood, like the desire to join an exclusive country club, cannot itself justify accepting a candidate. One must meet certain criteria. Whereas these criteria used to center on religion in both country clubs and the priesthood, the focus is now gender. This is not to suggest that a non-Catholic can become a priest but rather that a non-Catholic might be attracted to the priesthood on the basis of an old policy that excludes women.

How do we distinguish between a church and a country club, once the guiding admission criterion becomes gender? The deliberation required to finesse an answer suggests the difficulty of the question. It must be said that sympathy for women clerics continues to rise, even within exclusively male spheres. At the close of the twentieth century, Carlo Cardinal Montini of Milan, considered a frontrunner among possible successors to Pope John Paul II, called for a new Vatican Council, one in which the predicament of women would receive the attention it deserves. And in the United States, Jewish groups devoted more energy than ever before to advancing the ambitions of clerically minded women.

Breaking down gender barriers will transform religious groups and country clubs. Of course women can belong to either, but they have long had to allow men to run both. Gender inequality unites us to ancient

Greeks, Hebrews, and Christians. This inequality has shaped various social institutions, not just spiritual communities.

Greek gymnasia and Roman baths eventually gave way to restaurant culture, which in turn led to country club culture. Although country clubs revolve around sport and relaxation, they carefully police the forms relaxation may take. Of course the analogy to churches is not perfect, but a comparison to country clubs captures and highlights a shifting emphasis from spiritual to social orthodoxy.

BONA FIDE RELIGION

Some historians have treated particular beliefs as religious while dismissing other very similar ones as superstitious.[15] Classifying beliefs almost invariably involves ranking them in a hierarchy. According to most pecking orders, religious beliefs deserve more respect than merely superstitious ones. Atheists, of course, may question the difference between categories, but believers will reasonably insist on a working distinction.

This distinction is very much to the point as I try to argue that social beliefs have overtaken religious beliefs. Critics may scoff at the idea that religious beliefs amount to anything more than social ones. I am happy to privilege religious beliefs over social ones, such that religious devotion takes precedence over various social expectations (fasting during Ramadan, on Yom Kippur, or throughout Lent, for example, readily permits one to turn down dinner invitations). Beyond that, religious and social beliefs are linked in roughly the same way that I have paired churches with country clubs. Take, for example, the very requirement to attend church. Any country that obligates healthy people to go to church services every Sunday fuses a *religious* belief about what God wants his followers to do with a *social* belief about how upstanding citizens behave. I recognize that being religious entails acting in certain ways, for it is through our actions that we express our beliefs. And so on some level, every action of the believer is technically religious (unless, of course, he is breaking God's law). For the sake of simplifying unnecessarily complicated distinctions, I refer to religious beliefs as those that address in a fairly obvious way God's nature (that is, revelation), whereas social beliefs are those that dictate how people should treat one another (for example, smoking in public spaces).

As I have indicated, the strength or success of my overall argument relies on a workable distinction between honorable and dishonorable motives, between obeying religious rules and simply disliking a certain class of people. It would take another book to set out such distinctions in the analytical precision they deserve. Here, I simply take such admittedly imprecise differences on faith.

The Reformation stands as a good example of a genuinely religious controversy, as opposed to a sexual one posing as a theological dispute. Is Christ physically present in the Eucharist or is he not? Transubstantiation sharply divided ordinary citizens.[16] Even here, though, sex reared its head. Martin Luther objected to the infallibility of the pope and various other Catholic practices, one of which was enforcing the celibacy of the priesthood. A few decades later, Henry VIII broke with Rome, for reasons not entirely divorced from sexual roles.

What do properly religious sentiments look or sound like? This is a bit like asking an artist to paint someone of whom we have only verbal descriptions. The art historian Margaret Visser, a Roman Catholic who found her way back to the church after years away, writes of feeling profoundly moved in the catacombs of a Roman church some sixteen hundred years old. Visser ponders questions she considers natural to believers standing in such an old, sacred spot, Sant' Agnese fuori le Mura: "Who were they? How did they live? What did they look like? What would I have in common with [names taken from tombstones there]?" Her answer is a boldly confident one: "A twenty-first century Christian, after having thought for a moment, can reply: everything that is most important."[17] Visser, an educated believer, suggests that beliefs about Christ's divinity and presence in the Eucharist constitute the appropriate core of Catholic teachings worth fighting for. This strikes me as an entirely reasonable stance for Catholics to follow. What does not strike me as reasonable is placing sexual activity at the heart of Catholicism.

Another newly Catholic writer, returned to the fold he had deserted years earlier, summed up what makes the fellow parishioners of his London church Catholic:

> At Mass we sing together, and pray together; we ask forgiveness, and tell God that we are unworthy to enter under his roof; we sit and stand and kneel and give each other the sign of peace with a handshake or a kiss; we take that little white bread wafer with a sip of red wine, in amnesty and mercy for the time being—which is the only time we have. Our church is no New Jerusalem, but we believe Christ is with us in the priest, in the people, in the Word, and especially in the Eucharist—that piece of bread. His presence in the bread is a kind of language; like building the New Jerusalem, it is not a language we shall mange to learn in time.[18]

English journalist John Cornwell explains what makes the faithful of his Covent Garden Church true to Catholic teaching. This litmus test of fidelity could be applied to Catholics everywhere. Here someone might object that it is through obeying rules (for example, sexual ones) that we enact our beliefs. The problem with such thinking, no doubt largely sound, is that the particular practices, many of which come to seem arbitrary, eclipse in importance the beliefs which they purport to embody and thereby honor.

Christianity stands on a long history of debating what within the faith is true and properly central. In his survey *A History of Heresy* (1991), David Christie-Murray writes, "It has been rightly said that the Christian Church, while concerned with uniformity in religious practice, always made doctrine the central criterion of orthodoxy."[19] Whether one takes "the infallible Church" as doctrine (as Catholics are supposed to) or "the infallible Book" (the Bible, as Southern Baptists are supposed to), doctrine presumably turns on God—his nature and will. It is less and less clear that doctrine stands as the "central criterion of orthodoxy" these days. A long string of ecclesiastical documents instruct Catholics to take as the essential core of their faith an inherited tradition of worshiping God in a particular way. Thus, in a comment on the shortage of priests in the contemporary church, religious historian Jo Ann Kay McNamara writes, "The simple fact is that for the last two centuries large numbers of Catholics have been forced to do without reliable reception of the sacraments that define the spirituality of their church."[20] Catholics take these sacraments (there are seven of them) to be visible signs of God's presence in the world. One sacrament, marriage, has a lot to do with sex; another, holy orders, has a lot to do with gender. The other sacraments (baptism, confession, communion, confirmation, and blessing of the sick) have nothing explicit to do with sexuality or gender. Today the question is what defines the spirituality of the Catholic Church— religious or social beliefs.

A MAGNET FOR
CONSERVATIVE PROTESTANTS?

If you were a Protestant who really cared about holding the line against women and gays, where would you go? What would you do if your church suddenly started softening? The Roman Catholic Church might appeal to you. Although the church includes many different kinds of people who disagree on various topics, its teaching authority does not shy away from taking an increasingly unpopular stance on women and gay people.

Sympathetic to Rome is a British association called "Forward in Faith," composed of Anglican clergy and lay people who do not accept the ordination of women and worry about the possibility of female bishops. According to their Web site, "Forward in Faith was founded in November 1992, in the wake of the decision of the General Synod of the Church of England to proceed with the ordination of women to the priesthood. In 1995, it became a membership organisation and, in 1996, it became a Registered Charity." Members of "Forward in Faith" are likely to become Roman Catholic or Orthodox in part for another reason: these conservative Anglicans also view their Archbishop Runcie as entirely too permissive toward priests involved in stable gay relationships. "Forward in Faith" makes no such criticism of Runcie on its Web site, although such dissatisfaction is common knowledge in the United Kingdom.[21]

Unless someone explicitly declares that his interest in Roman Catholicism stems from the Vatican's hard line on sex and gender (as indeed a few have), it is quite difficult to prove that anyone has recently converted to Catholicism largely or exclusively because of the Pope's firm stance. And yet, we can legitimately wonder about conversions of conservative Protestants. Suspicion hovers over negative reasons for switching alliances: instead of pushing for a new church, disgruntled conservatives appear to be trying to escape from a suddenly more liberal home. If the next pope were to focus more on ecclesiology (or the theology of the church itself) than on sexual morals, conservative Protestants might show less enthusiasm for Rome. But for now, Catholicism stands ready to attract conservatives from other Christian communions.

Various writers have pointed to a growing coalition of conservatives from different religions.[22] Sociologist Gene Burns has noticed that "it is historically and sociologically inaccurate to argue that the politicization of the [Catholic] Church is without precedent. . . ."[23] Sitting ducks for ecclesiastical anxieties, women and gay people who will not sacrifice their views for official acceptance often claim to find themselves sacrificed instead. Homosexual heads on the cutting block can unite people of different religious allegiances as few other causes can. To cite but one instance, it was an alliance of Catholics, evangelicals, and Mormons that finally persuaded the voters of Hawaii to reject same-sex marriage in the late 1990s.[24] Some scholars have characterized "pro-family" or "antigay" proponents as largely Protestant.[25] Though this equation is largely correct, it is important to recognize a Catholic contribution here. Strange bedfellows indeed.

Of course it is possible to talk about sex in the context of genuine spiritual motivation, or "bona fide religion." Take Mormonism, for example, which gives a whole new dimension to being "pro-family." In Mormon belief, families are, quite literally, forever. Proxies are baptized on behalf of the dead, and families and relatives hope to go on living together and procreating in a celestial eternity. All children are baptized at age eight, and at twelve boys (no girls allowed) take their place of responsibility and status by entering the first level of the priesthood— the priesthood, according to Joseph Smith, having been restored by John the Baptist in upstate New York in 1829. While bar mitzvah among Jews and confirmation among Christians too often means that young people consider their religious responsibilities fulfilled, Mormon twelve-year-olds assume serious and clearly defined responsibilities within the community.

No wonder that Roman Catholic leaders fear a "thinning out" or "hollowing" of their tradition, for sexual practices and gender politics have overtaken concern for theology. According to a New York Times / CBS News poll published in April 1994, almost two-thirds of American Catholics believe that Christ is only symbolically present in the Eucharist.[26] Unbeknownst to them, these Catholics have theologically joined forces with Anglicans and Episcopalians. Gone are the days of heroic saints such as Thomas More and John Fisher, who accepted torture and death in the sixteenth century rather than accept Henry VIII as the supreme head of the English Church (as the king named himself in 1534). The English martyrs of Henry VIII's day believed that only the bishop of Rome, that is, the pope, could claim authority over the church. Today the world seems more complicated, as intellectual Catholics (for example, Garry Wills and John Cornwell) criticize the pope while pledging their allegiance to the church he represents.

Henry VIII also defied the theology of the Eucharist. The battle over defining sacred ritual in Catholicism is a good example of what it means to care about theology (to the extent that we can separate theology from sex). Whether the bread and wine on the altar are actually transformed into Christ's body and blood remained a burning issue for centuries. But mainstream Catholics don't seem to care much anymore, and, despite Paul VI's encyclical on transubstantiation, *Mysterium Fidei* (1965), the Vatican has yet to indicate that it cares as much about this remarkable trend as it does about thwarting the social advancement of gays, lesbians, and women seeking ordination. Of course, someone could argue that gone, too, are the days when people heroically overcame the temptation to have improper sex. But this objection does little more than to return us to the question of where the Vatican's priorities lie.

RELIGION AND THE DECLINE OF THEOLOGY

The Vatican today exercises little influence in global politics. It is no longer part of the ruling establishment of any nation. In fact, various Italians have so resented it that it now stands as a country of its own, an interior Island in Italy.[b] And yet, its remarkable longevity pays tribute to the Vatican's strategy for remaining relevant. As we argue over whether the Vatican creates or responds to cultural anxiety, God drifts to the margins.

This recentering in Catholicism, mirrored in some Protestant communions, came into focus in the debates preceding the birth control encyclical. *Humanae Vitae* (1968) disappointed Catholics around the world, many of whom soon left the church. Word had leaked that Pope Paul VI was likely to legalize birth control, as his cardinals had advised him to do, and yet he reaffirmed the forbidding stance of *Casti Connubii* (1930).[28] Paul VI understood the slippery slope leading from birth control to gay sex (and even masturbation). Once you allow the morality of sex for either pleasure or expressing love between two persons, it becomes harder to oppose what two men or two women might do in bed together. By outlawing birth control, Paul VI stunned and alienated many of the faithful. But by allowing it, he would have exposed the church to encroaching claims of the gay faithful.

In an effort to reverse the biting and corrosive accusations of Catholic cruelty to Jews not just in the Holocaust but through two millennia, John XXIII rallied the Second Vatican Council to allow Jews into heaven. This was not merely a political move, although it certainly was that. In allowing Jews into heaven, John risked making Catholic theology look incoherent. In his plea to make Catholics recognize the "signs of the times," John could scarcely have guessed just how vocal gay rights activists would become in the two short decades after his death. The sexual revolution had not yet swept through the United States when John died in June 1963. And yet, he may well have had some sense of how dramatically the cultural landscape of Europe and North America was about to change. A legalization of birth control seems consonant with his goal of updating the church, as does a careful exploration of blessing the unions of same-sex couples committed to fidelity and striving for permanence. Privileging reproductive goals over the physical expression of genuine love puzzles many non-Catholics and angers some who profess an allegiance to Rome. Why should fertility count for more than affection?

John XXIII and John Paul II would have disagreed on much, but not on outreach to Jews. Both pontiffs can claim a genuine concern for Jews. For Jews, Catholic acceptance may well be an uneasy truce—too little, too late—yet it must be considered remarkable historically. John XXIII put John Paul II into a curious bind, though. Because John Paul II has opposed publicly and strenuously the political advancement of gay people, his efforts collide with John XXIII's legacy of inclusion. Like Paul VI, who sensed danger rather than exhilaration in "the signs of the times," John Paul II finds himself in a difficult position. He can't possibly retreat from the effort to protect Jews, nor does he want to. But he has subsequently steered the church into confusing waters—disagreement over the divinity of Jesus can be tolerated, but acceptance of gay sex cannot. And in a bold move smacking of desperation, John Paul II has ordered Joseph Cardinal Ratzinger, prefect of the Congregation for the Doctrine of the Faith, to declare as infallible the papal assertion than the church cannot ordain women.

There is further evidence that the cloth of religious culture has started to fray. It's not just that a particular issue such as sex or race can eclipse the centrality of religion in a culture; religion may be so threatened that believers of different sorts find themselves united against nonbelievers. The threat of atheism or of religious indifference may compel religious groups otherwise at odds with one another to band together in order to safeguard the thinnest slice of religion. Instead of thinking of religion in "thick" terms, say in highly developed ways such as traditional Roman Catholicism or Reform Judaism, individuals may see the value of reducing religion to its most basic element of all: namely, belief in a higher, omnipotent being. Describing the broad outlines of American politics at the dawn of a new century, one observer stated, "The historic conflict was Protestant-Catholic, and although evangelicals were the last to get the word, that conflict is pretty much dead. The alignment today is the religiously intense against the secular, and with respect to that fight, evangelicals and conservative Catholics are now on the same side."[29] The coalition of believers includes Jews, it is important to note. Jeffrey Rosen, legal affairs editor of *The New Republic*, has observed:

> As Jews became more culturally assimilated, they felt less threatened by an increasingly tolerant Christian majority. And mainstream Christian religions in general became less sectarian and less threatening to religious minorities . . . sects that used to compete over whose vision of revealed truth would triumph in the public square began to see value in one another's work. In an age when everyone is a hyphenated American, religious identity became just one more prefix in the pluralistic mix.[30]

The trend Rosen and others have noticed is remarkable. Liberal Jews do not agree with evangelical Protestants and conservative Catholics on a number of social issues, yet the very belief in God—any God, it may seem—can unite historically opposed religious groups in a secular age. Seeing that a particular view of women or gays gains widespread currency may be a motivating reason to break down religious walls. What it takes to break down religious walls tells us something important about the vitality of a particular faith, as well as the seriousness of the issue involved. Increasingly, sexuality and gender delimit religious orthodoxy.

SEX SCANDALS IN THE PRIESTHOOD

The year 2002 will go down in history as one of the most painful for American Catholics. Some nine months after the *Boston Globe* had brought to light a sex scandal in the Roman Catholic priesthood that proceeded to unfold and reverberate throughout the United States, major newspapers were still printing front-page stories that read like soap operas. In late September 2002, the *Washington Post* featured a story on Bishop Wilton Gregory, the first African American to head the United States Conference of Catholic Bishops, that began as follows:

> BELLEVILLE, ILL.—When Wilton D. Gregory arrived here as bishop nearly a decade ago, this sprawling diocese of small towns and large cornfields was in the midst of a sex scandal that was truly American Gothic.
>
> Thirty-three people, including three priests, said they had been abused by priests. The local newspaper reported sex parties in rectories, a church-sponsored youth camp run by an alleged pedophile, a male prostitute who stole checks from a priest-client, a "homosexual ring" operating out of the National Shrine of Our Lady of the Snows, a priest who impregnated a 16-year-old and then gave her a voodoo potion to induce an abortion.[31]

Catholics, it seemed, had become their own worst enemies. Profoundly saddened and frightened by the steady stream of bad news, American Catholics ached for some ray of hope in 2002.

All Roman Catholics priests take a vow of celibacy (with the exception of certain converts and Eastern rite priests, as already discussed). And so a sexually active priest is a problem. Surveys and statistics may suggest that Catholic priests as a group have become less and less observant of the vow of celibacy, but I want only to highlight the obvious gap between theory and practice in religious leaders who do not practice what they preach.

Curiously, it took young victims to bring to light the staggering extent of clerical sexual transgressions. That certain priests were or had been sexually active didn't attract much attention; that priests were or had been sexually active with children and adolescents scandalized Catholics worldwide. *Time* magazine featured a cover story on April 1, 1985 about priestly sexual abuse of children; committed American Catholics waited for the media field day to die down, even as they worried about the extent of clerical misconduct.[32] After Thomas C. Fox published a lengthy expose of sexually abusive priests in the *National Catholic Reporter* on June 7, 1985, it became harder to pretend that the media were simply exaggerating.

In the early 1990s, the simmering scandal once again captured the attention of the American media.[33] Then, in January of 2002, came what seemed to be the worst blow yet. Cardinal Bernard Law of Boston reeled in the face of accusations that he had secretly shuffled a serial child abuser from one parish to another; a priest, this child abuser took victim after victim. This is not the place to detail all the events documented by the American media beginning in January 2002, nor the various books that delve into the sociological and psychiatric underpinnings of this crisis.[34] As devastated believers struggled to understand feelings of betrayal, Catholics realized anew the terrific power wielded by the church hierarchy and the unspoken, overriding importance attached to sexual matters.

At issue was sexual abuse of children, children of the faithful, no less. Sexual abuse by priests had been covered up by dioceses and bishops hoping to avoid scandal. The institutional church was protected in a way that other agencies (for example, a scout troop, a public school, or a day care center) were not. Whereas law suits would surely result against most or all other bodies, the church seemed immune from them. The paucity of law suits (the disputes brought by victims of sexual abuse were handled privately and settled out of court) stemmed from the church's power, certainly, but also from clauses in the First Amendment protecting religious freedom.

On March 8, 2002 , Bishop Anthony J. O'Connell of Palm Beach, Florida admitted past sexual conduct with a teenage seminarian and submitted his resignation to the pope, who accepted it on March 13. O'Connell's predecessor in Palm Beach, J. Keith Symons, had resigned in June 1998 after acknowledging that he had sexually abused at least five boys many years earlier. A month later, numerous angry Catholics in Boston publicly protested and called for the resignation of Cardinal Law, who steadfastly refused to step down from his postion.

The problem in Boston triggered public accusations in other dioceses throughout the country.[35] In May 2002, a sixty-four-year-old Connecticut priest hanged himself in a Maryland institute for troubled clergy after having been confronted by his bishop, who had interviewed two young men who claimed to have been sexually abused by the priest. Three days earlier, a Baltimore priest had been shot and seriously wounded by a young man who claimed to have been sexually molested by the priest some nine years before. And six weeks before that shooting, an Ohio priest had killed himself when he was accused of sexual abuse. In late May, Archbishop Rembert Weakland of Milwaukee asked the Vatican to act quickly on the resignation letter he had submitted weeks earlier. His affair with a male student some two decades earlier had suddenly come to light, and Weakland became the first archbishop to resign amid the sex abuse scandal of 2002 (Archbishop Eugene Marino of Atlanta had resigned in 1990 after admitting a relationship with a female parishioner). The same day Weakland found himself publicly accused, Bishop J. Kendrick Williams of Lexington, Kentucky temporarily relinquished his pastoral duties; he nonetheless denied charges of having molested an altar boy twenty-one years before. Meanwhile, exasperated Catholics pondered whether a soap opera script could exceed the drama contained in their daily newspapers.

The largely homosexual assaults reported in America prompted some Catholics to try to blame the scandal on gay culprits. Psychologists and psychiatrists debated whether abusive priests were just preying on the people closest at hand, the most vulnerable, or the victims most likely to maintain silence. Of course heterosexual men are equally capable of abusing young girls, and some heterosexual incidents found their way into the press as well. Nonetheless, national and ecclesiastical attention focused on gay priests. Bishop Wilton Gregory, as president of the U.S. Conference of Catholic Bishops, explained it was "a struggle to make sure that the Catholic priesthood is not dominated by homosexual men."[36] Joaquin Navarro-Valls, a Spanish psychiatrist who serves as the Vatican's spokesman, was quoted as saying, "People with these inclinations just cannot be ordained. That does not imply a final judgment on people with homosexuality. But you cannot be in this field."[37] He went on to compare gay men who enter the priesthood to gay men who enter traditional marriages. Just as marriage can be annulled by the church as invalid, he pointed out, so could the ordinations by revoked.

Some liberal Catholics seized the opportunity to urge the Vatican once again to lift the ban on married priests. For the first twelve centuries of its existence, the church allowed priests (but not monks and nuns) to marry. Pope John XXIII once remarked in the 1960s that he could repeal this rule with the stroke of his pen. But linking priestly abuse of children and adolescents to the celibacy dispute made little sense. Most people who abuse children are not celibate clergy, so removing the celibacy requirement would not likely affect the problem of priestly pedophilia. Pedophiles don't seek sexual contact with adults, in any event, but rather with teenagers or children. Priests who solicit sex from sixteen- or seventeen-year-olds present a different problem.

Despite the unclear nexus of the sex scandal to celibacy, the negative media coverage renewed popular skepticism about celibacy. So few men seem to be capable of it that Catholic culture appeared to doom its own clergy to misery and failure—and to endangering those on whom priests might prey. The memory of Rome's steadfast refusal to negotiate on the matters of ordaining women or permitting priests to marry burned in the minds of many Catholics, who came to understand viscerally the extent to which Rome cares about sex. Regulating sex, it seemed to some, mattered more than the psychological security of priests, more than the sadness of Catholics who had to do without a parish priest because there weren't enough to go around, and the safety of vulnerable people who trusted priests.

Between the outbreak of the scandal in January and the start of the national meeting of the American bishops in June, two hundred fifty accused priests had resigned or were dismissed.[38] Even more dramatically, four bishops had stepped down.[39] On the morning of June 13, 2002, the first day of the bishops' conference, the *Dallas Morning News* featured a headline proclaiming "Two-Thirds of Bishops Let Accused Priests Work"; not unlike an FBI "most wanted" list, the article posted mug shots of bishops alongside accounts of cover-ups in individual dioceses. At the Dallas meetings, presiding Bishop Wilton Gregory conceded that the negligence of bishops had exacerbated the scandal. Bravely, Gregory accepted responsibility for the egregious betrayal of the faithful and asked forgiveness from victims and their families. He requested that priests guilty of sexual abuse but still hiding from public censure turn themselves over to the Vatican. In the Fairmont Hotel, bishops meanwhile listened to adult survivors of priestly abuse and debated whether to adopt a zero-tolerance policy for pedophile priests.

Ultimately, the bishops voted to adopt a policy nearly as strict as zero tolerance. The Vatican had objected to a one-strike-and-you're-out regulation out of fear that accused priests might be denied due process and out of the conviction that forgiveness is necessary and rehabilitation possible (the day before the Dallas meeting began, a *Wall Street Journal* / NBC News poll found that 91 percent of American Catholics rejected the idea of giving fallen priests another chance). Despite the popular saying, "Once a cheater, always a cheater," the Vatican denied that this particular sin overcomes all efforts to stop it. Nonetheless, the American bishops voted in June 2002 to pull from the ministry any priest ever accused or convicted of child abuse. Victims cried out that the new policy did not go far enough, because guilty priests would not be defrocked; instead a priest with a past would be sent off to a monastery for the rest of his life. Bishops, in any event, do not wield the power to laicize a priest; only the Vatican can do that. What bishops can do is choose to resign their posts, out of a sense of responsibility for having contributed to the sexual abuse of children. No bishop stepped forward to accuse himself in Dallas.

What do sexually abusive priests have to do with a fertility cult? A fertility cult invests in mystery and sacrifice in order to control sex. Revered leaders call the shots while everyone worries about regeneration. High school teachers or coaches who take sexual advantage of minors incur our anger; but religious leaders who do this unleash a deeper, more raw kind of amazement. Anyone who proclaims the sacredness of sex but then proceeds to steal it from a vulnerable youth doesn't so much destroy what we hold sublime as dirty it. Some will argue that destroying ideals is almost preferable to dragging them through the dirt, leaving the faithful to clean up the mess. In any event, priests tap into a power source unavailable to high school teachers.

When the misconduct of Catholic priests seized public interest in 2002, a new generation learned about the forbidding culture of the priesthood and the subservient role of the laity. Despite the progressive changes of Vatican II, a powerful Roman hierarchy still controlled the sex lives of priests and the faithful to whom they ministered. Shrouded in secrecy, the Roman Curia and its international army of bishops worked quietly to patch up a sinking ship. In the name of upholding a ban on artificial birth control, gay sex, and female clerics, a network of priests and bishops covered up its own sexual transgressions. For the show had to go on, even at the expense of vulnerable children. Just as a permanently infertile woman threatened the power of a fertility cult, so did the sexual sins of a priest endanger the credibility of the institution he represented. Infertility is the worst thing that can happen in a community preoccupied with fertility; sexual sedition is the worst thing that can happen in a community deeply invested in sexual orthodoxy.

CONCLUSION: SEX IN THE VATICAN

Theology includes several branches, one of which is moral theology. This branch cultivates and maintains critical attention to sexual morality and social justice. It cannot be said that the other branches have died or fallen into abeyance simply because all questions pertaining to God's will or nature have been definitively resolved; it's rather the case that the world no longer seems to care terribly much about these other issues. What animates conservative and progressive Catholics alike is sex. In Catholicism, religious fervor seems to have waned; what remains of it rests on bodies and their political ramifications.

In addition to sex and gender, the church does try to combat other dangerous enemies: materialism, secularism, and individualism, for instance. But the task of policing debates over sex and gender roles has consumed the church since Vatican II. The church's teachings seem to come down to disputes over the morality of abortion, divorce, and same-sex relationships (even though there are certainly other encyclicals). Thrown into the spotlight have been the arrests of priests who had sexually abused children, the refusal to readmit to active service those priests who have married, and the restriction of priesthood to men (in late May of 1994 the pope decreed that faithful Catholics could no longer even discuss the ordination of women).

Men who must not procreate are called "Father" by followers whose every legal sex act aims at procreation. Women are not eligible for the role of "Father," even if they too swear off sex. Sex and gender both recede under a beguiling veil, upon which the faithful look with awe. Same as it ever was, or late-breaking news? I have argued that Catholicism is regressing to the state of a pagan fertility cult. Just as ancient fertility cults allowed the sacrifice of some of what they most wanted (that is, crops and animals), so have certain Catholic bishops tacitly allowed the sacrifice of the chastity of adolescents.

Perhaps Christianity never really defeated paganism, maybe paganism has been smoldering for nearly two thousand years. Neither of the three monotheistic traditions in the West has defeated lust, in any event. Lust and piety have coexisted, and lust may be regaining its upper hand not only in the secular sphere but the religious one as well.

Certain differences threaten to pollute or unsettle a religion. These threats change over time. I argue that sex and gender are the biggest threats today. This point will hardly seem controversial, yet various believers will resist my claim that religious morality has blended into sexual morality. This is not to say that God is dead, only that we have relegated God to the status of the madwoman in the attic. We haul God out in public whenever we need his authority to shore up opposition to women and gay people and to further the no longer urgent task of increasing the number of children born.

Meanwhile, the pressure on the infrastructure of Catholicism mounts. Mass defections from the priesthood (some one hundred thousand since the late 1960s) coincided with a precipitous drop in recruitments. In the United States alone, the number of men entering the priesthood has dropped from 58,600 in 1965 to 45,200 in 2001. Celibacy, abstaining from sex, no doubt accounts for much of the decline. Men who cannot have any sex instruct those who may how to do it. Those for whom fertility is irrelevant impose restrictions on those for whom it is virtually an obligation.

The number of priests per number of Catholics continues to drop, and not only in the United States. At the same time, Catholics around the globe shudder at the thought of their priests sexually abusing children. Negative publicity will not help attract new recruits to the clergy, and the price tag for settling cases against priests who molest children strains church coffers. In March 2002, the Archdiocese of Boston settled a lawsuit by agreeing to pay up to $30 million to eighty-six plaintiffs in a case involving just one priest (the Archdiocese later backed away from that promise). Since the 1980s, the church has faced hundreds of civil actions and turned over an estimated $1 billion in damages.

The more the Vatican refuses to allow married priests or to extend ordination to women, the odder an investment in an all-male, celibate clergy seems. And the more priests get caught in homosexual trysts, the more curious the Vatican's cold shoulder to marriage-hungry gays appears.

Fertility cults and country clubs differ significantly from monasteries and convents. The seriousness and integrity of a well-run house of prayer can still inspire genuine piety, which will concern sexuality on some level but not be subsumed by it. Blessing the attempts of gay and lesbian people to commit to monogamous unions, as opposed to smiling on pagan licentiousness, would represent a great leap forward for the Catholic Church today. In so doing, the church might manage to put sex back in its proper place, respectfully subservient to piety. In no way would a return to traditional religious devotion entail a return to anti-Semitism. Moreover, rapprochement between the Holy See and Jews worldwide might pave the way for better relations between the Vatican and gay people.

Meanwhile, there are apologies to make and fences to mend. In principle, it might have been a good idea for Catholics to maintain a convent of nuns to pray for those who perished at Auschwitz.[40] It would certainly be a good idea to dedicate a convent of nuns to pray for children sexually abused by a priest. There is no time like the present to own up to mistakes.

Heaven's Dominion

"There have been times," C. S. Lewis once wrote, "when I think we do not desire heaven but more often I find myself wondering whether, in our heart of hearts, we have ever desired anything else."[1] I myself have desired heaven. The reason why sin has haunted me since childhood must be heaven, or rather anxiety over losing it.

I picture heaven in fairly prescribed terms; what might seem a lack of imagination on my part stems as much from personal fascination with Catholicism as from a traditional upbringing in that faith. My parents, both devout, never saw fit to enroll me in Catholic school, and I am not a pious person. And yet Catholicism captivated me as no other force ever has.

I was born the day John XXIII died. My parents adopted me from the Sisters of Saint Joseph in Phoenix, having signed an oath to raise me Catholic. I took to the faith eagerly. Gradually, though, I knew better than to broadcast to other kids the saints' lore I had learned by heart. I certainly never told anyone about trying to live as a monk in my bedroom, fasting regularly, observing vows of silence, and setting my alarm at night to pray. Years later I had to defend this devotion. While in college, a Jewish friend referred obliquely to the ugliness of my spiritual heritage. We were both philosophy majors, and I admired her. I puzzled over why she blamed Catholics for enabling the Shoah.

I began searching for answers. Meanwhile, another college classmate challenged my loyalty to Catholicism. A gifted painter dying of AIDS in his mid-twenties, he saw hatred for gay men spewing from the Roman Curia (the Vatican's bureaucracy). He crafted letters to the editors of various national magazines, seizing every opportunity to criticize Roman Catholics. A friend I wanted to keep, he had stopped just short of calling me a traitor. I resolved to find out the very worst about Catholicism. Once I knew that, I could decide whether to stay.

I have stayed. To its credit, the Vatican has now apologized to Jews. It has yet to ordain women or embrace gay people, but I continue to hope. That hope led to this book. If the Church can get over its institutional dislike of the Jewish faith, the Church can get over its institutional distaste for gay marriage.

Heaven is what I'd focus on if doctors told me I only had one more year to live. I wouldn't fly to Disneyland, travel around the world, or deplete my bank account on trips to four-star restaurants. I would attend Mass daily and pray the rosary. I would prepare myself for death by contemplating heaven, much in the way I learned from Rilke years ago. As a student, these lines once seized me, "Be ahead of all parting, as though it were already behind you, like the winter that has just gone by."[2] Before dying, I would have already withdrawn from this world, resigned myself to the inevitable, and mentally begun the transition at hand. People I liked would still matter to me, but heaven would preoccupy my thoughts.

Is heaven a reward within the reach of any human being? Easy as it might seem to think about heaven's dominion in rosy terms, we apparently should not. For discrimination continues there, in the sense that superiority and inferiority will organize the souls in paradise. More importantly, we would proclaim equal access to heaven at our peril. Various groups here on earth have cast their eyes upward and claimed a monopoly on eternity. Grasping the enormity of the stakes in this rivalry, believers might feel the urgency of worshiping correctly. If only one religious tradition will prove to be right, than the rest of us become infidels, destined for a place no one wants.

Technically speaking, the scenario isn't really so dire as all that. Various traditions have included wiggle room in their theologies, such that the faithful of other traditions may nonetheless qualify for someone else's heaven. And certain creeds, such as Islam and Mormonism, allow for the possibility that we can work ourselves out of hell.

The struggle for control of heaven continues, even as sophisticated segments of the faithful lose interest. American Catholics today seem less concerned with securing salvation than with leading satisfying lives—perhaps because a number of Catholics are uncertain that there is a heaven. Simultaneously, the dividing lines between Catholics and Protestants blur and bleed. After ethnic assimilation, the old badges of Italian, Irish, Polish, or German heritage lost much of their luster. So too has old-fashioned religious identity drifted away from social status. For better or worse, educated Catholics today take less pride in Roman roots than their grandparents did.

At a time when movie plots seem no more complicated than an explosion or an orgasm, the drama of eternal salvation remains complex. The ending of the Roman story never came down simply to membership in the Catholic Church, nor does it now come down merely to sexual acts. The intricacy of heaven emerges from the path upward, including differing procedures for canonization or liturgical mention, different centuries of literary works, and religious artifacts.

Forfeiting heaven does not automatically follow from neglecting doctrinal or disciplinary rules. That said, confusion remains. For Saint Paul did leave us with a list of people who will not possess the kingdom of heaven (1 Cor. 6:10), and both "the effeminate" and sodomites make his list. And Cardinal Ratzinger does occasionally threaten to excommunicate dissident groups, such as pro-choice Catholics (for example, the German group Donum Vitae, in 2000). In popular imagination, excommunicating a person is akin to forfeiting him to hell.

Separating the wheat from the chaff today seems to come down to separating insiders from outsiders. The pope and the members of the Curia are willing to smile on non-Catholics because non-Catholics don't pose the threat of disobedience, of internal dissent. In the same way, some Orthodox Jewish rabbis can be perfectly charming to gay men while essentially shunning gay members of their own synagogues—precisely because gentile gays don't pose any challenge from within. Although the Vatican buzzes around the morality of sexual doctrines and practices, this preoccupation is not particularly linked to inter-religious or ecumenical efforts. This means that gay and lesbian Catholics are left in a puzzling position: they would be better off as Jews, particularly straight Jews. Rome would hold these misfits in higher regard.

Sex and gender have spiraled out of control in religious thinking. They should be pulled back into line. The Catholic Church now risks the loss of its salvific reach and transcendental purpose.

It is interesting and important that same-sex desire has become the site of some of our fiercest fights about religion (though not the only site, as I have indicated). Like the harlot saints fleeing sensual joy for desert asceticism, gays and lesbians must renounce their sexual history, or the possibility for one. It took a fight as Herculean as legalizing gay marriage to eclipse Roman furor over artificial birth control; who can guess at the enormity of the debate that will ever supercede gay rights. Historically, the goal of Christianity has been to foster faith, hope, and charity, but today the mission seems to be to promote orthodox sexuality.

It is also interesting and important that sex as a whole has come to occupy so much of the foreground of Catholic teaching and living. Ask Catholic university students today what makes their religion distinctive, and you will likely hear about the Virgin Mary, birth control, abortion, premarital sex, homosexuality, and an all-male, celibate priesthood. You may laugh or sneer, but it's not hard to understand why some Catholic students offer such an answer. Dramatically, John Paul II summoned the American cardinals to Rome in April 2002 to discuss a sex scandal. This most unusual move did have a precedent: the pontiff had called the American cardinals to the Vatican in 1989 to discuss widespread disregard for the teaching on birth control and to emphasize the unsuitability of women for the priest-hood. Sex fuels trips back to Rome; no other topic commands such attention or mobilizes the troops faster.

Sex maniacs are not just those who have sex all the time but also those who talk about it all the time. Maybe it's fitting that the Vatican speaks out forcefully on sexual issues, given that the modern media stirs the lust of the faithful everyday. But then why does the institutional stress lie on sex, as opposed to love? Why can't the Vatican pivot moral assessment on the love two people share instead of the sex they have? Sex counts for more than love in Rome. In this ranking of priorities, the Vatican is not alone.

But the real insights emerge when you ask, Why the clamoring over sex just now and in just this conceptual configuration? The Vatican has become principally a political fortress, one bent on shoring up social institutions now that fewer and fewer people care about worship protocol. It may seem that the Church is simply following the market here, catering to contemporary tastes. More likely, the Church needs to fight sex battles in order to win the war against irrelevance, or perhaps to maintain credibility in the face of past decisions. Today the Church fights three media battles: (1) against the ordination of women; (2) against a married clergy; and (3) against gay marriage. Losing any of these contests would change the church so profoundly that it might no longer recognize itself.

In the decades to come, the Catholic Church will try to prevent gay men from entering the priesthood, which means that a tiny clergy will grow even smaller. (We can only guess at the macho posturing candidates will resort to in order to calm fears about effeminate infiltrators.) Meanwhile, the scientific world will criticize Rome for equating pedo-philia with homosexuality and scholars will fault the church for its sad attempt to pin responsibility for a sex scandal on a vulnerable minority. Instead of relaxing the celibacy rule imposed in the twelfth century, the Magisterium will instead pray harder for male priests, and the ability to detect gay ones. The next pontiff will not likely reverse the ban on women priests. All in all, sex and sexuality will continue to dominate the agenda of heaven's gatekeepers.

There is much more to a moral life than promulgating and obeying sex rules. Turning away from sex, contemporary Catholics might strive to refine their religious identity based on the spiritual exercises and moral disciplines of, say, Saint John of the Cross, Saint Ignatius of Loyola, and Saint Teresa of Avila. Such a reorientation hardly amounts to a sabotage of tradition. Nor does it point emptily to a mere romanticization of a past long gone. It seems younger Catholics have yet to discover the intellectual, literary, musical, and artistic resources their ancient faith harbors (an adequate account of these riches would take another book). Catholicism, perhaps like any religion, can sweeten existence. Sex can as well, but it competes here with prayer and artistic reveries.

What matters to the Holy See does not necessarily matter so much to Catholics in the street. And yet there must be a vital connection between the two classes, however difficult it is to pin down. Ordinary Americans may shrug at official accounts of what it is to be an American (no flag burning, for instance), only to find feelings of patriotism welling up inside them when war breaks out, feelings that compel them to embrace the very signals they once disregarded. Similarly, religious Catholics may, during a mid-life crisis or on the occasion of the death of a friend or the birth of a child, reach out for a stronger connection to the religion that imbues their life with meaning.

Men together in bed, women touching between the sheets: the Church does not want that sex to happen. The very thought pains the Church, perhaps more than the idea of contraceptive sex between an unmarried man and woman. In any event, there are various kinds of sex the Church can't stand to think of, just as there are some roles it can't bear to see women play. I suspect it is much the same in other religions today, although I don't pretend to have proven it.

I have not taken up the sexist requirement for a Jewish *minyan,* nor have I turned to the Islamic customs of *purdah* (the separation of women from male society) or female infanticide. Nor have I attempted to count and categorize relevant papal encyclicals or documents issued by the

Congregation for the Doctrine of the Faith over the last four or five decades.

The world did not need a book to show that Christianity, Judaism, and Islam privilege men over women. What the world could use is a wake-up call. When an institution such as Catholicism encourages Jews to celebrate their Jewishness and at the same time denounces Catholic lesbians and gay men who publicly celebrate their sexuality, something dramatic has happened. God has taken a back seat to fertility. The Catholic Church, despite all its good works among the poor, in drug rehabilitation centers, orphanages, summer camps, and even hospitals specializing in the care of AIDS patients, seems profoundly worried about sex. To what extent do our worries define us? To a significant degree, no doubt. The more serious and complicated the worry, the more serious and complicated the person. The battles we choose to fight, like those we let slide, indicate depth and strength of character. A religion devoted to reproduction seems pretty shallow.

By definition, all practicing Christians, regardless of church affiliation, share a desire to get to heaven. And almost without exception, all human beings burn with sexual desire—some more, some less. The stage is set for drama in this world, where the two passions have been pitted against one another. Gender figures into the drama as well. In both Catholicism and Islam, we can spot male fingerprints on the blueprints for heaven.

Marriages between Christians and Jews, between Protestants and Catholics, have become increasingly commonplace. In this, we differ from previous centuries. It is tempting to conclude from this observation that religion is thus declining in importance. Because "interfaith" couples, as they're now called, may still teach the importance of religion to their children and may remain religiously observant, it would be misleading simply to say that religion counts for less now than it did before.

Birds of a feather have always flocked together. In an increasingly complex world where we embody shifting and competing identities, as

working mothers and corporate moguls, as school teachers and environ-
mental activists, as concert violinists and aspiring triathletes, it is not
particularly surprising that conservatives of various backgrounds would
band together, or that liberals would do the same. The wealthy have long
vacationed in the same spots and frequented the same restaurants and
opera houses, despite conflicting religious and political convictions.
Conservative stances on the rights of women and gay people now point
the way to an oasis; the faithful of various religions can gather around
the cool water and dedicate themselves to a fight against the new infidels.
Together, the old guard protects and sanctifies an ancient heterosexual
dance.

In a utopian song entitled "Imagine," John Lennon exhorts us to strive
for a world without a heaven or a hell, without religion at all. Then, there
would be "nothing to kill or die for." For many, heaven is too great a
price to pay for peace. Letting go of heaven is a thought worse than
nuclear war. If the only way to crack down on sex is to hold heaven
hostage, then so be it, the hardliners maintain. This just can't be right,
nor can Lennon.

Heaven waits for you.

NOTES

NOTES TO CHAPTER ONE

1. For accounts of how some Protestant groups prepare for the afterlife, see Paul Boyer, *When Time Shall be No More: Prophecy Belief in American Culture* (Cambridge, Mass.: Harvard University Press, 1992) and Kenelm Burridge, *New Heaven, New Earth: A Study of Millenarian Activities* (Oxford: Basil Blackwell, 1969).

2. Quoted in John Cornwell, *Hitler's Pope: The Secret History of Pius XII* (New York: Viking, 1999), p. 358.

3. See *Summa theologiae*, ed. and trans. Fathers of the English Dominican Province, 61 vols. (London: Blackfriars, 1964-81), 1-2 qq. 1-3. I thank Mark Jordan for pointing this out to me.

4. *Wall Street Journal,* January 30, 1996, p. A8. See also *U.S. News and World Report,* April 4, 1994, pp. 48-59.

5. Of course some people find the idea silly, even an impediment to the good life. Noël Coward, for one, thought it a waste of time to pine for a realm the very existence of which hovers in doubt. For his part, he preferred oblivion to heaven. See Graham Payne and Sheridan Morley, eds., *The Noël Coward Diaries* (Boston: Little, Brown, 1982), p. 260. See also footnote 4 in chapter 5 of this book: according to a 1995 poll, fewer than half of the Catholics in the city of Rome believe in an afterlife.

6. 1 Cor. 2.9, *Revised Standard Version. The New Oxford Annotated Bible,* ed. Bruce M. Metzger and Roland E. Murphy (New York: Oxford University Press, 1991). All biblical quotations in this book are taken from the *RSV,* unless otherwise indicated. Note well that Paul implies in 2 Cor. 12:1-4 that he has himself visited heaven.

7. For a good overview of Egyptian heaven, see John H. Taylor, *Death and the Afterlife in Ancient Egypt* (Chicago: University of Chicago Press, 2001).

8. For an good overview of Jewish heaven, see chapter 14, "Angels, Devils, and Judgment Day," in Daniel Jeremy Silver, *A History of Judaism,* vol. 1 (New York: Basic Books, 1974), p. 254. (This quotation comes from there.)

9. Eliezer David Rosenthal, "Yom Kippur," trans. Helena Frank in Philip Goodman, *The Yom Kippur Anthology* (Philadelphia: The Jewish Publication Society of America, 1971), pp. 293, 294, 296

10. Steve Stern, "Lazar Malkin Enters Heaven," in *The Oxford Book of Jewish Stories,* ed. Ilan Stavans (New York: Oxford University Press, 1998), pp. 397-406.

11. Quoted in Colleen McDannell and Bernhard Lang, *Heaven: A History* (New Haven: Yale University Press, 1988) p. 366, n. 39.

12. The scholar is Paul Henry; he is quoted in McDannell and Lang, p. 56.

13. Much of the summary from *Heaven: A History* can also be found in McDannell and Lang. See Jeffrey Burton Russell, *A History of Heaven: The Singing Silence* (Princeton: Princeton University Press, 1998). See also Peter J. Kreeft, *Everything You Ever Wanted to Know About Heaven* (San Francisco: Harper & Row, 1982).

14. For a comparison of Jewish hell to its Catholic counterpart, see John Portmann, *When Bad Things Happen to Other People* (New York: Routledge, 2000), pp. 152-158. Jewish thinkers come off looking kinder than Catholic ones.

15. See Richard McBrien, *Catholicism: Study Edition* (Minneapolis: Winston Press, 1981), pp. 1150-1152.

16. Historically, Catholics have sometimes regarded as proper saints deceased people yet to be canonized by the Vatican. See Aviad M. Kleinberg, *Prophets in Their Own Country: Living Saints and the Making of Sainthood in the Later Middle Ages* (Chicago: University of Chicago Press, 1992), especially chapter 2. Today, Catholics revere Padre Pio and Pope John XXIII as though these two were already bona fide saints (Padre Pie was canonized as I wrote this book). While still living, Mother Teresa of India (d. 1997) seemed to command the reverence due a saint. American Catholics now rally around the cause of Father Mychal Judge, an openly gay priest who volunteered with the New York Police Department and died at the World Trade Center on September 11, 2002. Supporters have organized a Web site to promote Judge's canonization: www.saintmychal.com.

17. Listed in Majid Fakhry, *A History of Islamic Philosophy* (New York: Columbia University Press, 1987), pp. 313-314.

18. For an overview of the harsh moral/social rules enforced by the Taliban before its fall, see Amy Waldman, "More No-Nos Than You Can Shake a Stick At," *New York Times,* December 2, 2001, D7.

19. Listed in Julius Guttmann, *Philosophies of Judaism, the History of Jewish Philosophy from Biblical Times to Franz Rosenzweig,* trans. David W. Silverman (New York: Holt, Rinehart and Winston, 1964), pp. 178-179. See also Karen Armstrong, *A History of God: The 4,000 Year Quest of Judaism, Christianity, and Islam* (New York: Ballantine, 1994), pp. 194-195. The preceding two lists appeared there.

20. Jacob Katz, *Exclusiveness and Tolerance: Studies in Jewish-Gentile Relations in Medieval and Modern Times* (New York: Schocken, 1961), p. 174.

21. William Shakespeare, *Twelfth Night,* I.5.

22. Foucault speculates that part of the reason why eighteenth-century French people subjected criminals to brutal torture in public was to cleanse the guilty of their sins and speed them to heaven. See Michael Foucault, *Discipline and Punish,* trans. Alan Sheridan (New York: Vintage, 1979), p. 46. For more on medieval Spanish religious beliefs, see Carlos Eire, *From Madrid to Purgatory: The Art and Craft of Dying in Sixteenth-Century Spain* (Cambridge: Cambridge University Press, 1995). See also Mary C. O'Connor, *The Art of Dying Well: The Development of the Ars Moriendi* (New York: Columbia University Press, 1942); the *Ars Moriendi* circulated widely throughout the Middle Ages. O'Connor describes it as "a complete and intelligible guide to the business of dying, a method to be learned while one is in good health and kept at one's fingers' ends for use in that all-important and inescapable hour" (p. 5).

23. From *The Imitation of Christ.* Quoted in Brad S. Gregory, *Salvation at Stake: Christian Martyrdom in Early Modern Europe* (Cambridge, Mass.: Harvard University Press, 1999), p. 52.

24. For a clear account of this point, see Bernhard Lang, "The Sexual Life of the Saints: Towards an Anthropology of Christian Heaven," *Religion* 17 (April 1987): 149-171, p. 156. According to Lang, "the whole range of traditional Christian ideas about life after death can be understood from its axiom, that there is no sex in heaven. This idea reflects the early Christian charismatic neglect of worldly matters as well as the rejection of established society to which one relates through a sexually active and child-bearing body." In his response to the Saducee's question about the true husband of the woman who took seven successive brothers as her spouse (Luke 20: 34-6), Jesus denied the very idea of marriage in heaven—not necessarily out of disdain for sex, but rather to emphasize that family ties will be radically rearranged in the next world.

25. Colleen McDannell and Bernhard Lang, "Modern Heaven . . . And a Theology," in *Mormons and Mormonism: An Introduction to an American World Religion*, ed. Eric A. Eliason (Urbana: University of Illinois Press, 2000), p. 143. This essay on Mormon beliefs in the afterlife seems to supplement the coverage of Mormon beliefs in an earlier joint effort, *Heaven: A History*, particularly pp. 313-322.

26. This belief comes from a Hadith, not the Koran. (The Hadith collections record in minute detail what the prophet did and said.) See Ibn Warraq, "Virgins, What Virgins?" in *The Guardian* (London), January 12, 2002, p. 3. Particularly since September 11, 2001, scholars have debated the translation of "*houri*," which may mean "chilled raisin." The implications would be large and obvious. Still other scholars believe that *houris* will be both male and female, thereby giving Muslim women something special as well.

27. Abdelwahab Bouhdiba, *Sexuality in Islam*, trans. Alan Sheridan (London: Routledge & Kegan Paul, 1985), p. 18

28. McDannell and Lang, *Heaven: A History*, p. 240.

29. David Herlihy, *Medieval Households* (Cambridge, Mass.: Harvard University Press, 1985), p. 118.

30. Tertullian, *Apology and De Spectaculis*, trans. T. R. Glover (Cambridge, Mass.: Harvard University Press, 1966), *Apology* section 50, p. 227.

31. See the fictional account of this aspect of Jewish culture in Anita Diamant, *The Red Tent* (New York: St. Martin's Press, 1997). For women in Islam see Janet Bauer, "Sexuality and the Moral 'Construction' of Women in an Islamic Society," *Anthropological Quarterly* 58 (July 1985), p. 121. In regards to Christianity, see Ute Ranke-Heinemann's discussion of "churching" in *Eunuchs for the Kingdom of Heaven: Women, Sexuality, and the Catholic Church*, trans. Peter Heinegg (New York: Penguin, 1991), especially pp. 21-26. On the Christian origins of this practice, see James A. Brundage, *Law, Sex, and Christian Society in Medieval Europe* (Chicago: University of Chicago Press, 1987), pp. 155-156. Mary Douglas discusses the idea of "female pollution" outside of the three major monotheistic traditions in *Purity and Danger: An Analysis of the Concepts of Pollution and Taboo* (London: Routledge, 1995), pp. 147-149.

32. The scriptural basis for this belief must be Matthew 19:3-13. Jesus urges all those who are able to make themselves "eunuchs for the Kingdom of God." Catholics have differed from Protestants in interpreting this passage, which echoes through ascetic works.

33. Margaret Visser, *The Geometry of Love: Space, Time, Mystery and Meaning in an Ordinary Church* (New York: North Point, 2001), pp. 133-134.

34. Robert McClory, *Turning Point: The Inside Story of the Papal Birth Control Commission* (New York: Crossroads, 1995), p. 78. Quoted in Garry Wills, *Papal Sin: Structures of Deceit* (New York: Doubleday, 2000), p. 93.

35. Marina Warner, *Alone of All Her Sex: The Myth and the Cult of the Virgin Mary* (New York: Vintage, 1983), p. 232. This paragraph is adapted from Warner, chapter 15. For an engaging account of the Magdalene's sexuality, see Katharine Ludwig Jansen, *The Making of the Magdalene: Preaching and Popular Devotion in the Later Middle Ages* (Princeton: Princeton University Press, 2000), pp. 130-134 and 169-172. For more on the harlot saints generally, see Benedicta Ward, *Harlots of the Desert: A Study of Repentance in Early Monastic Sources* (Kalamazoo, Mich.: Cistercian Publications, 1987). See also Jocelyn Wogan-Browne, *Saints' Lives and Women's Literary Culture c. 1150-1300* (Oxford: Oxford University Press, 2001), pp. 132-150. There is also Philip Gavitt, *Charity and Children in Renaissance Florence: The Ospedale degli Innocenti 1410-1536* (Ann Arbor: University of Michigan Press, 1990). For more on Saint Mary of Egypt, see Ruth Mazo Karras, *Common Women: Prostitution and Sexuality in Medieval England* (Oxford: Oxford University Press, 1996), pp. 123-125.

36. Sad to say, Roman Catholic canon lawyers allowed that poverty would excuse a man's thievery but not a woman's prostitution. Saint Mary never charged men, out of fear of discouraging anyone who could satisfy her "mad desire." She nonetheless incurred the additional wrath of various theologians, who judged her guilty of facilitating the sin of men she bedded.

37. James A. Brundage, "Sex and Canon Law," in *Handbook of Medieval Sexuality*, ed. Vern L. Bullough and James A. Brundage (New York: Garland Publishing, 1996), p. 44.

38. See Sherrill Cohen, *The Evolution of Women's Asylums Since 1500: From Refuges for Ex-Prostitutes to Shelters for Battered Women* (Oxford: Oxford University Press, 1992); Charles Chauvin, *Les chrétiens et la prostitution* (Paris: Les Editions du Cerf, 1983); and R. C. Trexler, "La prostitution florentine au XVe siècle," *Memoria* 17 (1986): 983-1015. See also James A. Brundage, *Law, Sex, and Christian Society in Medieval Europe*, pp. 395- 96, 529-30. Finally, see Jo Ann Kay McNamara, *Sisters in Arms: A History of Nuns* (Cambridge, Mass.: Harvard University Press, 1997), p. 459.

39. For a chronicle of one such, see Lynne Vallone's account of eighteenth-century England's Magdalen Hospital for penitent prostitutes in chapter 1 of *Disciplines of Virtue: Girls' Culture in the Eighteenth and Nineteenth Centuries* (New Haven: Yale University Press, 1995). Homes for unwed mothers resemble this model, and Vallone discusses in chapter 6 the Florence Crittendon Homes for unwed mothers of late nineteenth-century America. See also Katharine Ludwig Jansen's account "Convents for Repentant Women" in *The Making of the Magdalene*, pp.177- 184.

40. Irving B. Tebor, "Male Virgins: Conflicts and Group Support in American Culture," *Family Life Coordinator* 9, nos. 3-4, (March-June 1961). Quoted in Julia A. Eriksen, *Kiss and Tell: Surveying Sex in the Twentieth Century* (Cambridge, Mass.: Harvard University Press, 1999), p. 70.

41. Eugene Kennedy, *The Unhealed Wound: The Church and Human Sexuality* (New York: St. Martin's, 2001), p. 60.

42. Luther wrote, "Know, my dear Christian, and do not doubt that next to the devil you have no enemy more cruel, more venomous and virulent, than a true Jew." And later: "They are for us a heavy burden, the calamity of our being; they are a

pest in the midst of our lands." Salo Wittmayer Baron, *A Social and Religious History of the Jews*, vol. 13 (New York: Columbia University Press / Jewish Publication Society), p. 227.

43. See chapter 5 and chapter 6 of this work.

44. Other non-Christian groups were also barred from heaven. See Hans Urs von Balthasar, *Dare We Hope "That All Men Be Saved"?*, trans. David Kipp and Lothar Krauth (San Francisco: Ignatius Press, 1988). A prominent Catholic theologian, von Balthasar published the original text in 1986 under the title *Was dürfen wir hoffen?*

45. Examples here include Garry Wills and James Carroll. Each writes as a committed Catholic, and each laments the anti-Semitic sins of the Vatican. Garry Wills heaped praise on David Kertzer's book *The Popes Against the Jews: The Vatican's Role in the Rise of Modern Anti-Semitism* (New York: Knopf, 2001) in the *New York Times Book Review*, September 23, 2001.

46. Susan Zuccotti, *Under His Very Windows: The Vatican and the Holocaust in Italy* (New Haven: Yale University Press, 2001), p. 10.

47. Alessandra Stanley, "In Ukraine, Pope Tries to Heal Rift with Orthodox Church," *New York Times*, June 24, 2001, p. A8.

NOTES TO CHAPTER TWO

1. Augustine, *The City of God*, trans. John Healey (London: E.P. Dutton & Co, 1934), 22:1,2. In chapter 17, Augustine writes of heavenly bliss: "But we being made partakers of His peace, according to the measure of our capacity, shall obtain a most excellent peace in us, and amongst us, and with Him, according to the quantity of our excellency. In this manner the Holy angels according to their measure do know the same . . ." (p. 253). Later, Augustine writes that "no inferior shall envy his superior: even as now the other angels do not envy the archangels . . ." (p. 263). Thus we will understand but not resent the hierarchy that rewards us with a rank lower than other people.

Roughly eight centuries later, Saint Thomas Aquinas will fill out this notion in his *Summa theologiae*. Like Augustine does, Aquinas refers to the heavenly amphitheater as a "beatific vision" in which some people have better seats than others. Heaven is the reward for those who have performed good works (for example, works of charity). Those who demonstrate superior merits enjoy better seats in heaven, even though everyone there enjoys a vision of the Holy Trinity and the Virgin Mother.

The seating analogy fails after a point, because the beatific vision does not itself admit of degrees. Rather, some people have greater skill at maximizing the benefits afforded by the beatific vision. Everyone in heaven is a saint, and all of them will see God. It's just that some will see him more perfectly.

Some eight centuries after Aquinas, George Orwell would conclude his satirical work *Animal Farm* with the related insight that all animals are equal, but some are more equal than others.

2. Saint Thomas Aquinas elucidates the beatific vision in his *Summa theologiae* (Ia.12; and IaIIae 1-5).

3. Graham Greene, *The Power and the Glory* (1940; New York: Penguin, 1971), p. 210; Saint Jerome, *Against Jovinian*, 2.33. See http//www.ccel.org/fathers2/ and search "Nicene and Post-Nicene Fathers/Second series, vol. 6, St. Jerome." See

also Margaret Visser's discussion "Rape and Virginity," in *The Geometry of Love: Space, Time, and Mystery in an Ordinary Church* (New York: North Point, 2001), pp. 252-257

4. Jo Ann Kay McNamara, *Sisters in Arms: Catholic Nuns Through Two Millennia* (Cambridge, Mass.: Harvard University Press, 1996). The first extracted quote is found on pp. 579-580, the second on p. 581, and the quote above is found on p. 591.

5. John O'Malley, *The First Jesuits* (Cambridge, Mass.: Harvard University Press, 1993), p. 189. See also McNamara, *Sisters in Arms,* pp. 589-590:

> A common religion could not heal the deep differences among the immigrants. German congregations resisted the recruitment of Irish sisters, condemning them as ill-bred and (perhaps worse) English speaking. Swiss Benedictines hesitated to join the American Congregation of Saint Scholastica descended from the German community of Eichstätt.

For more on the presence of slaves in American convents, see pp. 579-580 and 597-598. See also *American Catholics and Slavery: 1789-1866: An Anthology of Primary Documents,* ed. Kenneth J. Zanca (Lanham, Maryland: University Press of America, 1994) and, for a slanted account, Richard Roscoe Miller's baldly anti-Catholic work *Slavery and Catholicism* (Durham, North Carolina: North State Publishers, 1957).

6. Some art historians claim that Titian's *Gloria* features the Holy Roman Emperor and his wife floating within heaven. Others have claimed to see Michelangelo's heavenly portrait in the *Last Judgment,* which dominates the Sistine Chapel. Thanks to Paul Barolsky for both these points.

7. See Winifred Gallagher, *Spiritual Genius: The Mastery of Life's Meaning* (New York: Random House, 2001), chapter 4.

8. That's to say that canonization rates have long favored men, a point Kenneth Woodward nails down in *Making Saints: How the Catholic Church Determines Who Becomes a Saint, Who Doesn't, and Why* (New York: Simon & Shuster, 1990). For specific examples of overlooked holy women, see Jocelyn Wogan-Browne, *Saints' Lives and Women's Literary Culture c. 1150- 1300,* (Oxford: Oxford University Press, 2001), pp. 192-193. For another account of possible canonization bias, see chapter 14 "The Science and Politics of Saints" in John Cornwell, *Breaking Faith: The Pope, the People, and the Fate of Catholicism* (New York: Viking, 2001).

9. See Nicholas Lemann, *The Big Test: The Secret History of the American Meritocracy* (New York: Farrar Straus & Giroux, 1999).

10. Peter Brown, *The Body And Society: Men, Women, and Sexual Renunciation in Early Christianity* (New York: Columbia University Press, 1988), p. 383.

11. A. N. Wilson, *God's Funeral* (New York: W.W. Norton, 1999), p. 142.

12. This is explicitly true of some racists writing from the American South during the segregation struggles. See Adam Nossiter, *Of Long Memory: Mississippi and the Murder of Medgar Evers* (Reading, Mass.: Addison-Wesley, 1994), p. 119. Nossiter quotes Byron de la Beckwith:

> I believe in segregation like I believe in God. I shall combat the evils of integration and shall bend every effort to rid the USA of the integrationist, whoever and wherever he may be." And later: "And furthermore, when I die I'll

be buried in a SEGREGATED cemetery. When you get to Heaven you'll find me in the part of Heaven that has a sign saying, "FOR WHITE ONLY!" and, if I go to Hades—I'm going to raise Hell all over Hades 'til I get in the WHITE SECTION OF HADES!

I thank Charles Marsh for these citations.

13. *Peace on Earth*, 1963. For this and other Catholic encyclicals, see the official Web site of the Vatican, www.vatican.va.

14. Edward Walsh, "Presbyterian Board Alters Gay Policy," *Washington Post*, June 16, 2001, pp. A1, A7.

15. Jane Gross, "In Stamford, Scout Troop is Evicted, but Prepared," *New York Times*, June 30, 2001, p. A24.

16. *Washington Post*, June 16, 2001, B7.

17. Woodward, *Making Saints*, p. 401.

18. Eugene Kennedy, *The Unhealed Wound: The Church and Human Sexuality* (New York: St. Martin's Press, 2001), p. 35.

19. See Michael Ford, *Mychal Judge: An Authentic American Hero* (New York: Paulist Press, 2002).

20. See John Boswell on Saints Serge and Bacchus in *Same-Sex Unions in Premodern Europe* (New York: Vintage, 1994), pp. 146-147 and pp. 151-154.

21. Fyodor Dostoevsky, *The Brothers Karamazov* (New York: W. W. Norton & Company, 2002), chapter 5.

22. *The Collected Works of Ralph Waldo Emerson*, Vol. 2: *Essays: First Series* (Cambridge: Harvard University Press, 1979), p. 94

NOTES TO CHAPTER THREE

1. Sarah Bradford, *America's Queen: A Life of Jacqueline Kennedy Onassis* (New York: Viking, 2000), pp. 275-276. For a portrait of JFK as a modern-day "sex addict," see Seymour M. Hersh, *The Dark Side of Camelot* (Boston: Little, Brown and Company, 1997), especially p. 238.

2. Calvin Trillin, *Remembering Denny* (New York: Farrar, Strauss, Giroux, 1993), pp. 170- 171.

3. Andrew Holleran, "The Sense of Sin" in *Wrestling with the Angel: Faith and Religion in the Lives of Gay Men*, ed. Brian Bouldrey (New York: Riverhead, 1995), p. 86.

4. Sigmund Freud, *Civilization and Its Discontents*, trans. James Strachey (New York: W. W. Norton, 1989), p. 59.

5. In his study *Bodies of Knowledge: The Psychological Significance of the Nude in Art* (London: Weidenfeld & Nicholson, 1982), Liam Hudson laments, "What a misfortune it is that so profoundly influential a theorist . . . should have had so slight a sexual interest in his own wife!" (p. 15).

6. See Deborah Solomon, *Utopia Parkway: The Life and Work of Joseph Cornell* (New York: Farrar, Straus, Giroux, 1997).

7. W. H. Auden, *Collected Poems*, ed. Edward Mendelson (New York: Random House, 1976), p. 114.

8. Janet L. Bauer, "Sexuality and the Moral 'Construction' of Women in Islamic Society" in the *Anthropological Quarterly* 58: 3 (July 1985), p. 122.

9. *Encyclopedia Judaica* (Jerusalem, 1972), vol. 14, p. 1206.

10. See for example Pierre J. Payer, *Sex and the Penitentials: The Development of a Sexual Code 550 - 1150* (Toronto: University of Toronto Press, 1984), especially pp. 52-53.

11. Hammed Shahidian, "Gender Relations in Persia" in *Encyclopedia Iranica,* ed. Ehsan Yarshater (New York: Biblioteca Persica Press), Vol. X, p. 405. I thank Farzaneh Milani for bringing this entry to my attention. See also Norman Roth, "A Research Note on Sexuality and Muslim Civilization" in *Handbook of Medieval Sexuality,* ed. Vern L. Bullough and James A. Brundage (New York: Garland Press, 1996).

12. Elizabeth Abbott, *A History of Celibacy* (New York, Scribner, 2000), p. 293. Abstention emphatically differs from intercourse with birth control; Bjorn Borg may have overlooked this difference when, early in our new millennium, he took out ads urging Europeans to have more sex. See "Bjorn Borg Urges Europe to Have More Sex," Reuters, March 9, 2001, available at http://www.iol.co.za. It seems Borg worried about having a new generation of workers to pay for our generation's social security, but increasing sexual frequency will do little to achieve this goal if couples use birth control.

13. Paul Rudnick, *Jeffrey* (Los Angeles: Orion Pictures, 1995), starring Nathan Lane, Sigourney Weaver, and Olympia Dukakis.
    Abstinence and chastity are sometimes taken to be synonymous, although technically they are not. For a brief indication of how ancient Romans and early Christians distinguished between chastity (avoidance of fornication) and continence (avoidance of sex altogether), see Kate Cooper, *The Virgin and the Bride: Idealized Womanhood in Late Antiquity* (Cambridge, Mass.: Harvard University Press, 1996), p. 56. For an account of the degrees of chastity, see Jocelyn Wogan-Browne, *Saints's Lives and Women's Literary Culture* (Oxford: Oxford University Press, 2001), pp. 44-47.

14. Cited in Richard Posner, *Aging and Old Age* (Chicago: University of Chicago Press, 1995), p. 86.

15. Ronald De Sousa, *The Rationality of the Emotions* (Cambridge, Mass.: MIT Press, 1987), p. 219.

16. Anton Gill, *Art Lover: A Biography of Peggy Guggenheim* (New York: HarperCollins, 2002); Lisa Zeidner, *Layover* (New York: Random House, 1999), p. 28.

17. See the story of former Jesuit Joe Kramer in David Guy, *The Red Thread of Passion: Spirituality and the Paradox of Sex* (Boston: Shambala, 1999), especially p. 209.

18. Peter Kurth, *Isadora: A Sensational Life* (New York: Little Brown & Company, 2001). The kind of sexual confidence we find in Duncan surfaces in other biographies, from Nureyev to Iris Murdoch.

19. Arthur Rimbaud, *Rimbaud Complete,* ed. Wyatt Mason (New York: Modern Library, 2002), pp. 62-64.

20. C. S. Lewis, *Mere Christianity* (New York: Macmillan, 1952), p. 75.

21. Michel Foucault, *The History of Sexuality, Volume I: An Introduction,* trans. Robert Hurley (New York: Random House, 1978), p. 156. In *The Sexual Fix* (New York: Schoken, 1982), British writer Stephen Heath identifies a "new sexual orthodoxy," one every bit as oppressive as older, Western sexual codes. According to Heath, culture has now changed in such a way that we *must* think of sexual fulfillment as a primary goal.

22. The first statement and others can be found on the Internet at: http://www.newadvent.org. The second is quoted in Ranke-Heinemann, *Eunuchs for the Kingdom of Heaven*, p. 337.

23. Mary Pipher, *Reviving Ophelia: Saving the Selves of Adolescent Girls* (New York: Ballantine Books, 1994); Wendy Shalit, *A Return to Modesty: Discovering the Lost Virtue* (New York: Free Press, 1999).

24. Nathan Englander, "For the Relief of Unbearable Urges" in *For the Relief of Unbearable Urges* (New York: Knopf, 1999), p. 180.

25. Bernadette Brooten, *Love Between Women: Early Christian Responses to Female Homoeroticism* (Chicago: University of Chicago Press, 1996), p. 191. See Dyan Elliott, *Spiritual Marriage: Sexual Abstinence in Medieval Wedlock* (Princeton: Princeton University Press, 1993), especially chapter 4, "The Conjugal Debt and Vows of Chastity." In another work, Elliott maintains that the very idea of a conjugal debt benefits men, not women. She holds, "the husband was the most obvious beneficiary of the sex-on-demand policy advocated by theoreticians of the conjugal debt." See *Fallen Bodies: Pollution, Sexuality, and Demonology in the Middle Ages* (Philadelphia: University of Pennsylvania Press, 1999), p. 75. See also her essay "Bernardino of Siena versus the Marital Debt," in *Desire and Discipline: Sex and Sexuality in Premodern Europe*, ed. Jacqueline Murray and Konrad Eisenbichler (Toronto: University of Toronto Press, 1996), pp. 168-200. See also Elizabeth M. Makowski, "The Conjugal Debt and Medieval Canon Law," *Journal of Medieval History* 3 (1977), pp. 99-114.

26. Citing John Noonan's study *Contraception: A History of Its Treatment by Catholic Theologians and Canonists* (Cambridge, Mass.: Harvard University Press, 1966), Garry Wills has pointed out the patristic view that "women, as the weaker sex, are more the prisoners of lust than men are." See Garry Wills, *Papal Sin: Structures of Deceit* (New York: Doubleday), p. 86, n. 5. *Coitus interruptus* became morally acceptable (in order to quench a wife's lust), provided that a husband did not ejaculate.

27. Italo Svevo, *Zeno's Conscience*, trans. William Weaver (New York: Knopf, 2001), p. 102.

28. David Chase, *The Sopranos* (New York: HBO Home Video, 1999), Season I, Episode 5.

29. Geraldine Brooks, *Nine Parts of Desire: The Hidden World of Islamic Women* (New York: Anchor, 1995), pp. 38-39. I follow Brooks closely here.

30. Abbott, pp. 192-195.

31. Andrew Greeley, *Sex and the Catholic Experience* (Allen, TX: Thomas More, 1994), pp. 26, 161.

32. Laura Doyle, *The Surrendered Wife: A Practical Guide to Finding Intimacy, Passion, and Peace with Your Man* (New York: Fireside, 2001), p. 206.

33. Studies cited in Helen Fisher, *Anatomy of Love: The Natural History of Monogamy, Adultery, and Divorce* (New York: W.W. Norton, 1992), p. 185.

34. In Phyllis Theroux, ed., *The Book of Eulogies: A Collection of Memorial Tributes, Poetry, Essays, and Letters of Condolence* (New York: Scribner, 1997), p. 208.

35. Sam Mendes, *American Beauty* (Dreamworks, 2000), starring Kevin Spacey and Annette Bening.

36. Peter McDonough and Eugene C. Bianchi, *Passionate Uncertainty: Inside the American Jesuits* (Berkeley and Los Angeles: University of California Press, 2002), p. 95.

NOTES TO CHAPTER FOUR

1. Alessandra Stanley, "Pope Declares His 'Bitterness' Over Gay Event," *New York Times,* July 10, 2000, p. A11. See also Alessandra Stanley, "Gay Parade, Opposed by Vatican, Passes Peacefully in Rome," *New York Times,* July 9, 2000, p. A5; and Alessandra Stanley, "Duelling Festivals: Gay Pride and Vatican Collide," *New York Times,* June 3, 2000, p. A4.

2. John Boswell, *Christianity, Social Tolerance, and Homosexuality* (Chicago: University of Chicago Press, 1980), pp. 15-16. For corroborating views, see Didi Herman, *The Antigay Agenda: Orthodox Vision and the Christian Right* (Chicago: University of Chicago Press, 1997), pp. 85-86 and pp. 125-128; and Elaine Pagels, *The Origin of Satan* (New York: Random House, 1996), pp. 102-105.

3. Pius XII, "Address to the Supreme Council of the Arab People of Palestine." Cited in John Cornwell, *Hitler's Pope: The Secret History of Pius XII* (New York: Viking, 1999), p. 197.

4. Gary Wills, *Papal Sin: Structures of Deceit* (New York: Doubleday, 2000), p. 66.

5. "American Catholics: A Church Divided," *New York Times,* June 1, 1994, pp. A1, B8.

6. Former Catholic priest Eugene Kennedy explains the way the world looks to a priest: "Such ecclesiastical leaders truly believe that they are carrying out a divinely imposed duty in a divinely ordained way in a hierarchically deployed Church in which they view the playing field from the equivalent of sky boxes. They mean well; they are, by their lights, doing the 'right' thing because they are carrying out their providential obligation to ensure and promote what they understand, in a famous phrase, as 'the good of the Church.'" See Kennedy, *The Unhealed Wound: The Church and Human Sexuality* (New York: St. Martin's Press, 2001), p. 67.

7. Saint Thomas Aquinas, *Summa theologiae,* III.47.5. In *Hitler's Pope,* Cornwell writes of a boyhood teacher of the future Pope Pius XII, "The most enduring form of antipathy focused on the 'obstinacy' of the Jews, the theme of Pacelli's [Pius XII's] ranting schoolmaster, Signore Marchi" (p. 26).

8. David I. Kertzer, *The Kidnapping of Edgardo Mortara* (New York: Vintage, 1998).

9. Austin Flannery, O. P., ed., *Vatican II: The Conciliar and Post Conciliar Documents* (Collegeville, Indiana, 1992), p. 741.

10. John Paul II also reached out to Muslims. On March 11, 1999 he greeted in his private library Hojjat ol-Islam Muhammed Khatami, president of the Islamic Republic of Iran. In his first meeting ever with a Shi'i Muslim national leader, the pope blessed the religious representative. In 2001 John Paul II became the first pope to enter a mosque (in Damascus).

11. See James Shapiro, *Oberammergau: The Troubling Story of the World's Most Famous Passion Play* (New York: Pantheon, 2000).

12. *Le Monde,* September 22, 1997, p. 1.

13. *Corriere della Sera,* March 16, 1998, p. 15.

14. Melinda Henneberger, "Vatican Says Jews' Wait for Messiah is Validated by the Old Testament," *New York Times,* January 18, 2002, p. A8.

15. See, for example, Keith Hartman, *Congregations in Conflict: The Battle Over Homosexuality* (New Brunswick, NJ: Rutgers University Press, 1996), p. 155.

16. John McNeill, *The Church and the Homosexual* (Boston: Beacon Press, 1993), p. xv.

17. Charles Morris, *American Catholic: The Saints and Sinners Who Built America's Most Powerful Church* (New York: Times Books, 1997), p. 354.
18. E. J. Dionne, Jr., "America and the Catholic Church: Conflicts with Rome and Within" in *The New York Times*, December 24, 1986, p. A1.
19. James Carroll, *Constantine's Sword: The Church and the Jews: A History* (New York: Houghton Mifflin, 2001), pp. 316-317.
20. Even here, nuances emerge. See Alan Unterman, "Judaism and Homosexuality: Some Orthodox Perspectives" in *Jewish Quarterly* (Autumn 1993): 5-9; see also Arthur Waskow and Daniel Landes, "Down-to-Earth Judaism: Sexuality" in *Jewish Explorations of Sexuality*, ed. Jonathan Magonet (Providence, RI: Berghahn Books, 1995).
21. *Trembling Before G-d*, dir. Sandi Simcha DuBowski (New York: New Yorker Films, 2001).
22. Eugene Borowitz, "On Homosexuality in the Rabbinate" in *Exploring Jewish Ethics* (Detroit: Wayne State University Press, 1990), p. 277. On the subtlety of Jewish responses to the morality of same-sex erotic relationships, see Tivka Frymer-Kensky, "Law and Philosophy: The Case of Sex in the Bible," in *Jewish Explorations of Sexuality*.
23. Samuel G. Freedman, *Jew vs. Jew: The Struggle for the Soul of American Jewry* (New York: Simon & Schuster, 2000), p. 356
24. Robert Kirschner, "Halakhah and Homosexuality: A Reappraisal," in *Judaism* 37.3 (Fall 1988), p. 450.
25. Helen Carter, "Lambeth Conference: Intervention by Carey Helps Sway Bishops," *The Guardian* (London), August 6, 1998, p. 10; Walter C. Righter, *A Pilgrim's Way* (New York: Knopf, 1998).
26. Cathy Lynn Grossman, "Protestants Face Annual Sexual Divide: Same-Sex Unions, Gay Clergy, Female Leaders Divide Faithful," *USA Today*, June 6, 2001, p. 1D.
27. David Van Biema, "Episcopal Turf War," *Time*, July 9, 2001, p. 41.
28. Gustav Niebuhr, "Episcopal Dispute in Maryland Spills into Federal Court," *New York Times*, August 14, 2001, p. A10.
29. Nicholas Pyke, "The Church Militant; C of E: the New Archbishop Will Face a Church Riven by Warring Tribes," *The Independent on Sunday*, July 28, 2002, p. 20.
30. Ruth Gledhill, "Evangelicals Warn that Williams in Canterbury Would Split the Church," *The Times* (London), June 21, 2002. According to the article, "The evangelicals claimed that Dr Williams's support for the ordination of homosexuals flew 'in the face of Holy Scripture' and would lead to the split in the Anglican Communion only narrowly averted by Dr Carey [the previous Archbishop of Canterbury] four years ago."
31. Salman Rushdie, "In Good Faith," in *Imaginary Homelands: Essays and Criticism 1981-1991* (New York: Viking, 1991).
32. See the Vatican's Web site for this and other encyclicals (www.vatican.va).
33. Flannery, *Vatican II*, p. 367.
34. Ibid.
35. Monika K. Hellwig, *Understanding Catholicism* (New York: Paulist Press, 1981), p. 113.
36. See Laurie Goodstein, "Women Taking Active Role to Study Orthodox Judaism," *New York Times*, December 21, 2000, p. A1; Laurie Goodstein, "Unusual, but

Not Unorthodox; Causing a Stir, 2 Synagogues Hire Women to Assist Rabbis," *New York Times,* February 6, 1998, p. B1; and Nadine Brozan, "Annulling a Tradition; Rabbis Stir Furor by Helping 'Chained Women' to Leave Husbands," *New York Times,* August 13, 1998, p. B1.

37. See David W. Dunlop, "Reform Rabbis Vote to Back Gay Marriage," *New York Times* March 29, 1996, p. B9. The vote "underscored a stark division in Judaism over the place of homosexuals in society."

38. Mark D. Jordan, *The Invention of Sodomy in Christian Theology* (Chicago: University of Chicago Press, 1997), p. 1.

39. Carroll, *Constantine's Sword,* p. 583.

40. I am grateful to Carl Archaki and Martin Calkins, S. J., for helpful discussions of the material in this chapter.

NOTES TO CHAPTER FIVE

1. The idea caught on. According to a *New York Times* article, the American bishops who convened in Dallas in June 2002 "had spent thousands on public relations consultants who were working both behind the scenes and quite publicly at the Dallas conference." See Laurie Goodstein, "U.S. Bishops Let Public Opinion Guide Them This Time," June 16, 2002.

2. Alan Cooperman, "U.S. Catholic Bishops Disown Efforts to Convert Jews," *Washington Post,* August 17, 2000, p. B9. The statement lies in the Catholic portion of a document, "Reflections on Covenant and Mission," issued jointly by the bishops' Ecumenical and Interreligious Affairs Committee and the National Council of Synagogues.

3. The representative in question was Jim Sibley, coordinator of Jewish ministries for the Southern Baptist Convention. See Jerry Filteau, "Catholic-Jewish Statement on Conversion Draws Heat," *The Catholic Virginian,* September 2, 2002, pp. 1 and 9. The national director of the Anti-Defamation League, Abraham H. Foxman, called Sibley's accusation "completely absurd."

4. "Rome's Catholics Gone Astray, Study Shows," *National Catholic Reporter,* May 26, 1995, p. 6. Quoted in Thomas J. Reese, *Inside the Vatican: The Politics and Organization of the Catholic Church* (Cambridge, Mass.: Harvard University Press, 1996), p. 12.

5. See Stephanie Flanders, "Demonstrators at U.N. Accuse Priests of Abusing Nuns in Africa," *New York Times,* July 15, 2001, p. A27.

6. John Cornwell, *Breaking Faith: The Pope, the People, and the Fate of Catholicism* (New York: Viking, 2001), p. 3.

7. John W. Fountain, "Shock Over Accusations in Milwaukee," *New York Times,* May 24, 2002, p. A18.

8. *New York Times,* March 9, 2002, p. A26.

9. Quoted in Susan Zuccotti, *Under His Very Windows: The Vatican and the Holocaust in Italy* (New Haven: Yale University Press), p. 8.

10. *American Sermons: the Pilgrims to Martin Luther King, Jr.* (New York: Library of America, 1999), p. 349

11. Rabbi Arthur Gilbert, "Jews, Prejudice and Catholic Practice," in Maerican Catholics: A Protestant-Jewish View, ed. Philip Scharper (New York: Sheed & Ward, 1959): 159-192.

12. David Kertzer, *The Kidnapping of Edgardo Mortara* (New York: Knopf, 1997), pp. 55- 57.

13. James Carroll, *Constantine's Sword: The Church and the Jews: A History* (New York: Houghton Mifflin, 2001), p. 275.

14. Kertzer, *The Kidnapping of Edgardo Mortara*, p. 56. That Saint Thomas Aquinas decried the practice did not stop all Catholics from secretly baptizing Jewish infants anyway.

15. A religious order of nuns founded by a Jewish convert in the nineteenth century, the Sisters of Sion long claimed converting Jews as its mission. Still in existence, the order now strives to fight anti-Semitism and no longer focuses on conversions.

16. Ute Ranke-Heinemann, *Eunuchs for the Kingdom of Heaven: Women, Spirituality, and the Catholic Church,* trans. Peter Heinegg (New York: Penguin, 1991), pp. 335-338. See also David Herlihy, *Medieval Households* (Cambridge: Harvard University Press), pp. 80-81.

17. Leslie Stainton, *Lorca: A Dream of Life* (New York: Farrar, Strauss, Giroux, 1999), pp. 136-136.

18. See Bill Carter, "Killing Poses Hard Questions about Talk TV," *New York Times,* March 14, 1995, p. A1; and David A. Dunlap, "Shameless Homophobia and the 'Jenny Jones' Murder," *New York Times,* March 19, 1995, p. D16.

19. *Kansas City Star* series by Judy L. Thomas, January 2000. Two-thirds of the eight hundred priests surveyed said they knew at least one priest who had already died of AIDS; one-third claimed to know a priest who was fighting the disease.

20. Garry Wills, *Papal Sin: Structures of Deceit* (New York: Doubleday, 2000), p. 195. Later Wills writes, "Humane modern laws respecting the dignity of gays and lesbians will not erase prejudices of long standing. They will just infuriate some. That is why I feel that only their resentment of gays will change their minds on other things—like the admission of women and married heterosexuals to the priesthood. Even those will be less abominated than a gay priesthood" (p. 200).

21. Matthew Arnold, *Culture and Anarchy,* ed. J. Dover Wilson (Cambridge University Press, 1966), pp. xxxi-xxxii; see also p. 181.

22. Bernard Häring, *Das Gesetz Christi,* trans. *The Law of Christ* by Edwin G. Kaiser, 3 vols. (Westminster: Newman Press, 1966), vol. 1, p. 376.

23. Cornwell, *Hitler's Pope: The Secret History of Pius XII* (New York: Viking, 1999), p. 27.

24. Noël Coward, *Private Lives* in *Noël Coward Collected Plays: Two,* introduced by Sheridan Morley (London: Methuen, 1986), pp. 42-43.

25. Eugenio Zolli, *Why I Became a Catholic* (previously titled *Before the Dawn*) (Fort Collins, Colo.: Roman Catholic Books, 1954).

26. Bernard Lewis, "What Went Wrong?" in *The Atlantic Monthly,* vol. 298, No. 1, January 2002: p. 43. See also his book of the same name (New York: Oxford University Press, 2002). On Western media and its interpretative lens with regard to Islamic civilization, see Edward Said, *Covering Islam: How the Media and the Experts Determine How We See the Rest of the World* (New York: Vintage, 1997). Said writes, "Of no other religion or cultural grouping can it be said so assertively as it is now said of Islam that it represents a threat to Western civilization" (p. lii). According to Said, the success of books, journals, and public figures that argue for a reoccupation of the Persian Gulf region relies on a belief in Islamic barbarism.

27. Lewis, "What Went Wrong?," p. 43.

28. Rosemary Curb and Nancy Manahan, eds., *Lesbian Nuns: Breaking Silence* (Tallahassee, FL: Naiad Press, 1985).
29. Thomas Reese, *Inside the Vatican: The Politics and Organization of the Catholic Church* (Cambridge: Harvard University Press, 1996), p. 236.
30. Ibid., p. 243.

NOTES TO CHAPTER SIX

1. William James examines conversion in his 1902 classic *The Varieties of Religious Experience* (New York: New American Library, 1958), pp. 157-206.
2. "Baptist Head Urges Prayers for Muslim Conversion," *New York Times,* November 27, 2001, p. A10.
3. Stephen J. Dubner, *Turbulent Souls: A Catholic Son's Return to His Jewish Roots* (New York: William Morrow, 1998). For an intelligent account of converting to Catholicism despite unresolved doubt, see Robert Clark, *My Grandfather's House: A Genealogy of Doubt and Faith* (New York: Picador, 1999).
4. Eugene Pogany, *In My Brother's Image: Twin Brothers Separated by Faith After the Holocaust* (New York: Viking, 2000). See especially Chapter 17, "Jew Priest."
5. Ronda Chervin, ed., *Bread from Heaven: The Stories of 23 Jews Who Found the Messiah in the Catholic Church* (New Hope, KY: Remnant of Israel, 1995).
6. G. K. Chesterton, *The Catholic Church and Conversion* (New York: Macmillan, 1926), pp.57-66.
7. Jaroslav Pelikan, *The Riddle of Roman Catholicism* (New York: Abingdon Press, 1959), pp.205, 208-9.
8. Graham Greene, "On Becoming a Catholic," in *Commonweal Confronts the Century,* ed. Patrick Jordan and Paul Baumann (New York: Touchstone, 1999), p. 291.
9. Cornwell, *Breaking Faith: The Pope, the People, and the Fate of Catholicism* (New York: Viking, 2001), p. 98.
10. Thomas C. Fox, *Sexuality and Catholicism* (New York: George Braziller, 1995), p. 183.
11. Eugene V. Gallagher, "Conversion and Community in Late Antiquity" in *The Journal of Religion,* vol. 73, no. 1 (January 1993), pp. 1-15.
12. The pivotal moment of adopting a new allegiance recurs throughout "a lifelong process in which the meaning of the initial experience is constantly revised and transferred, both by converts themselves and by others who tell their stories" (Gallagher, "Conversion and Community in Late Antiquity," pp. 2-3). He in turn refers us to James A. Beckford, "Accounting for Conversion," in *British Journal of Sociology* 29 (1978): 249-62, particularly p. 260.
13. Mark Jordan, *The Silence of Sodom: Homosexuality in Modern Catholicism* (Chicago: University of Chicago Press, 2000), p. 6.
14. Unlike Judaism or Catholicism, many Protestant communions don't require formal conversions, which means the whole question of official admittance never arises, at least not in the same juridical sense.
15. Louise Erdrich, *The Last Report on the Miracles at Little No Horse* (New York: HarperCollins, 2001), pp. 55-56, 71, 81.
16. Patrick Allitt, *Catholic Converts: British and American Intellectuals Turn to Rome* (Ithaca, NY: Cornell University Press, 1997).

17. David J. O'Brien, "What Happened to the Catholic Left?," in *What's Left? Liberal American Catholics,* ed. Mary Jo Weaver (Bloomington: Indiana University Press, 1999), p. 256.

18. Ellis Hanson, *Decadence and Catholicism* (Cambridge, Mass.: Harvard University Press, 1997), p. 127. Writing at the end of the century he chronicles, Hanson notes, ". . . I might add that Roman Catholicism is doing remarkably well on the international market for converts" (p. 370).

19. Richard McBrien, *HarperCollins Encyclopedia of Catholicism* (New York: Harper-Collins, 1995), n. 3, pp. 242-243.

20. Taken from Austin Flannery, O. P., ed., *Vatican II: The Conciliar and Post Conciliar Documents* (Collegeville, Indiana, 1992), n. 14.

21. Tracy Early, "Jewish Group Wants Holocaust Honor for Pope John XXIII," *Catholic New York,* September 14, 2000, p. 4. The article includes a picture of Cardinal Angelo Sodano, the Vatican secretary of state, accepting a sculpture presented to him by Baruch Tenembaum, founder of the International Raoul Wallenberg Foundation, and Abraham Foxman, president of the Anti-Defamation League. Rabbi Simon Moguilesky of Argentina is looking on.

22. As reported in Christopher Buckley's June 3, 1996 *New Yorker* piece about the memorial service, p 56. Compare a similar remark Oskar Pfister made about his friend Sigmund Freud. Pfister, a Protestant Pastor in Zurich, called Jesus the first psychoanalyst and Freud a good Christian ("a better Christian never was"). See Peter Gay, *Freud: A Life for Out Time* (New York: W.W. Norton, 1988) pp. 191-192.

23. See Chapters 10 and 13 in A. D. Nock, *Conversion: The Old and the New Religion from Alexander the Great to Augustine of Hippo* (Oxford: Oxford University Press, 1969).

24. "Future of Catholicism Worries Many of the Church's Leaders," *New York Times,* June 1, 1994, pp. A1, B8. On the Eucharist as a unifying symbol fraught with tension, see especially Miri Rubin, *Corpus Christi: The Eucharist in Late Medieval Culture* (Cambridge: Cambridge University Press, 1991).

25. Jordan, *The Silence of Sodom,* p. 245.

26. Gay, *Freud,* p. 601.

27. Most liberal and moderate theologians now reject the view that missing weekly Mass (that is, failing to fulfill the Sunday obligation) amounts to a mortal sin.

28. Bernard Häring, "The Encyclical Crisis," in *Commonweal Confronts the Century,* p. 272. Häring nevertheless maintains that responsible couples whose consciences allow them to use birth control need not even mention the fact in confession.

29. For a sociological account of how far American Catholics believe they can stray from the teachings of the church and still legitimately call themselves "Catholic," see Michelle Dillon, *Catholic Identity: Balancing Reason, Faith, and Power* (Cambridge: Cambridge University Press, 1999).

30. A. N. Wilson recounts the story of one Maude Petre: "The fact that she came of one of the oldest English Catholic families, and that she had a robust temperament, gave Miss Petre the confidence to continue attending Mass, even when the Prior of Storrington did his best to tell her she was excommunicated. Doughty champion for the truth, she lived on until the Second World War." See *God's Funeral* (New York: Doubleday, 2000), p. 352.

31. Kevin Sullivan, "Thoroughly Modern Martha: Mexico's new First Lady is a Career Woman, A Conservative Catholic—and a Force for Change," *Washington Post,* September 4, 2001, p. C1.

32. Syllabus of Errors, prop. 80 (Henricus Denzinger and Adolphus Schöetzer. eds., *Enchiridion Symbolorum,* editio XXXII [Rome: Herder, 1963], no. 1780). Quoted in Joseph A. Komonchak, "The Encounter Between Catholicism and Liberalism," in *Catholicism and Liberalism: Contributions to American Public Philosophy,* ed. Bruce Douglass and David Hollenbach (New York: Cambridge University Press, 1997), p. 78..

33. Keith Hartman, *Congregations in Conflict: The Battle Over Homosexuality* (New Brunswick, NJ: Rutgers University Press, 1996), p. 167. See also Michelle Dillon, *Catholic Identity,* chapter 5 ("Gay and Lesbian Catholics: 'Owning the Identity Differently'").

34. Bernard Häring, "The Encyclical Crisis," in *Commonweal Confronts the Century,* pp. 262-263.

35. The satisfaction of these converts contrasts with other stories. Take George Tyrell, for example, an Anglican who converted to Catholicism a century ago, only to find himself rejected by his (Jesuit) Order and expelled by his church. Accused of heretical writings, in which he attacked a "perverted" devotion to the idea of hell, Tyrell returned to the Anglican faith, exclaiming, "Church of my baptism! Why did I ever leave you?" See A. N. Wilson, *God's Funeral,* pp. 348-352.

36. *The Daily Telegraph,* August 3, 2001, p. 31. See also the British newspapers *The Times,* August 7, 2001; and *The Independent,* August 4, 2001, p. 6.

37. Stephen Ryan, "Episcopal Priest Becomes Catholic Laywoman," in *National Catholic Register,* August 1, 2001.

38. See "News Briefs" of May 7, 1999 at www.episcopalchurch.org/ens/99-066.html.

39. Elisaberth Abbott, *A History of Celibacy* (New York: Scribner), p. 382.

40. "The Question of the Ordination of Lay Men and Women to the Priesthood in the Catholic Church" (on-line: http://christ-usrex.org/www/CDHN/kephas.html [30 August 1996]), quoted in Abbott, *A History of Celibacy,* p. 382.

41. Ibid., p. 383.

42. It is not clear that they do. See Patrick Shaw, "On Worshipping the Same God" in *Religious Studies,* vol. 28, No. 4 (December 1992): 511-522.

NOTES TO CHAPTER SEVEN

1. Mircea Eliade, *Patterns in Comparative Religion,* trans. Rosemary Sheed (Lincoln, Nebraska: University of Nebraska Press, 1996). See especially chapter 9, "Fertility and Fertility Cults." See also *Keith Thomas, Religion and the Decline of Magic: Studies in Popular Belief in Sixteenth- and Seventeenth-Century England* (New York: Scribners, 1971) and John M. Allegro, *The Sacred Mushroom and the Cross: A Study of the Nature and Origins of Christianity Within the Fertility Cults of the Ancient Near East* (New York: Doubleday, 1970), particularly chapter 7, "The Man-child Born of a Virgin."

2. Eliade, *Patterns in Comparative Religion,* p. 354.

3. See for example *Death and the Regeneration of Life,* ed. Maurice Bloch and Jonathan Parry (Cambridge: Cambridge University Press, 1994).

4. *New Catholic Encyclopedia* (San Francisco: McGraw-Hill, 1967), 19 vols., vol. 2, p. 2.

5. *New Catholic Encyclopedia*, vol. 5, p. 897.

6. According to Shaker doctrine and practice, new souls are gained only by adopting children, since Shakers forbid sexual intercourse.

7. See Rebecca L. Spang, *The Invention of the Restaurant* (Cambridge, Mass.: Harvard University Press, 2000), especially pp. 30-32 and 80-83.

8. Richard J. Moss, *Golf and the American Country Club* (Urbana, IL: University of Illinois Press, 2001), pp. 5-6. See especially chapter 1: "The Country Club and American Experience."

9. Thorstein Veblen, *The Theory of the Leisure Class* (Boston: Houghton Mifflin, 1973).

10. See *The Stories of John Cheever* (New York: Knopf, 1978), a collection of shorter works put out just before his death.

11. James M. Mayo, *The American Country Club: Its Origins and Development* (New Brunswick: Rutgers University Press, 1998), p. 30.

12. Daniel Oren, *Joining the Club: A History of Jews and Yale* (New Haven: Yale University Press, 1985).

13. Ibid, p. 1.

14. In a *New Yorker* article cleverly titled "Slim for Him," Rebecca Mead describes the ascent of Gwen Shamblin, a leader in the Christian weight loss movement (January 15, 2001, pp. 48-57). Shamblin blames modern (Protestant) churches for becoming too comfortable, for failing to terrorize people who come to church. In this regard, Shamblin speaks for a vocal coalition of conservative Christians who insist that we must reinstate an anxious consciousness of sin in our neighbors if we are to correct the social ills of the modern West.

15. See for example Keith Thomas, *Religion and the Decline of Magic* (New York: Scribner's, 1971), pp. 625-628, 663-668.

16. On the Eucharist as a unifying symbol fraught with tension, see Miri Rubin, *Corpus Christi: The Eucharist in Late Medieval Culture* (Cambridge: Cambridge University Press, 1991).

17. Margaret Visser, *The Geometry of Love: Space, Time, Mystery, and Meaning in an Ordinary Church* (New York: North Point), pp. 25-26.

18. John Cornwell, *Breaking Faith: the Pope, the People, and the Fate of Catholicism* (New York: Viking Penguin, 2001), p. 12.

19. David Christie-Murray, *A History of Heresy* (New York: Oxford University Press, 1991), p. 8.

20. *Sisters in Arms*, p. 634.

21. See Christopher Morgan, "Anglican Rebels Build New Church," *Sunday Times*, November 9, 1997. Sympathy toward gays was only one sticking point; the ordination of women was another. Disgruntled Anglicans were converting to Catholicism out of protest. According to Morgan, "High-profile Anglicans who defected [to Catholicism] included the Duchess of Kent, John Gummer, the former environment secretary, and Anne Widdecombe, the former prisons minister."

22. See, for example, Robert D. Cross, *The Emergence of Liberal Catholicism in America* (Cambridge, Mass.: Harvard University Press, 1958); Mary Fulbrook, *Piety and Politics* (Cambridge: Cambridge University Press, 1983); Mary Hanna, *Catholics and American Politics* (Cambridge, Mass..: Harvard University Press, 1979); and Eric Hanson, *The Catholic Church in World Politics* (Princeton: Princeton University Press, 1987). See also Bruce Bawer's discussion of legalism v.

nonlegalism in *Stealing Jesus: How Fundamentalism Betrays Christianity* (New York: Crown, 1997); Martin E. Marty and R. Scott Appleby, eds., *Fundamentalisms Observed* (Chicago: University of Chicago Press, 1991); and James Davison Hunter's account of "culture wars" in his book of the same name (New York: Basic Books, 1992). In an epilogue to *Being Right: Conservative Catholics in America*, Scott Appleby observes, "Catholic intellectuals and activists often seem more comfortable with their ideological counterparts in other denominations than with their fellow Catholics. . . ." See *Being Right: Conservative Catholics in America*, edited by Mary Jo Weaver and R. Scott Appleby (Bloomington, IN: University of Indiana Press, 1995), p. 325.

23. Gene Burns, *The Frontiers of Catholicism* (Berkeley, CA: University of California Press), p. 2.

24. See Lisa Schiffren, "Gay Marriage: An Oxymoron," *New York Times*, March 23, 1996, p. A21. For an account of the subsequent vote of the House of Representatives, see Jerry Gay, "House Votes to Ban Gay Marriages," *New York Times*, July 14, 1996, p. D2. Gay quotes the Reverend Lou Shelton, chairman of the Traditional Values Coalition, as saying, "There is no other issue on the American landscape where there is such a strong political consensus—Americans oppose homosexual marriages."

25. Didi Herman, *The Antigay Agenda*, pp. 10-11. It might be thought that we would do better to describe these movements as "Christian" ones. However, conservative Protestants seem to have arrogated this title or description, excluding liberal Protestants and, certainly, Roman Catholics. See Bruce Bawer, *Stealing Jesus: How Fundamentalism Betrays Christianity* (New York: Crown, 1997).

26. John Cornwell has maintained, "At the dawn of the twenty-first century . . . few Catholics have even a remote sense of this specifically Catholic concept. Of the estimated 30 percent of Catholics who retain a devotion to the real presence in the Eucharist, few, according to most surveys, are even aware of the terrors of the transubstantiation argument." See *Breaking Faith*, p. 44.

27. Most of Vatican territory was absorbed into Italy during the struggle for Italian unification, from 1860 to 1870. An Italian law of May 13, 1871 abrogated the temporal power of the pope and confined the territory of the papacy to the Vatican and Lateran palaces and the villa of Castel Gandolfo. The popes consistently refused to recognize this arrangement and, by the Lateran Treaty of February 11, 1929, between the Vatican and the kingdom of Italy, the exclusive dominion and sovereign jurisdiction of the Holy See over Vatican City was again recognized, thus restoring the pope's temporal authority over the area.

28. *On Christian Marriage*, 1930. See www.vatican.va

29. Douglas Laycock, as quoted in Jeffrey Rosen, "Is Nothing Secular?," *The New York Times Magazine*, January 30, 2000, p. 42.

30. Rosen, p. 43.

31. Alan Cooperman, "The Bishop, the Scandal and His Plan," *Washington Post*, September 28, 2002, p. A1. The article goes on to praise Gregory's leadership in Belleville and states that it is "the first diocese in the country to disclose exactly how much money it has spent over the years on legal fees, counseling and settlements in [sexual] abuse cases: $3,156,414 from 1993 through 2001."

32. See Elinor Burkett and Frank Bruni, *A Gospel of Shame: Children, Sexual Abuse, and the Catholic Church* (New York: Viking, 1993).

33. See Thomas C. Fox, *Sexuality and Catholicism* (New York: George Braziller, 1995), pp. 184-197.

34. See Philip Jenkins, *Pedophiles and Priests: Anatomy of a Contemporary Crisis* (New York: Oxford University Press, 1996); Samuel Laeuchli, *Power and Sexuality: The Emergence of Canon Law at the Synod of Elvira* (Philadelphia: Temple University Press, 1972); A.W. Richard Sipes, *A Secret World: Sexuality and the Search for Celibacy* (New York: Brunner/Mazel, 1990); and Sipes, *Sex, Priests, and Power: Anatomy of a Crisis* (New York: Brunner/Mazel, 1995).

35. The *Boston Globe* constructed a Web site dedicated to covering child sexual abuse among the Catholic clergy: www.boston.com/globe/spotlight/abuse. Reporters from the same newspaper published a comprehensive account of the Boston sex scandal in *Betrayal: The Crisis in the Catholic Church* (Boston: Little Brown & Company, 2002).

36. Melinda Henneberger, "Scandals in the Church: the Overview; Pope Offers Apology to Victims of Sex Abuse by Priests," *New York Times,* April 24, 2002, p. A1.

37. Melinda Henneberger, "Vatican Weighs Reaction to Accusations of Molesting by Clergy," *New York Times,* March 3, 2002, p. A30. See also John Tagliabue, "A Doctor-Spokesman Attends to Papal Image," *New York Times,* June 29, 2002, p. A1.

38. According to a survey by the *Washington Post,* 355 priests had been removed from ministry because of sex abuse allegations before the scandal of 2002 erupted. See Alan Cooperman and Lena H. Sun, "Hundreds of Priests Removed Since '60s," *Washington Post,* June 9, 2002, pp. A1, A18. While the *Post* publicized the fact that thirty-four past offenders remained in ministry, the paper also made clear that American bishops had indeed taken some actions to remove sexual predators from the ranks of the priesthood.

39. Bishops in Ireland, Poland, Canada, and Australia also stepped down, for the same reason.

40. The Carmelite nuns ultimately had to leave the Auschwitz convent. The presence of the convent at the camp where more than two million Jews were killed by the Nazis deeply offended many Jews and strained Jewish-Catholic relations in the late 1980s. See "Upheaval in the East; Nuns Are to Quit Site at Auschwitz," *New York Times,* February 17, 1990, p. A8. That same year, many Jews sharply criticized the Vatican for having beatified Edith Stein, a Jewish philosopher who converted to Catholicism. Although Stein had become a Carmelite nun, the Nazis killed her as a Jew. See "Edith Stein, Jewish Catholic Martyr." *Carmelite Studies 4* (Washington, D.C.: ICS Publications, 1987), pp. 310-327.

NOTES TO CONCLUSION

1. C. S. Lewis, *The Problem of Pain* (New York: Macmillan, 1962), p. 145.

2. *The Selected Poetry of Rainer Maria Rilke,* ed. and trans. by Stephen Mitchell (New York: Vintage, 1984), p. 245.

SELECT BIBLIOGRAPHY

Abbott, Elizabeth. *A History of Celibacy.* New York: Scribner, 2000.

Allegro, John M. *The Sacred Mushroom and the Cross: A Study of the Nature and Origins of Christianity Within the Fertility Cults of the Ancient Near East.* New York: Doubleday, 1970.

Allitt, Patrick. *Catholic Converts: British and American Intellectuals Turn to Rome.* Ithaca, NY: Cornell University Press, 1997.

Aquinas, Saint Thomas. *Summa theologiae.* Ed. and trans. Fathers of the English Dominican Province. 61 vols. London: Blackfriars, 1964-81.

Armstrong, Karen. *A History of God: The 4,000 Year Quest of Judaism, Christianity, and Islam.* New York: Ballantine, 1994.

Arnold, Matthew. *Culture and Anarchy.* Ed. J. Dover Wilson. New York: Cambridge University Press, 1966.

Auden, W. H. *Collected Poems.* Ed. Edward Mendelson. New York: Random House, 1976.

Augustine, *The City of God.* Trans. John Healey. London: E. P. Dutton & Co., 1934.

Baron, Salo Wittmayer. *A Social and Religious History of the Jews.* New York: Columbia University Press / Jewish Publication Society, 18 volumes, 1960 -.

Bauer, Janet. "Sexuality and the Moral 'Construction' of Women in an Islamic Society." *Anthropological Quarterly* 58:3 (July 1985).

Bawer, Bruce. *Stealing Jesus: How Fundamentalism Betrays Christianity.* New York: Crown Publishers, 1997.

Beckford, James A. "Accounting for Conversion." In *British Journal of Sociology* 29 (1978): 249-62.

Bloch, Maurice and Jonathan Parry, eds. *Death and the Regeneration of Life.* Cambridge: Cambridge University Press, 1994.

Borowitz, Eugene. *Exploring Jewish Ethics.* Detroit: Wayne State University Press, 1990.

Boswell, John. *Christianity, Social Tolerance, and Homosexuality.* Chicago: University of Chicago Press, 1980.

———. *Same-Sex Unions in Premodern Europe.* New York: Vintage, 1994.

Boston Globe Investigative Staff. *Betrayal: The Crisis in the Catholic Church.* Boston: Little, Brown & Company, 2002.

Bouhdiba, Abdelwahab. *Sexuality in Islam.* Trans. Alan Sheridan. London: Routledge & Kegan Paul, 1985.

Bouldrey, Brian, ed. *Wrestling with the Angel: Faith and Religion in the Lives of Gay Men.* New York: Riverhead, 1995.

Boyer, Paul. *When Time Shall Be No More: Prophecy Belief in American Culture.* Cambridge: Harvard University Press, 1992.

Bradford, Sarah. *America's Queen: A Life of Jacqueline Kennedy Onassis.* New York: Viking, 2000.

Brooks, Geraldine. *Nine Parts of Desire: The Hidden World of Islamic Women.* New York: Anchor, 1995.

Brooten, Bernadette. *Love Between Women: Early Christian Response to Female Homoeroticism.* Chicago: University of Chicago Press, 1996.

Brown, Peter. *The Body and Society: Men, Women, and Sexual Renunciation in Early Christianity.* New York: Columbia University Press, 1988.

Brozan, Nadine. "Annulling a Tradition: Rabbis Stir Furor by Helping 'Chained Women' to Leave Husbands." *New York Times,* August 13, 1998, p. B1.

Brundage, James A. *Law, Sex, and Christian Society in Medieval Europe.* Chicago: University of Chicago Press, 1989.

————. "Sex and Canon Law," in *Handbook of Medieval Sexuality,* ed. Vern L. Bullough and James A. Brundage. New York: Garland Publishing, 1996.

Buckley, Christopher. "Taps," in *New Yorker,* June 3, 1996, p. 56.

Burkett, Elinor and Frank Bruni. *A Gospel of Shame: Children, Sexual Abuse, and the Catholic Church.* New York: Viking, 1993.

Burridge, Kenelm. *New Heaven, New Earth: A Study of Millenarian Activities.* Oxford: Basil Blackwell, 1969.

Burns, Gene. *The Frontiers of Catholicism.* Berkeley and Los Angeles, CA: University of California Press, 1992.

Carroll, James. *Constantine's Sword: The Church and the Jews: A History.* New York: Houghton Mifflin, 2001.

Chauvin, Charles. *Les chrétiens et la prostitution.* Paris: Les editions du Cerf, 1983.

Chervin, Ronda, ed. *Bread from Heaven: The Stories of 23 Jews Who Found the Messiah in the Catholic Church.* New Hope, KY: Remnant of Israel, 1995.

Chesterton, G. K. *The Catholic Church and Conversion.* New York: Macmillan, 1926.

Christie-Murray, David. *A History of Heresy.* New York: Oxford University Press, 1991.

Clark, Robert. *My Grandfather's House: A Genealogy of Doubt and Faith.* New York: Picador, 1999.

Cohen, Sherill. *The Evolution of Women's Asylums since 1500: from Refuges for Ex-prostitutes to Shelters for Battered Women.* New York: Oxford University Press, 1992.

Cooper, Kate. *The Virgin and the Bride: Idealized Womanhood in Late Antiquity.* Cambridge: Harvard University Press, 1996.

Cooperman, Alan. "The Bishop, the Scandal and His Plan." *Washington Post,* September 28, 2002, p. A1.

————. "U.S. Catholic Bishops Disown Efforts to Convert Jews." *Washington Post,* August 17, 2002, p. B9.

Cooperman, Alan and Lena H. Sun. "Hundreds of Priests Removed Since '60s." *Washington Post,* June 9, 2002, pp. A1, A 18.

Cornwell, John. *Breaking Faith: The Pope, the People, and the Fate of Catholicism.* New York: Viking, 2001.

————. *Hitler's Pope: The Secret History of Pius XII.* New York: Viking, 1999.

Coward, Noël. *The Noël Coward Diaries.* Eds. Graham Payne and Sheridan Morley. Boston: Little, Brown, 1992.

————. *Private Lives.* In *Noël Coward Collected Plays: Two.* London: Methuen, 1986.

Cross, Robert D. *The Emergence of Liberal Catholicism in America.* Cambridge: Harvard University Press, 1958.

deSousa, Ronald. *The Rationality of the Emotions.* Cambridge: MIT Press, 1987.

Diamant, Anita. *The Red Tent.* New York: St. Martin's, 1997.

Dillon, Michelle. *Catholic Identity: Balancing Reason, Faith, and Power.* Cambridge: Cambridge University Press, 1999.

Dionne, E. J., Jr. "America and the Catholic Church: Conflicts with Rome and Within." *New York Times,* December 24, 1986, p. A1.

Douglas, Mary. *Purity and Danger: An Analysis of the Concepts of Pollution and Taboo.* London: Routledge, 1995.

Douglass, Bruce and David Hollenbach, eds. *Catholicism and Liberalism: Contributions to American Public Philosophy.* New York: Cambridge University Press, 1997.

Doyle, Laura. *The Surrendered Wife: A Practical Guide to Finding Intimacy, Passion, and Peace with Your Man.* New York: Fireside, 2001.

Dubner, Stephen J. *Turbulent Souls: A Catholic Son's Return to His Jewish Roots.* New York: William Morrow, 1998.

DuBowski, Sandi Simcha. *Trembling Before G-d.* New York: New Yorker Films, 2001.

Dunlop, David W. "Reform Rabbis Vote to Back Gay Marriage." *New York Times,* March 29, 1996, p. B9.

Early, Tracy. "Jewish Group Wants Holocaust Honor for John XXIII." *Catholic New York,* September 14, 2000, p. 4.

Eire, Carlos. From Madrid to Purgatory: *The Art and Craft of Dying in Sixteenth-Century Spain.* Cambridge: Cambridge University Press, 1995.

Eliade, Mircea. *Patterns in Comparative Religion.* Trans. Rosemary Sheed. Lincoln, NE: University of Nebraska Press, 1996.

Elliott, Dyan. "Bernadino of Siena versus the Marital Debt." In *Desire and Discipline: Sex and Sexuality in Premodern Europe.* Ed. Jacqueline Murrary and Konrad Eisenbichler. Toronto: University of Toronto Press, 1996.

———. *Fallen Bodies: Pollution, Sexuality, and Demonology in the Middle Ages.* Philadelphia: University of Pennsylvania Press, 1999.

——— *Spiritual Marriage: Sexual Abstinence in Medieval Wedlock.* Princeton: Princeton University Press, 1993.

Englander, Nathan. *For the Relief of Unbearable Urges.* New York: Knopf, 1999.

Erdrich, Louise. *The Last Report on the Miracles at Little No Horse.* New York: HarperCollins, 2001.

Eriksen, Julia A. *Kiss and Tell: Surveying Sex in the Twentieth Century.* Cambridge: Harvard University Press, 1999.

Fakhry, Majid. *A History of Islamic Philosophy.* New York: Columbia University Press, 1987.

Filteau, Jerry. "Catholic-Jewish Statement on Conversion Draws Heat." *Catholic Virginian,* September 2, 2002, pp. 1 and 10.

Fisher, Helen. *Anatomy of Love: The Natural History of Monogamy, Adultery, and Divorce.* New York: Knopf, 1999.

Flanders, Stephanie. "Demonstrators at U.N. Accuse Priests of Abusing Nuns in Africa." *New York Times,* July 15, 2001, p. A27.

Flannery, Austin, O. P., ed. *Vatican II: The Conciliar and Post Conciliar Documents.* Collegeville, Ind., 1992.

Foucault, Michel. *Discipline and Punish.* Trans. Alan Sheridan. New York: Vintage, 1979.

———. *The History of Sexuality, Volume I: An Introduction.* Trans. Robert Hurley. New York: Random House, 1978.

Fountain, John. "Shock Over Accusations in Milwaukee." *New York Times,* May 24, 2002, p. A18.

Fox, Thomas C. *Sexuality and Catholicism.* New York: George Braziller, 1995.

Freedman, Samuel G. *Jew vs. Jew: The Struggle for the Soul of American Jewry.* New York: Simon & Schuster, 2000.

Freud, Sigmund. *Civilization and Its Discontents.* Trans. James Strachey. 1929; New York: W.W. Norton, 1989.

Frymer-Kensky, Tivka. "Law and Philosophy: The Case of Sex in the Bible." In *Jewish Explorations of Sexuality,* ed. Jonathan Magonet. Providence: Berghahn Books, 1995.

Fulbrook, Mary. *Piety and Politics.* Cambridge: Cambridge University Press, 1983.

Gallagher, Eugene V. "Conversion and Community in Late Antiquity." In *The Journal of Religion* 73 (1993): 1-15.

Gallagher, Winifred. *Spiritual Genius: The Mastery of Life's Meaning.* New York: Random House, 2001.

Gavitt, Philip. *Charity and Children in Renaissance Florence: The Ospedale degli Innocenti 1410-1536.* Ann Arbor, Mich.: University of Michigan Press, 1990.

Gay, Jerry. "House Votes to Ban Gay Marriages." *New York Times,* July 14, 1996, p. D2.

Gay, Peter. *Freud: A Life for Our Time.* New York: W.W. Norton, 1988.

Gill, Anton. *Art Lover: A Biography of Peggy Guggenheim.* New York: HarperCollins, 2002.

Gledhill, Ruth. "Evangelicals Warn that Williams in Canterbury Would Split the Church." *The Times* (London). June 21, 2002.

Goodstein, Laurie. "Unusual, but Not Unorthodox; Causing a Stir, 2 Synagogues Hire Women to Assist Rabbis." *New York Times,* February 6, 1998, p. B1.

———. "U.S. Bishops Let Public Opinion Guide Them This Time." *New York Times,* June 16, 2002, p. A1.

———. "Women Taking Active Role to Study Orthodox Judaism." *New York Times,* December 21, 2000, p. A1.

Greeley, Andrew M. *Sex and the Catholic Experience.* Allen, Texas: Thomas More, 1994.

Greene, Graham. "On Becoming a Catholic." In *Commonweal Confronts the Century,* ed. Patrick Jordan and Paul Baumann. New York: Touchstone, 1999.

———. *The Power and the Glory* [1940]. New York: Penguin, 1971.

Gregory, Brad S. *Salvation at Stake: Christian Martyrdom in Early Modern Europe.* Cambridge: Harvard University Press, 1999.

Gross, Jane. "In Stamford, Scout Troop is Evicted, but Prepared." *New York Times,* June 30, 2001, p. A24.

Grossman, Cathy Lynn. "Protestants Face Annual Sexual Divide: Same-sex Unions, Gay Clergy, Female Leaders Divide Faithful." *USA Today,* June 6, 2001, p. 1D.

Guttmann, Julius. *Philosophies of Judaism, the History of Jewish Philosophy from Biblical Times to Franz Rosenzweig.* Trans. David W. Silverman. New York: Holt, Rinehart, and Winston, 1964.

Guy, David. *The Red Thread of Passion: Spirituality and the Paradox of Sex.* Boston: Shambala, 1999.

Hanna, Mary. *Catholics and American Politics.* Cambridge: Harvard University Press, 1979.

Hanson, Ellis. *Decadence and Catholicism.* Cambridge: Harvard University Press, 1997.

Hanson, Eric. *The Catholic Church in World Politics.* Princeton: Princeton University Press, 1987.

Häring, Bernard. "The Encyclical Crisis," in *Commonweal Confronts the Century.* Ed. Patrick Jordan and Paul Baumann. New York: Touchstone Books, 1999.

———. *The Law of Christ. (Das Gesetz Christi)* 3 vols.. Trans. Edwin G. Kaiser [1956]. Westminster: Newman Press, 1966.

Hartman, Keith. *Congregations in Conflict: The Battle Over Homosexuality.* New Brunswick, N.J.: Rutgers University Press, 1996.

Heath, Stephen. *The Sexual Fix.* New York: Schoken, 1982.

Hellwig, Monika. *Understanding Catholicism.* New York: Paulist Press, 1981.

Henneberger, Melinda. "Scandals in the Church: the Overview; Pope Offers Apology to Victims of Sex Abuse by Priests." *New York Times,* April 24, 2002, p. A1.

————. "Vatican Says Jews' Wait is Validated by the Old Testament." *New York Times,* January 18, 2002, p. A8.

————. "Vatican Weighs Reaction to Accusations of Molesting by Clergy." *New York Times,* March 3, 2002, p. A30.

Herlihy, David. *Medieval Households.* Cambridge: Harvard University Press, 1985.

Herman, Didi. *The Antigay Agenda: Orthodox Vision and the Christian Right.* Chicago: University of Chicago Press, 1997.

Hersh, Seymour M. *The Dark Side of Camelot.* Boston: Little, Brown and Company, 1997.

Holleran, Andrew. "The Sense of Sin" in *Wrestling with the Angel: Faith and Religion in the Lives of Gay Men.* New York: Riverhead, 1995.

Hudson, Liam. *Bodies of Knowledge: The Psychological Significance of the Nude in Art.* London: Weidenfeld & Nicholson, 1982.

James, William. *The Varieties of Religious Experience.* 1902; New York: New American Library, 1958.

Jansen, Katharine Ludwig. *The Making of the Magdalene: Preaching and Popular Devotion in the Later Middle Ages.* Princeton: Princeton University Press, 2000.

Jenkins, Philip. *Pedophiles and Priests: Anatomy of a Contemporary Crisis.* New York: Oxford University Press, 1996.

Jordan, Mark. *The Invention of Sodomy in Christian Theology.* Chicago: University of Chicago Press, 1997.

————. *The Silence of Sodom: Homosexuality in Modern Catholicism.* Chicago: University of Chicago Press, 2000.

Jordan, Patrick and Paul Baumann, eds. *Commonweal Confronts the Century.* New York: Touchstone, 1999.

Karras, Ruth Mazo. *Common Women: Prostitution and Sexuality in Medieval England.* Oxford: Oxford University Press, 1996.

Katz, Jacob. *Exclusiveness and Tolerance: Studies in Jewish-Gentile Relations in Medieval and Modern Times.* New York: Schocken, 1961.

Kennedy, Eugene, *The Unhealed Wound: The Church and Human Sexuality* (New York: St. Martin's Press, 2001.

Kertzer, David. *The Kidnapping of Edgardo Mortara.* New York: Vintage, 1998.

————. *The Popes Against the Jews: The Vatican's Role in the Rise of Modern Anti-Semitism.* New York: Knopf, 2001.

Kirschner, Robert. "Halakhah and Homosexuality: A Reappraisal." In *Judaism* 37.3, 1988.

Kleinberg, Aviad M. *Prophets in Their Own Country: Living Saints and the Making of Sainthood in the Later Middle Ages.* Chicago: University of Chicago Press, 1992.

Kreeft, Peter J. *Everything You Ever Wanted to Know About Heaven.* San Franciso: Harper & Row, 1982.

Kurth, Peter. *Isadora: A Sensational Life.* New York: Little Brown & Company, 2001.

Laeuchli, Samuel. *Power and Sexuality: The Emergence of Canon Law at the Synod of Elvira.* Philadelphia: Temple University Press, 1972.

Lang, Bernhard. "The Sexual Life of Saints: Towards an Anthropology of the Christian Heaven." *Religion* 17 (April 1987): 149-171.

Lemann, Nicholas. *The Big Test: The Secret History of the American Meritocracy.* New York: Farrar, Straus, Giroux, 1999.

Lewis, C. S. *Mere Christianity.* New York: Macmillan, 1952.

————. *The Problem of Pain.* New York: Macmillan, 1962.

Makowski, Elizabeth M. "The Conjugal Debt and Medieval Canon Law." In *Journal of Medieval History* 3 (1977): 99-114.

Mayo, James M. *The American Country Club: Its Origins and Development.* New Brunswick, NJ: Rutgers University Press, 1998.

McBrien, Richard. *Catholicism: Study Edition.* Minneapolis: Winston Press, 1981.

McBrien, Richard. *HarperCollins Encyclopedia of Catholicism.* New York: HarperCollins, 1995.

McClory, Robert. *Turning Point: The Inside Story of the Papal Birth Control Commission.* New York: Crossroads, 1995.

McDannell, Colleen and Bernhard Lang. *Heaven: A History.* New Haven: Yale University Press, 1988.

————. "Modern Heaven . . . And a Theology." In *Mormons and Mormonism: An Introduction to an American World Religion.* Ed. Eric A. Eliason. Urbana, Ill.: University of Illinois Press, 2000.

McDonough Peter and Eugene C. Bianchi. *Passionate Uncertainty: Inside the American Jesuits.* Berkeley and Los Angeles: University of California Press, 2002.

McNamara, Jo Ann Kay. *Sisters in Arms: Catholic Nuns Through Two Millennia.* Cambridge: Harvard University Press, 1996.

McNeill, John. *The Church and the Homosexual.* Boston: Beacon Press, 1993.

Mead, Rebecca. "Slim for Him." *New Yorker,* January 15, 2001.

Mendes, Sam. *American Beauty.* Los Angeles: Dreamworks, 2000.

Miller, Richard Roscoe. *Slavery and Catholicism.* Durham, N.C.: North State Publishers, 1957.

Morgan, Christopher. "Anglican Rebels Build New Church." *Sunday Times,* November 9, 1997.

Morris, Charles. *American Catholic: The Saints and Sinners Who Built America's Most Powerful Church.* New York: Times Books, 1997.

Moss, Richard J. *Golf and the American Country Club.* Urbana, IL: University of Illinois Press, 2001.

Murray, Jacqueline and Konrad Eisenbichler, eds. *Desire and Discipline: Sex and Sexuality in Premodern Europe.* Toronto: University of Toronto Press, 1996.

Niehbur, Gustav. "Episcopal Dispute in Maryland Spills into Federal Court." *New York Times,* August 14, 2001, p. A10.

Nock, A. D. *Conversion: The Old and the New Religion from Alexander the Great to Augustine of Hippo.* Oxford: Oxford University Press, 1969.

Noonan, John. *Contraception: A History of Its Treatment by Catholic Theologians and Canonists.* Cambridge: Harvard University Press, 1966.

Nossiter, Adam. *Of Long Memory: Mississippi and the Murder of Medgar Evers.* Reading, Mass.: Addison-Wesley, 1994.

O'Brien, David J. "What Happened to the Catholic Left?," in *What's Left? Liberal American Catholics.* Ed. Mary Jo Weaver. Bloomington, IN: Indiana University Press, 1999.

O'Connor, Mary C. *The Art of Dying Well: The Development of the* Ars Moriendi. New York: Columbia University Press, 1942.

O'Malley, John. *The First Jesuits.* Cambridge: Harvard University Press, 1993.

Pagels, Elaine. *The Origin of Satan.* New York: Random House, 1996.

Payer, Pierre J. *Sex and the Penitentials: The Development of a Sexual Code 550-1150.* Toronto: University of Toronto Press, 1984.

Payne, Graham and Sheridan Morley, eds. *The Nöel Coward Diaries.* Boston: Little, Brown, 1992.

Pelikan, Jaraslov. *The Riddle of Roman Catholicism.* New York: Abingdon Press, 1959.

Pipher, Mary. *Reviving Ophelia: Saving the Selves of Adolescent Girls.* New York: Ballantine Books, 1994.

Pogany, Eugene. *In My Brother's Image: Twin Brothers Separated by Faith After the Holocaust.* New York: Viking, 2000.

Portmann, John. *When Bad Things Happen to Other People.* New York: Routledge, 2000.

Posner, Richard. *Aging and Old Age.* Chicago: University of Chicago Press, 1995.

Ranke-Heinemann, Ute. *Eunuchs for the Kingdom of Heaven: Women, Spirituality, and the Catholic Church.* Trans. Peter Heinegg. New York: Penguin, 1991.

Reese, Thomas. *Inside the Vatican: The Politics and Organization of the Catholic Church.* Cambridge: Harvard University Press, 1996.

Rilke, Rainer Maria. *The Selected Poetry of Rainer Maria Rilke.* Trans. and Ed. Stephen Mitchell. New York: Vintage, 1984.

Rimbaud, Arthur. *Rimbaud Complete.* Ed. Wyatt Mason. New York: Modern Library, 2002.

Righter, Walter C. *A Pilgrim's Way.* New York: Knopf, 1988.

Rosen, Jeffrey. "Is Nothing Secular?" *New York Times Magazine,* January 30, 2000, p. 40.

Rosenthal, Eliezer David. "Yom Kippur," trans. Helena Frank. In *The Yom Kippur Anthology,* ed. Philip Goodman. Philadelphia: The Jewish Publication Society of America, 1971.

Roth, Norman. "A Research Note on Sexuality and Muslim Civilization," in *Handbook of Medieval Sexuality,* ed. Vern L. Bullough and James A. Brundage. New York: Garland Press, 1996.

Rubin, Miri. *Corpus Christi: The Eucharist in Late Medieval Culture.* Cambridge: Cambridge University Press, 1991.

Rudnick, Paul. *Jeffrey.* Los Angeles: Orion Pictures, 1995.

Rushdie, Salman. *Imaginary Homelands: Essays and Criticism 1981-1991.* New York: Viking, 1991.

Russell, Jeffrey Burton. *A History of Heaven: The Singing Silence.* Princeton: Princeton University Press, 1998.

Ryan, Stephen. "Episcopal Priest Becomes Catholic Laywoman." *National Catholic Register,* July 29 - August 4, 2001: pp. 1 and 10.

Said, Edward. *Covering Islam: How the Media and the Experts Determine How We See the Rest of the World.* New York: Vintage, 1997.

Schiffrin, Lisa. "Gay Marriage: An Oxymoron." *New York Times,* March 23, 1996: A21.

Shalit, Wendy. *A Return to Modesty: Discovering the Lost Virtue.* New York: Free Press, 1999.

Shapiro, James. *Oberammergau: The Troubling Story of the World's Most Famous Passion Play.* New York: Pantheon, 2000.

Shaw, Patrick. "On Worshipping the Same God," in *Religious Studies,* December 1992: 511-522.

—, Daniel Jeremy. *A History of Judaism*, 2 volumes. New York: Basic Books, 1974.

A. W. Richard. *A Secret World: Sexuality and the Search for Celibacy.* New York: Brunner/Mazel, 1990.

—n, Deborah. *Utopia Parkway: The Life and Work of Joseph Cornell.* New York: Farrar, Straus, Giroux, 1997.

—ebecca L. *The Invention of the Restaurant.* Cambridge: Harvard University Press, 2000.

Leslie. *Lorca: A Dream of Life.* New York: Farrar, Straus, Giroux, 1999.

—essandra. "Duelling Festivals: Gay Pride and Vatican Collide." *New York Times,* —ne 3, 2000, p. A4.

—ay Parade, Opposed by Vatican, Passes Peacefully in Rome." *New York Times,* July 9, 2000, p. A5.

———. "In Ukraine, Pope Tries to Heal Rift with Orthodox Church." *New York Times,* June 24, 2001, p. A8.

———. "Pope Declares His 'Bitterness' Over Gay Event." *New York Times,* July 10, 2000, p. A11.

Stavans, Ilan. *The Oxford Book of Jewish Stories.* New York: Oxford University Press, 1998.

Stern, Steve, "Lazar Malkin Enters Heaven" in *The Oxford Book of Jewish Stories,* ed. Ilan Stavans. New York: Oxford University Press, 1998.

Sullivan, Kevin. "Thoroughly Modern Martha: Mexico's new First Lady is a Career Woman, a Conservative Catholic – and a Force for Change." *Washington Post,* September 4, 2001, p. C1.

Svevo, Italo. *Zeno's Conscience.* Trans. William Weaver. 1923; New York: Knopf, 2001.

Tagliabue, John. "A Doctor-Spokesman Attends to Papal Image." *New York Times,* June 29, 2002, p. A1.

Taylor, John H. *Death and the Afterlife in Ancient Egypt.* Chicago: University of Chicago Press, 2001.

Tebor, Irving B. "Male Virginis: Conflicts and Group Support in American Culture." *Family Life Coordinator* 9, March-June 1961.

Tertullian. *Apology, De Spectaculis.* Trans. T. R. Glover. Cambridge: Harvard University Press, 1966.

Thomas, Keith. *Religion and the Decline of Magic: Studies in Popular Belief in Sixteenth- and Seventeenth-Century England.* New York: Scribner, 1971.

Thurber, James and E. B. White. *Is Sex Necessary? or Why You Feel the Way You Do.* New York: Harper & Brothers, 1929.

Trexler, R. C. "La prostitution florentine au XVe Siècle." In *Memoria* 17 (1986): 983-1015.

Trillin, Calvin. *Remembering Denny.* New York: Farrar, Strauss, Giroux, 1993.

Trilling, Diana. "Marilyn Monroe." In *The Book of Eulogies: A Collection of Memorial Tributes, Poetry, Essays, and Letters of Condolence.* Ed. Phyllis Theroux. New York: Scribner, 1997.

Unterman, Alan. "Judaism and Homosexuality: Some Orthodox Perspectives." In *Jewish Quarterly,* 1993.

Vallone, Lynne. *Disciplines of Virtue: Girls' Culture in the Eighteenth and Nineteenth Centuries.* New Haven: Yale University Press, 1995.

Van Biema, David. "Episcopal Turf War." *Time,* July 9, 2001, p. 41.

Veblen, Thorstein. *The Theory of the Leisure Class.* Boston: Houghton Mifflin, 1973.

Visser, Margaret. *The Geometry of Love: Space, Time, and Mystery in an Ordinary Church.* New York: North Point, 2001.

von Balthasar, Hans Urs. *Dare We Hope "That All Men Be Saved?"* Trans. David Kipp and Lothar Krauth. San Francisco: Ignatius Press, 1988.

Waldman, Amy. "Taboo Heaven: More No-Nos Than You Can Shake a Stick at." *New York Times,* December 2, 2001, p. D7.

Walsh, Edward. "Presbyterian Board Alters Gay Policy." *Washington Post,* June 16, 2001, p. A1.

Ward, Benedicta. *Harlots of the Desert: A Study of Repentance in Early Monastic Sources.* Kalamazoo, Mich.: Cistercian Publications, 1987.

Warner, Marina. *Alone of All Her Sex: The Myth and Cult of the Virgin Mary.* New York: Vintage, 1983.

Warraq, Ibn. "Virgins, What Virgins?" *The Guardian* (London). January 12, 2002, p. 3.

Waskow, Arthur and Danile Landes. "Down-to-Earth Judaism: Sexuality." In *Jewish Explorations of Sexuality,* Ed. Jonathan Magonet. Providence, R.I.: Berghahn Books, 1995.

Weaver, Mary Jo, ed. *What's Left? Liberal American Catholics.* Bloomington, IN: Indiana University Press, 1999.

Weaver, Mary Jo and R. Scott Appleby, eds. *Being Right: Conservative Catholics in America.* Bloomington, IN: University of Indiana Press, 1995.

Wills, Garry. *Papal Sin: Structures of Deceit.* New York: Doubleday, 2000.

Wilson, A. N. *God's Funeral.* New York: W.W. Norton, 1999.

Wogan-Browne, Jocelyn. *Saints' Lives and Women's Literary Culture c. 1150-1300.* Oxford: Oxford University Press, 2001.

Woodward, Kenneth. *Making Saints: How the Catholic Church Determines Who Becomes a Saint, Who Doesn't, and Why.* New York: Simon & Schuster, 1990.

Yarshater, Ehsan, ed. *Encyclopedia Iranica.* New York: Biblioteca Persica Press.

Zanca, Kenneth J., ed. *American Catholics and Slavery: 1789-1866: An Anthology of Primary Documents.* Lanham, Md.: University Press of America, 1994.

Zeidner, Lisa. *Layover.* New York: Random House, 1999.

Zolli, Eugenio. *Why I Became a Catholic.* Fort Collins, Colo.: Roman Catholic Books, 1954.

Zuccotti, Susan. *Under His Very Windows: The Vatican and the Holocaust in Italy.* New Haven: Yale University Press, 2000.

INDEX